William Davies

Foreword by Aditya Chakrabortty

The Limits of Neoliberalism

Authority, Sovereignty and the Logic of Competition

REVISED EDITION

Los Angeles | London | New Delhi
Singapore | Washington DC | Melbourne

Los Angeles | London | New Delhi
Singapore | Washington DC | Melbourne

SAGE Publications Ltd
1 Oliver's Yard
55 City Road
London EC1Y 1SP

SAGE Publications Inc.
2455 Teller Road
Thousand Oaks, California 91320

SAGE Publications India Pvt Ltd
B 1/I 1 Mohan Cooperative Industrial Area
Mathura Road
New Delhi 110 044

SAGE Publications Asia-Pacific Pte Ltd
3 Church Street
#10-04 Samsung Hub
Singapore 049483

Editor: Natalie Aguilera
Editorial assistant: Delayna Spencer
Production editor: Victoria Nicholas
Marketing manager: Sally Ransom
Cover design: Tristan Tutak
Typeset by: C&M Digitals (P) Ltd, Chennai, India
Printed and bound by CPI Group (UK) Ltd,
Croydon, CR0 4YY

Library of Congress Control Number: 2016953513

British Library Cataloguing in Publication data

A catalogue record for this book is available from the
British Library

ISBN 978-1-5264-0352-0 (pbk)

At SAGE we take sustainability seriously. Most of our products are printed in the UK using FSC papers and boards.
When we print overseas we ensure sustainable papers are used as measured by the PREPS grading system.
We undertake an annual audit to monitor our sustainability.

CONTENTS

ABOUT THE AUTHOR

William Davies is a Reader in Political Economy at Goldsmiths, University of London, where he is also Co-Director of the Political Economy Research Centre. He is author of *The Happiness Industry: How the government and big business sold us wellbeing* (Verso, 2015) and his writing has appeared in *The New York Times, New Left Review, The Atlantic* and *The Guardian*. He blogs at www.potlatch.org.uk and is on twitter as @WillDavies.

ACKNOWLEDGEMENTS

Many of the ideas, concerns and arguments contained in this book began as part of my doctoral research, carried out between 2005–2009, at Goldsmiths, University of London, which resulted in my thesis, 'Competition and Competitiveness: A Cultural Political Economy'. For this reason, I owe particular thanks to my two PhD supervisors, Scott Lash and Michael Keith. I would also like to thank the various friends I made during those years, both at Goldsmiths and via the NYLON research network that brings together graduate students in London and New York.

I was able to carry on developing ideas and reading widely, thanks to the opportunity afforded by a two-year post-doctoral fellowship at the Institute for Science Innovation & Society (InSIS), University of Oxford, between 2009–2011. This was followed by a year spent at Kellogg College, University of Oxford, when I began working on this manuscript. I would like to thank all those who provided a supportive intellectual and collegial environment during those years, especially my InSIS colleagues Javier Lezaun and Lisa Stampnitzky, with whom I shared an interest in policy expertise and from whom I learnt a lot.

I finished the manuscript following a move to the Centre for Interdisciplinary Methodologies, University of Warwick. Again, I'd like to thank colleagues there, and Celia Lury in particular, for providing a stimulating environment and enough time to help me complete this book. Emma Uprichard, Gurminder Bhambra, Alice Mah and Claire Blencowe offered valuable feedback on Chapter 1. Nate Tkacz offered useful references for Chapter 2. At Sage's request, Nicholas Gane read the manuscript, and offered some excellent comments and suggestions; I was very fortunate to have such a thoughtful and knowledgeable reader.

Elements of Chapter 3 have already been published, as 'Economics and the "Nonsense" of Law: the Case of the Chicago Antitrust Revolution' in *Economy & Society*, and as 'Economic Advice as a Vocation: Symbioses of Scientific and

Political Authority', in *The British Journal of Sociology*. The main arguments within Chapter 5 have appeared as 'The Emerging Neocommunitarianism' in *Political Quarterly* (which subsequently won the Bernard Crick award for best *Political Quarterly* article of 2012) and as 'When is a Market not a Market?: "Exemption", "Externality" and "Exception" in the case of European State Aid Rules' in *Theory, Culture & Society*. I am grateful to the editors and reviewers of those journals for helping me develop this work and building my confidence in it.

Monika Krause has read various pieces of my work over the years, including some which have found their way into Chapters 4 and 5. She's been an excellent friend and critic, including at those moments when one gets stuck with a piece of writing. Henry Paker is partly responsible for me becoming fascinated by the latent absurdity of competition (specifically 5-a-side football) in the first place.

I would also like to thank my family and friends for always being supportive of my academic ambitions and career over the past eight years. Finally, I would like to express my love and thanks to Lydia, my wife, and Martha our daughter. It is my hope that Martha will one day live in a society which offers more choices than merely 'winning' or 'losing' in a competitive game.

FOREWORD

Through the autumn of 2008, a steady stream of obituaries flowed into my inbox. They came from think tanks, from academics and from small publishers of books and journals. All announced the same death and all were gleeful. 'Neoliberalism is dead!' they crowed. Wasn't it obvious? The banks had collapsed, governments had stepped in and the workings of the system had been exposed for all to see on the *Ten O'Clock News*. No longer could politicians, economists and businesspeople gesture to a curtain that marked off the political from the economic. That veil had been torn down after the death of Lehman Brothers – then buried deep under the trillions dispensed in bailouts, underwriting and quantitative easing.

Neoliberalism had had its plutocrats' funeral; now for the replacement.

Needless to say, things haven't worked out like that. Just why has become the key question in liberal-left discourse, albeit one that is put in a variety of ways and registers. For dilute Keynesians such as Paul Krugman, the central argument is why austerity still stalks Europe. For the old left-wing parties of government, it is why they aren't in power. For campaigners, it is about what became of the energy and imagination shown by Occupy and UK Uncut. At the bottom of all these questions is the big one: why haven't we won?

What's important to note is that the original prediction was half right. This economic and political system has failed. Neoliberalism is dead – but, zombie-like, it staggers on.

Across the rich countries, growth remains mediocre. In Britain, workers are still getting paid less after inflation than they were almost a decade ago. This is happening despite years of an austerity programme that was meant to have a purgative effect; despite the state dreaming up ever more lending schemes and chucking billions at the housing market; despite the Bank of England pumping over £400bn into money markets.

Whether at the Treasury or on Threadneedle Street, our economic policy makers now bear the exhausted look of tutors who have rifled through every page of the textbook – and yet still can't find the right answers for the restive students. What they've done instead is give cash to homeowners, to bond-holders and to the asset-rich. The Bank of England admits that its quantitative-easing programme has done precisely this.

The crash has sharpened the central contradiction in neoliberal economics: it has become purely a system that rewards dead money even while it fails to create new money. No ideology can survive unless it has something to offer the young and the almost young. You can't keep winning elections if you can't promise reasonable jobs, wage rises, affordable groceries and housing. Put another way, you can have neoliberalism but you can't have democratic validity.

This is the contradiction over which mainstream politicians wedded to neoliberalism – both Left and Right – keep stumbling. Where they can, they rely on the old tricks to get by: operating party machinery, access to big money funders, consulting the manual of TV presentability. But the formula isn't reliable, as the New Labour generation can tell you. And where it can deliver majorities it doesn't confer legitimacy, as David Cameron and Hilary Clinton now know.

Faced with this mess, the obituarists for neoliberalism are out again. Some I recognise from 2008 – the definition of a left-wing economist being one who has spotted ten out of the last two crises of capitalism. Others have joined them, perhaps spurred on by the Brexit vote, or the rise of Donald Trump or the nice-sounding promises made by Theresa May.

I understand the thinking and I certainly get the thinking. But to imagine that an ideology that has ruled Britain for longer than Yugoslavia was communist will now just fall apart is sheer fantasy. It is to mistake word for deed, symbolism for policy. In Brexit Britain, not much has changed yet except for rhetoric. The Treasury continues with its austerity programme; the government presses on with its privatisations of whatever is left in public hands, from social housing to the Green Investment Bank; the establishment still hankers after those grand free-trade deals such as the Transatlantic Trade and Investment Partnership (TTIP). True, there is more talk now about those 'left behind' by globalization, but the very phrasing gives away how shallow the concern is – this is *your* fault for not keeping up.

Besides, politics is never a simple test of logic. Winning or exercising power is not a chess game. As Will Davies points out in this book, neoliberalism began as, and largely remains, an elite project. What four decades of neoliberalism in practice have achieved is the bulldozing of many sites of dissent. To see what I mean, visit any of the places in Britain that have done worst out of it – from the North East to South Wales. The regional business elites have nearly all died or fled to London. The trade unions are a shadow of their former selves, as are the fierce tenants' associations. The universities are now largely anodyne. The local newspapers are typically mere repositories of agency copy and local advertisements, while the regional BBC studios have either shrunk or consolidated elsewhere. Without such civic institutions there is no hope of building an alternative.

The answer to neoliberalism isn't another ideology. It certainly isn't a Mont Pelerin Society of the Left, which would surely be as ghastly as it sounds. No, the answer is democracy. Without that, we will continue with the same bankrupt ideology – expecting failure, and not being surprised or even angry any more when it comes.

Aditya Chakrabortty
Senior Economics Commentator, The Guardian

PREFACE

Plucking pivotal years from history can be a deceptive enterprise. Certain dates can accrue a reputation for being decisive, which is then very difficult to dislodge from the historical imaginary. On the other hand, if we're ever to offer a name or description for a given epoch, it is reasonable to also give some suggestion of when it began and when it ended. With the economic epoch known as 'neoliberalism', 1979 is viewed as a pivotal year – the year of Margaret Thatcher's first General Election victory, with Ronald Reagan's election to President the year after. But, in a number of ways, things were also much more complicated than that.

When exploring paradigm shifts in political economy, maybe it makes more sense to identify how protracted crises were book-ended historically than to seek specific turning points. Consider the crisis of Keynesianism, which provided the opening for the neoliberal take-over and overhaul of economic policy, including those Thatcher and Reagan victories. 1968 was a critical year, not only for the civic unrest that swept the world, but also for the early signs that the US economy would be unable to sustain its role in the global financial system on which Keynesian domestic policies depended. A slow-down in US productivity growth that year, combined with the fiscal costs of an escalation of the Vietnam war, meant that the dollar started to come under increased strain. The 'Bretton Woods' system of fixed exchange rates, with the dollar (convertible to gold) at its centre, struggled on for another five years, before being abandoned under Richard Nixon.

It was a further three years before the final death-knell of Keynesianism was sounded, most loudly in Britain. In 1976, Britain's Labour government had to turn to the IMF for a loan, and agreed to adopt a new monetarist, *neoliberal* strategy for restoring the public finances. That September, Jim Callaghan, the leader of the Labour Party, famously addressed his party conference with the words:

We used to think that you could spend your way out of a recession, and increase employment by cutting taxes and boosting Government spending. I tell you in all candour that that option no longer exists.

While 'book-ending' a crisis runs its own risk of over-simplification, it is perhaps more helpful to see paradigm shifts as lengthy, torturous and confusing affairs. As summarised here, the end of Keynesianism was a crisis that lasted eight years.

When Lehman Brothers collapsed in September 2008, the drama of the following days and months produced a sense of history suddenly accelerating. More specifically, it produced a sense that neoliberalism had suddenly gone off the rails, and a new paradigm would have to be grasped. This later turned out not to be the case, a matter that became an object of scholarly enquiry in its own right (Crouch, 2011; Mirowski, 2013). Several years passed, with governments bailing out banks, central banks slashing interest rates and pumping new money into the economy via quantitative easing, and social policies in Europe being decimated under the pretext of rescuing confidence in the financial and monetary system. The result of all this was economic stagnation but also a perpetuation of the status quo. In a sense, we've been waiting for the second 'book-end' of the crisis. Might 2016 – also eight years after the first 'book-end' – have been just that?

The economic news of 2016 was much like that of 2015 or 2014. Still not much economic growth. Further rounds of quantitative easing. More rising asset prices benefiting the rich. But the political events were incendiary. In the form of Brexit, and Donald Trump, we witnessed popular movements diametrically opposed to the economic common sense that has held sway in the UK and US since the 1970s. These movements are fervently anti-neoliberal, not in the sense that they rest on a coherent critique of monetarism, say, or a specific ambition to regulate markets differently. But inasmuch as neoliberalism embeds particular forms of economic rationality (overseen by economic experts) as the governing principles of nearly all public policy, the very fact that this rationality (and those experts) are being defied or ignored is evidence that something has come unstuck.

'Neoliberalism' is a term that some – especially busy journalists – deem meaningless, on the basis that nobody describes *themselves* as a 'neoliberal'. This has never struck me as an adequate reason not to use a category (nobody describes themselves as 'C1 lower middle class' yet election strategists will discuss how to attract such demographic segments). But it is nevertheless important to be explicit about how concepts are applied.

In this book, I provide a somewhat cumbersome definition of neoliberalism and a pithier one, both of which inform the argument running throughout this book. The cumbersome one is as follows: 'the elevation of marked-based principles and techniques of evaluation to the level of state-endorsed norms'. What this intends to capture is that, while neoliberal states have extended and liberated markets in certain areas (for instance, via privatisation and anti-union legislation), the neoliberal era has been marked just as much by the reform of non-market institutions, so as to render them *market-like* or *business-like*. Consider how competition is deliberately injected into socialised healthcare systems or universities. Alternatively, how protection of the environment is pursued by calculating a proxy price for natural public goods, in the expectation that businesses will then value them appropriately (Fourcade, 2011). It is economic calculation that spreads into all walks of life under neoliberalism, and not markets as such. This in turn provides the pithier version: neoliberalism is 'the disenchantment of politics by economics'.

Brexit was the revenge of politics on economics. The UK government assumed that the more they repeated expert economic analysis in favour of European Union (EU) membership, and the more economists, technocrats and world leaders they could find to agree with them (such as Christine Lagarde of the IMF), the more people would vote to remain in the EU. This now appears to have been the opposite of the case. Bizarrely, regions that do seem to benefit the most from EU membership – such as the North East and South Wales – recorded some of the highest votes in favour of leaving the EU. This flies in the face of the 'rational choice' dogma of the Chicago School of economics or Virginia School of public choice, both of which assume on methodological principle, that individuals behave rationally in pursuit of their own best interests, understood in an economic sense.

Such apparent political 'irrationality' is a more familiar phenomenon in the US, where the 'culture wars' have generated a strand of moral-economic conservatism, in which white working-class voters have repeatedly backed Republican policy platforms that benefit the very wealthy at the expense of everyone else (Frank, 2007). However, the rise of Trump represented something more drastic, whereby the Republican Party was no longer representing the economic interests of *anyone*. Trump's disregard for plausibility of policy or factual credibility signalled a new level of political hysteria, which seemed hostile to the very idea of measured, economically-rational government. 2016 was awash with talk of 'post-truth' politics and 'populist' uprising against 'elites'. Whether or not one subscribes to the idea of 'neoliberalism', there has evidently been a widespread reaction against the edifices of technocratic and managerial power, of the sort that (as I argue in this book) neoliberalism depends on, if economic calculation is to be extended into as many walks of social and economic life as possible.

POPULAR REVOLTS

In one sense, the 'book-ends' of this recent crisis are the inverse of the ones that killed Keynesianism. 1968 was a year of political and civic uprisings, under circumstances of rising prosperity and a still relatively coherent paradigm for economic policy making, albeit one that was showing early signs of deterioration. It was a public and political crisis, which posed a threat to a society of rising prosperity and falling inequality. The technical failings of Keynesianism only really emerged subsequently, before snowballing to the point where the macroeconomic paradigm could simply not be sustained any longer.

The crisis of neoliberalism has reversed this ordering. 2008 was an implosion of technical capabilities on the part of banks and financial regulators, which was largely unaccompanied by any major political or civic eruption, at least until the consequences were felt in terms of public sector cuts that accelerated after 2010, especially in Southern Europe. The economic crisis was spookily isolated from any accompanying political crisis, at least in the beginning. The eruptions of 2016 therefore represented the long-awaited politicisation and publicisation of a crisis that, until then, had been largely dealt with by the same cadre of experts whose errors had caused it in the first place.

Faced with these largely unexpected events and the threat of more, politicians and media pundits have declared that we now need to listen to those people 'left behind by globalisation'. Following the Brexit referendum, in her first speech as Prime Minister, Theresa May made a vow to the less prosperous members of society, 'we will do everything we can to give you more control over your lives. When we take the big calls, we'll think not of the powerful, but you.' This awakening to the demands and voices of marginalised demographics may represent a new recognition that economic policy cannot be wholly geared around the pursuit of 'national competitiveness' in the 'global race', a pursuit that in practice meant seeking to prioritise the interests of financial services and mobile capital. It signals mainstream political acceptance that inequality cannot keep rising forever. But it is still rooted in a somewhat economistic vision of politics, as if those people 'left behind by globalisation' simply want more material wealth and 'opportunity', plus fewer immigrants competing for jobs. What this doesn't do is engage with the distinctive political and cultural sociology of events such as Brexit and Trump, which are fuelled by a spirit of rage, punishment and self-punishment, and not simply by a desire to get a slightly larger slice of the pie.

This is where, I think, we need to pay close attention to a key dimension of neoliberalism, which I focus on at length in this book, namely competition. One of my central arguments here is that neoliberalism is not simply reducible to 'market fundamentalism', even if there are areas (such as financial markets) where markets have manifestly attained greater reach and power since the mid-1970s. Instead, the neoliberal state takes the principle of competition and the ethos of competitiveness (which historically have been found in and around markets), and seeks to reorganise society around them. Quite how competition and competitiveness are defined and politically instituted is a matter for historical and theoretical exploration, which is partly what *The Limits of Neoliberalism* seeks to do. But at the bare minimum, organising social relations in terms of 'competition' means that individuals, organisations, cities, regions and nations are to be tested in terms of their capacity to out-do each other. Not only that, but the tests must be considered fair in some way, if the resulting inequalities are to be recognised as legitimate. When applied to individuals, this ideology is often known as 'meritocracy'.

The appeal of this as a political template for society is that, according to its advocates, it involves the discovery of brilliant ideas, more efficient business models, naturally talented individuals, new urban visions, successful national strategies, potent entrepreneurs and so on. Even if this is correct (and the work of Thomas Piketty on how wealth begets wealth is enough to cast considerable doubt on it) there is a major defect: it consigns the majority of people, places, businesses and institutions to the status of 'losers'. The normative and existential conventions of a neoliberal society stipulate that success and prowess are things that are earned through desire, effort and innate ability, so long as social and economic institutions are designed in such a way as to facilitate this. But the corollary of this is that failure and weakness are also earned: when individuals and communities fail to succeed, this is a reflection of inadequate talent or energy on their part.

This has been critically noted in how 'dependency' and 'welfare' have become matters of shame since the conservative political ascendency of the 1980s. But this is just one example of how a culture of obligatory competitiveness exerts a damaging moral psychology, not only in how people look down on others, but in how they look down on themselves. A culture which valorises 'winning' and 'competitiveness' above all else provides few sources of security or comfort, even to those doing reasonably well. Everyone could be doing better, and if they're not, they have themselves to blame. The vision of society as a competitive game also suggests that anyone could very quickly be doing worse.

Under these neoliberal conditions, remorse becomes directed inwards, producing the depressive psychological effect (or what Freud termed 'melancholia') whereby people search inside themselves for the source of their own unhappiness and imperfect lives (Davies, 2015). Viewed from within the cultural logic of neoliberalism, uncompetitive regions, individuals or communities are not just 'left behind by globalisation', but are discovered to be inferior in comparison to their rivals, just like the contestants ejected from a talent show. Rising household indebtedness compounds this process for those living in financial precarity, by forcing individuals to pay for their own past errors, illness or sheer bad luck (Davies, Montgomerie & Wallin, 2015).

In order to understand political upheavals such as Brexit, we need to perform some sociological interpretation. We need to consider that our socio-economic pathologies do not simply consist in the fact that opportunity and wealth are hoarded by certain industries (such as finance) or locales (such as London) or individuals (such as the children of the wealthy), although all of these things are true. We need also to reflect on the cultural and psychological implications of how this hoarding has been represented and justified over the past four decades, namely that it reflects something about the underlying moral worth of different populations and individuals.

Hardship itself doesn't necessarily lead to the hopelessness and fury of which Donald Trump seemingly speaks. But when hardship feels both permanent and deserved, the psychological appeal of demagogues promising to divert blame elsewhere, be it towards Muslims, 'experts', immigrants, the Chinese, Brussels or wherever, becomes irresistible. Seemingly irrational or even nihilistic popular upheavals make some sense, if understood in terms of the relief they offer for those who have felt trapped by their own impotence for too long, with nobody available to blame but themselves.

One psychological effect of this is authoritarian attitudes towards social deviance: Brexit and Trump supporters both have an above-average tendency to support the death penalty, combined with a belief that political authorities are too weak to enforce justice (Kaufman, 2016). However, it is also clear that psychological and physical pain have become far more widespread in neoliberal societies than has been noticed by most people. Statistical studies have shown how societies such as Britain and the United States have become afflicted by often inexplicable rising mortality rates amongst the white working class, connected partly to rising suicide rates, alcohol and drug abuse (Dorling, 2016). *The Washington Post* identified close geographic correlations between this trend and support for Donald Trump (Guo, 2016). In sum, a moral-economic system aimed at identifying and empowering the most competitive people, institutions and places has become targeted, rationally or otherwise, by the vast number of people, institutions and places that have suffered not only the pain of defeat but the *punishment* of defeat for far too long.

NEOLIBERALISM: DEAD OR ALIVE?

The question inevitably arises, is this thing called 'neoliberalism' now over? And if not, when might it be and how would we know? In the UK, the prospect of Brexit combined with the political priority of reducing immigration means that the efficient movement of capital (together with that of labour) is being consciously impeded in a way that would have been unthinkable during the 1990s and early 2000s. The re-emergence of national borders as obstacles to the flow of goods, finance, services and above all people, represents at least an interruption in the vision of globalisation that accompanied the heyday of neoliberal policy making between 1989–2008. If events such as Brexit signal the first step towards greater national mercantilism and protectionism, then we may be witnessing far more profound transformations in our model of political economy, the consequences of which could become very ugly.

Before we reach that point, it is already possible to identify a reorientation of national economic policy making away from some core tenets of neoliberal doctrine. One of the main case studies of this book is antitrust law and policy, which has been a preoccupation for neoliberal intellectuals, reformers and lawyers ever since the 1930s. The rise of the Chicago School view of competition (which effectively granted far greater legal rights to monopolists, while also being tougher on cartels) in the American legal establishment from the 1970s onwards, later repeated in the European Commission, meant that market

regulation became a more expert, esoteric and ostensibly non-\
of power. One of the ideals of neoliberal scholars, both in the Au\
of Friedrich Hayek and the Chicago School of Milton Friedmai\
economic 'rules of the game' be established beyond the reach \
politics, where they might be manipulated to suit particular short-_ _ _ _ intellectual, social or political agendas. Independent central banks are one of the
more prominent examples of this, but the establishment of rational, apolitical
and European-wide antitrust and state aid rules would be another.

As I explore in Chapter 5, the banking crisis caused some immediate damage to
this vision of apolitical, permanent rules of competitive economic activity. The
need to rescue the financial system at all costs saw EU state aid rules being
overlooked, at least for a few months, suggesting that neoliberalism entered a
state of 'exception' where the state took rapid executive decisions, wherever they
were deemed necessary. Takeover rules were suspended to allow banks to buy
failing competitors, again on the basis that this was necessary to secure the
existential viability of the economy as such. But as is common in the state of
'exception', this was all done to preserve the status quo on the basis that an emergency had struck. It wasn't done with the aim of transforming the economic
paradigm.

While anti-trust and state aid are only one small area of European Commission
powers, they are symbolically very important. Competition regulations represent the normative ideal of the marketplace, which – in the case of post-war
Europe – is imagined as an international, even *post*-national space of freedom,
transcending cultural, linguistic and political differences. The liberal vision of
cosmopolitan Europe becomes realised in economic institutions such as the
single currency, but also the rules that govern market competitors. For these
reasons, Britain's post-Brexit opportunity to withdraw from European anti-trust
and state-aid regulations is symbolic of the new post-liberal or post-neoliberal
era that is emerging. Already, Theresa May has used her first few speeches as
UK Prime Minister to push for a more interventionist state, that seeks to shape
economic outcomes around national, political and social priorities (a reduction
of immigration above all else) no doubt mindful of the fact that the British state
will soon have far more discretion to do this, once it is no longer bound by state
aid rules.

At the time of writing, the odds are against Trump becoming President of the
United States, though one lesson of 2016 is not to be too confident regarding
political odds. This means that the prospect of the United States abandoning its

commitments to neoliberal policy goals is still less than likely. Free trade areas such as NAFTA, policies designed to attract and please mobile capital, the search for global hegemony surrounding international markets (as opposed to naked, mercantilist self-interest) may then continue for a few more years. But the collapse of legitimacy or popularity of these agendas will not be reversed. Meanwhile, the inability of the Republican Party to defend these policies any longer signals the ultimate divorce between the political and economic wings of neoliberalism: the conservative coalition that came into being as Keynesianism declined post-1968, and which got Ronald Reagan to power, no longer functions in its role of rationalising and de-politicising economic policy making.

If neoliberalism is the 'disenchantment of politics by economics', then economics is no longer performing its role in rationalising public life. Politics is being re-enchanted, by images of nationhood, of cultural tradition, of 'friends' against 'enemies', of race and religion. One of the many political miscalculations that led to Brexit was to under-estimate how many UK citizens would vote for the first time in their lives, enthralled by the sudden sovereign power that they had been granted in the polling booth, which was entirely unlike the ritual of representative democracy with a first-past-the-post voting system that renders most votes irrelevant. The intoxication of popular power and of demagoguery is being experienced in visceral ways for the first time since 1968, or possibly longer. Wendy Brown argues that neoliberalism is a 'political rationality' that was born in direct response to Fascism during the 1930s and '40s (Brown, 2015). While it would be an exaggeration to say that the end of neoliberalism represents the re-birth of Fascism, clearly there were a number of existential dimensions of 'the political' that the neoliberals were right to fear, and which we should now fear once more.

While there is plenty of evidence to suggest that 2016 is a historic turning point – indeed as I've argued here, possibly the second 'book-mark' in the crisis of neoliberalism – we need also to recognise how the seeds of this recent political rupture were sown over time. Indeed, we can learn a lot about policy paradigms from the way they go into decline, for they always contain, tolerate and even celebrate the very activities that later overwhelm or undermine them. Clearly, the 2008 financial crisis was triggered by activities in the banking sector that were not fundamentally different from those which had been viewed as laudable for the previous 20 years. Equally, as we witness the return of mercantilism, protectionism, nationalism and charismatic populism, we need to remember the extent to which neoliberalism accommodated some of this, up to a point.

The second major case study in this book, in addition to anti-trust policy, is of strategies for 'national competitiveness'. The executive branch of government has traditionally been viewed as a problem from the perspective of economic liberalism, seeing as powerful politicians will instinctively seek to privilege their own territories vis-à-vis others. This is the threat of mercantilism, which can spin into resolutely anti-liberal policies such as trade tariffs and the subsidisation of indigenous industries and 'national champions'. These forms of mercantilism may now be returning, however, the logic of neoliberalism was never quite as antipathetic to them as orthodox market liberals might have been. Instead, I suggest in Chapter 4, rather than simply seek to thwart or transcend nationalist politics, neoliberalism seizes and reimagines the nation as one competitive actor amongst many, in a global contest for 'competitiveness', as evaluated by business gurus such as Michael Porter and think tanks such as the World Economic Forum. To be sure, these gurus and think tanks have never been anything but hostile to protectionism; but nevertheless, they have encouraged a form of mild nationalism as the basis for strategic thinking in economic policy. As David Harvey has argued, 'the neoliberal state needs nationalism of a certain sort to survive': it draws on aspects of executive power and nationalist sentiment, in order to steer economic activity towards certain types of competitive strategies, culture and behaviours and away from others (Harvey, 2005: 85).

There is therefore a deep-lying tension within the politics of neoliberalism between a 'liberal' logic, which seeks to transcend geography, culture and political difference, and a more contingent, 'violent' logic that seeks to draw on the energies of nationhood and combat, in the hope of diverting them towards competitive, entrepreneurial production. These two logics are in conflict with each other, but the story I tell in this book is of how the latter gradually won out over the long history of neoliberal thought and policy making. Where the neoliberal intellectuals of the 1930s had a deep commitment to liberal ideals, which they believed the market could protect, the rise of the post-war Chicago School of economics and the co-option of neoliberal ideas by business lobbies and conservatives, meant that (what I term) the 'liberal spirit' was gradually lost. There is thus a continuity at work here, in the way that the crisis of neoliberalism has played out.

Written in 2012–13, the book suggests that neoliberalism has now entered a 'contingent' state, in which various failures of economic rationality are dealt with through incorporating an ever broader range of cultural and political resources. The rise of behavioural economics, for example, represents an attempt to preserve a form of market rationality in the face of crisis, by incorporating expertise provided by psychologists and neuroscientists. A form of 'neo-communitarianism' emerges, which takes seriously the role of relationships, environmental conditioning and empathy in the construction of independent, responsible subjects. This remains an economistic logic, inasmuch as it prepares people to live efficient, productive, competitive lives. But by bringing culture, community and contingency within the bounds of neoliberal rationality, one might see things like behavioural economics or 'social neuroscience' and so on as early symptoms of a genuinely post-liberal politics. Once governments (and publics) no longer view economics as the best test of optimal policies, then opportunities for post-liberal experimentation expand rapidly, with unpredictable and potentially frightening consequences. It was telling that, when the British Home Secretary, Amber Rudd, suggested in October 2016 that companies be compelled to publicly list their foreign workers, she defended this policy as a 'nudge'.

The Limits of Neoliberalism is a piece of interpretive sociology. It starts from the recognition that neoliberalism rests on claims to legitimacy, which it is possible to imagine as valid, even for critics of this system. Inspired by Luc Boltanski, the book assumes that political-economic systems typically need to offer certain limited forms of hope, excitement and fairness in order to survive, and cannot operate via domination and exploitation alone. For similar reasons, we might soon find that we miss some of the normative and political dimensions of neoliberalism, for example the internationalism that the EU was founded to promote and the cosmopolitanism that competitive markets sometimes inculcate. There may be *some* elements of neoliberalism that critics and activists need to grasp, refashion and defend, rather than to simply denounce: this book's Afterword offers some ideas of what this might mean. But if the book is to be read in a truly post-neoliberal world, I hope that in its interpretive aspirations, it helps to explain what was internally and normatively coherent about the political economy known as 'neoliberalism', but also why the system really had no account of its own preconditions or how to preserve them adequately. The attempt to reduce all of human life to economic calculation runs up against limits. A political rationality that fails to recognise politics as a distinctive sphere of human existence was always going to be dumbfounded, once that sphere took on its own extra-economic life. As Bob Dylan sang to Mr Jones, so one might now say to neoliberal intellectuals or technocrats: 'something is happening here, but you don't know what it is'.

1

THE DISENCHANTMENT OF POLITICS

Neoliberalism, sovereignty and economics

Friedrich Von Hayek believed that the intellectual, political and organizational forces of liberalism began a downward trajectory around 1870 (Hayek, 1944: 21). In place of the decentralized structure of the Victorian marketplace and British classical economics, came trends towards bureaucratization, management and the protection of the 'social' realm, all accompanied by a growing authority for German institutionalist and historicist ideas. By the 1940s this had reached the point of emergency. Having witnessed a financial crisis usher in Fascism, Keynesianism and then a world war, Hayek viewed the choices of political modernity in starkly binary terms:

> We have in effect undertaken to dispense with the forces which produced unforeseen results and to replace the impersonal and anonymous mechanism of the market by collective and "conscious" direction of all social forces to deliberately chosen goals. (1944: 21)

Reversing this trend would mean restoring the political authority of 'impersonal' and 'anonymous' mechanisms, and of 'individual' and 'unconscious' forces in public life, which lack any 'deliberately chosen goals'. When Hayek looked back to the high period of British liberalism, what he mourned was a society that had no explicitly collective or public purpose, and whose direction could not be predicted or determined. The central function of markets in this nostalgic vision was to coordinate social activity without intervention by political authorities or 'conscious' cooperation by actors themselves. And if there were other ways of coordinating individuals' unconscious goals, impersonally and anonymously, these might be equally welcome as markets. The virtue of markets, for Hayek, was their capacity to replace egalitarian and idealist concepts of the common good that he believed could lead to tyranny.

Hayek's thought is widely recognized to have played a key role in inspiring and co-ordinating the intellectual and political movement which came to be known as 'neoliberalism' (Mirowski & Plehwe, 2009; Stedman-Jones, 2012; Bergin, 2013). This movement achieved a number of significant political and policy victories from the late 1970s onwards, resulting in a roughly coherent paradigm that spread around the world over the subsequent thirty years. Its major crisis, if that is what it actually was, began in 2007, when it emerged that Western investment banks had drastically under-calculated the risks attached to the US housing market, the fall-out from which was a macro-economic stagnation more enduring than any since the 1880s. While the neoliberal policy era was punctuated by unusually frequent financial crises (Harvey, 2005), what was most significant about the 2007–09 banking crisis – in addition to its scale – was the fact that it originated in Wall Street, bringing vast fiscal and social costs to a nation that had played a key role in propagating neoliberal policies. But the fact that this policy paradigm appears largely intact, several years after the dawning of the financial crisis, is now an object of scholarly interest in its own right (Crouch, 2011; Engelen et al., 2011; Mirowski, 2013).

Running in parallel to this economic breakdown was a series of events that raised widespread moral concerns about the coherence of key public institutions and society more generally. Britain, for example, saw a succession of disturbances, apparently affected by forms of hedonistic self-interest: in 2009 Members of Parliament were discovered to be routinely lying about their expenses in order to inflate their pay; in 2011 journalists were discovered to be engaged in the criminal hacking of phones, possibly beknown to the police; in August 2011 disparate riots erupted across English cities, featuring seemingly hedonistic acts of destruction and the widespread looting of branded goods, with scarce collective or political grievance; and in 2012 it emerged that individuals working in major high street banks had conspired to alter the 'LIBOR' rate, which dictates the price at which banks lend to each other, and influences the rate at which banks will lend to customers, and questions were raised as to whether government officials had actively encouraged this. These unconnected events seem to suggest a normative and political crisis, whereby the very possibility of deliberate collective action is thrown into question. A form of *institutionalized anti-institutionalism* seemed to have become established. The routine nature of so much of this activity made it impossible to dismiss as mere 'corruption' or 'criminality'. Meanwhile, concerns about the effects of 'consumerism', inequality and loneliness upon health and mental health (which in turn bring major economic costs) have begun to raise elite concerns about the sustainability of the contemporary political-economic model (Davies, 2011a). 'Epidemics' of depression, anxiety, obesity and addictive behaviour register as an indictment on societies that have made calculated self-interest and competitiveness tacitly constitutional principles (Davies, 2012).

The inability to achieve a new political settlement or new economic paradigm is by some measures a testimony to the success of the neoliberal project. Hayek's complaint could now even be reversed: we have in effect undertaken to dispense with the forces which produced foreseen results and to replace the collective and 'conscious' direction of all social forces towards deliberately chosen goals by the impersonal and anonymous mechanism of the market (or market-like behaviour). Having consciously opened ourselves up to spontaneous and uncertain processes, we are now unable to escape from them again. The powerlessness of political or moral authorities to shape or direct society differently demonstrates how far the neoliberal critique of economic planning has permeated. Whether Hayek would have still trusted 'unconscious' social forces, when confronted with the libidinous, destructive rush of contemporary consumerism and financialization, is another question. The framing of neoliberal crises – including financial crises – in psychological and neurological terms (discussed in Chapter 5) can be seen partly as a last ditch effort to distinguish *which* 'unconscious' forces are to be trusted and which ones are not.

Defining neoliberalism

Neoliberalism is clearly not a unified doctrine to the extent that Keynesianism is. While Hayek is one of the obvious figureheads of the neoliberal 'thought collective' (Mirowski & Plehwe, 2009) his work is at odds with many other neoliberal forms of policy and governance. The origins of the neoliberal movement can be traced to the contributions of Hayek and Ludwig Von Mises to the 'socialist calculation debate' of the 1920s and 1930s (Mises, 1990; Hayek, 2009). The intellectual project of reinventing liberalism was scattered between London, New York, Chicago, Freiburg and Vienna, up until the 1970s (Peck, 2010). The application and adaptation of these ideas spread no less haphazardly, serving various masters as they went. But what, I suggest, is the common thread in all of this – and what makes the term 'neoliberalism' a necessary one – is an attempt to replace political judgement with economic evaluation, including, but not exclusively, the evaluations offered by markets. Of course, both political and economic logics are plural and heterogeneous. But the central defining characteristic of all neoliberal critique is its hostility to the ambiguity of political discourse, and a commitment to the explicitness and transparency of quantitative, economic indicators, of which the market price system is the model. Neoliberalism is the *pursuit of the disenchantment of politics by economics.*

The language of politics, unlike the language of economics, has a self-consciously performative dimension. It is used with a public in mind, and an awareness that the members and perspectives contained in that public are plural and uncertain. The praxis and aesthetics of discourse are acknowledged in what we consider to be 'political' situations. These include legal process, in which text and speech resonate in public settings, and seek to *do* something as much as represent something. This doesn't mean that economics as a discipline is not performative, requires no public or has no praxis. On the contrary, a great deal of recent scholarship has demonstrated that economics is often powerfully performative (Callon, 1998; Mitchell, 2002; MacKenzie, 2006; MacKenzie et al., 2007) and employs political rhetorics (McCloskey, 1985). Quantification and measurement have their own affective and aesthetic qualities (Porter, 1995), but the example of market price indicates to an economic sensibility that ambiguity and performativity can be beneficially minimized or constrained. From a neoliberal perspective, price provides a logical and phenomenological ideal of how human relations can be mediated without the need for rhetorical, ritualized or deliberately performative modes of communication. Indeed, price *may* even suggest that peaceful human interaction is feasible without speech at all. The reduction of complex and uncertain situations to a single number, as achieved by a market, appears as a route out of the hermeneutic pluralism and associated dangers of politics. Whether generated by markets or by economics, a price is an example of what Poovey terms the 'modern fact', a simple 'preinterpretive' or 'noninterpretive' representation of a state of affairs (Poovey, 1998).

If today politics and public institutions appear to have disintegrated into merely calculated and strategic behaviour, one response would be to view this as a side-effect of 'modernity' or 'advanced capitalism' or plain 'greed'. But perhaps a more fruitful one would be to examine this as a self-conscious project of rationalization on the part of intellectuals and policy elites. The disenchantment of politics by economics involves a deconstruction of the language of the 'common good' or the 'public', which is accused of a potentially dangerous mysticism. In the first instance, as manifest in the work of Mises and Hayek, this is an attack on socialism and the types of state expertise that enact it, but it is equally apparent in a critique of the liberal idea of justice, as in the work of Richard Posner and others. With some reservations, it is also manifest as a critique of executive political authority which is contrasted unfavourably with the economically rational authority of the manager. The targets of neoliberal critique are institutionally and ontologically various, which elicits different styles of critique. In each case, substantive claims about political authority and the public are critically dismantled and replaced with technical economic substitutes. These substitutes may need to be invented from scratch, hence the constructivist and often experimental dimensions of neoliberalism, a selection of which will be explored in detail in subsequent chapters.

As the more observant critics of neoliberalism have noted, it did not, therefore, seek or achieve a shrinking of the state, but a re-imagining and transformation of it (Peck, 2010; Mirowski, 2013). In the seventy years separating the golden age of Victorian liberalism and the intellectual birth of neoliberalism, the character of the state and of capitalism had changed markedly. The rise of American and German industrial capitalism had been achieved thanks to new economies of scale and organizational efficiencies associated with large corporations and hierarchical structures, including the birth of management (Chandler, 1977; Arrighi, 2009). Science and expertise were now formally channelled into business. Technical advancements in the fields of statistics and national accounts, followed by the birth of macroeconomics in the 1930s, meant that 'the economy' had appeared as a complex object of political management (Mitchell, 1998; Suzuki, 2003). And the on-going growth of a 'social' realm, measured and governed by sociology, social statistics, social policy and professions, meant that the American and European states of the 1930s had far more extensive capacities and responsibilities for audit and intervention than the British liberal state of the 1860s (Donzelot, 1991; Desrosieres, 1998).

The pragmatism of the neoliberal pioneers prevented them from proposing a romantic return to a halcyon age of classical liberalism, instead committing them to a reinvention of liberalism suitable for a more complex, regulated, Fordist capitalism. Hayek believed that 'the fundamental principle that in the ordering of our affairs we should make as much use as possible of the spontaneous forces of society, and resort as little as possible to coercion, is capable of an infinite variety of applications' (1944: 17). Victorian laissez-faire was only one empirical manifestation of the liberal *idea*. Restoring economic freedom would not be achieved simply through withdrawing the state from 'the market', but through active policy interventions, to remould institutions, state agencies and individuals, in ways that were compatible with a market ethos (however defined) and were amenable to economic measurement. The state is therefore a powerful instrument of neoliberalism, though also an object of its constant critique; this is one of many contradictions of neoliberalism, and one which has been raised to new heights since the banking crises of 2007–09.

Hayek's own interpretations of both liberalism and the political public sphere were highly idiosyncratic. Liberalism is associated primarily with the uncertainty of outcomes. Freedom, by this account, requires ignorance of the future, and the preservation of freedom requires a dogmatic agnosticism on the part of public institutions.[1] By contrast, political activity is interpreted as a project of determining outcomes and reducing uncertainty. At least in the modern era, politics is viewed as an instrument of planning and the pursuit of certainty, though this is concealed by the deceptive nature of political language. This pessimistic view directly inverts the (equally pessimistic) perspective of Hannah Arendt, for example, who saw liberal governance of the economic and 'social' realm as a poor, expertly managed substitute for the inherent uncertainty and vitality of political action (Arendt, 1958). Both positions celebrate, and arguably romanticize, uncertainty, but see its rationalist enemies in different places – the Hayekian neoliberal fears the politician, while the Arendtian political actor fears the economist.

Most analyses of neoliberalism have focused on its commitment to 'free' markets, deregulation and trade. I shan't discuss the validity of these portrayals here, although some have undoubtedly exaggerated the similarities between 'classical' nineteenth-century liberalism and twentieth-century neoliberalism. The topic addressed here is a different one – the character of neoliberal *authority*: on what basis does the neoliberal state demand the right to be obeyed, if not on substantive political grounds? To a large extent, it is on the basis of particular economic claims and rationalities, constructed and propagated by economic experts. The state does not necessarily (or at least, not always) cede power to markets, but comes to justify its decisions, policies and rules in terms that are commensurable with the logic of markets. Neoliberalism might therefore be defined as *the elevation of market-based principles and techniques of evaluation to the level of state-endorsed norms* (Davies, 2013: 37). The authority of the neoliberal state is heavily dependent on the authority of economics (and economists) to dictate legitimate courses of action. Understanding that authority – and its present crisis – requires us to look at economics, economic policy experts and advisors as critical components of state institutions.

Max Weber argued that modernity disenchants the world through positivist science and bureaucratization, subsuming the particular within the universal, reducing qualities to quantities. In Weber's analysis, modern science and bureaucracy lack any 'outward' or public sense of their own intrinsic value to humanity, making them cold, impersonal and anonymous forces – those same characteristics of markets that Hayek deemed valuable (Weber, 1991a, 1991b). Both the scientist and the bureaucrat run the risk of nihilism, but counter this through holding on to private, 'inward' vocations which condition and sustain their practices of empty rationalization. In this respect, 'disenchantment' can never be complete, as it depends for its progress on unspoken ethical commitments on the parts of those who propagate it. To some extent these ethical commitments must be shared, if rationalist depictions of the world are to hold together as a consensually shared reality. This becomes self-evident where the question of scientific and social scientific 'methodology' arises. In order for objective representations to be generated, certain presuppositions and practical procedures must be adhered to that have a normatively binding force. The stronger the claim to value neutrality, the more rigidly these presuppositions and procedures must bind, so, for example, neo-classical economists are bound by far tighter rules of conduct than social anthropologists. Paradoxically, therefore, value neutrality is an ethos in its own right (Du Gay, 2000), and efforts to eradicate *all* values are ultimately as dangerous to rationalization as they are to ethics, as Nietzsche recognized.

What is distinctive about neoliberalism as a mode of thought and government, however, is its acute desire to invert the relationship between technical rationality and substantive ethos. Where Weber saw modern rationalization and capitalism as dependent on certain ethical precepts, Hayek and his followers believed that various technical forms of quantitative evaluation could provide the conditions and guarantee of liberal values. This technocratic turn diverts the attention of the liberal away from moral or political philosophy and towards more mundane technical and pragmatic concerns. Prosaic market institutions and calculative devices become the harbinger of unspoken liberal commitments. This style of political reasoning survives, for example, in Thomas Friedman's 'golden arches theory of conflict prevention', which observes that no two nations possessing a McDonalds' outlet within their borders have ever gone to war with each other: the Kantian liberal ideal of 'perpetual peace' comes to be pursued via the mundane technologies of hamburger production (Friedman, 2000).

This offers one route to understanding the contradictory nature of neoliberal authority. Whether in the work of the Chicago School of economics, the 'New Public Management' and 'shareholder value' movements of the 1980s or the 'national competitiveness' evaluations that framed policy debates in the 1990s, neoliberalism has sought to eliminate normative judgement from public life to the greatest possible extent. In the tradition of Jeremy Bentham, intrinsic values are to be replaced by extrinsic valuation (i.e. measurement). Converting qualities into quantities removes ambiguity, emptying politics of its misunderstandings and ethical controversies, over which, Milton Friedman believed, 'men can ultimately only fight' (Friedman, 1953). Just as Bentham reduced all forms of experience to different quantities of utility, Friedman and his colleagues reduced all values, tastes, beliefs and political ideals to the status of 'preferences', eliminating the distinction between a moral stance and a desire. In this respect, they shared the anti-metaphysical ethos of behaviourism which permeated much of American social science over the first half of the twentieth century (Mills, 1998). Neoliberalism has been an acutely modernizing force, in the Weberian sense of rationalization.

But this form of rationalization, this disenchantment of politics by economics still rests on certain vocational commitments and intrinsic notions of the common good, albeit unarticulated ones. The rendering of economy, state and society as explicit and as quantified as possible is an implicitly moral agenda, which makes certain presuppositions about *how and what to value*. These presuppositions are, by their very nature, ambiguous and tacit – but without them, any technical evaluation or measurement becomes arbitrary and nihilistic. No methodology or measurement device can provide empirical evidence for its own validity. Neoliberalism is not only conflicted in its relationship to the state, but also in its relationship to its own prerequisite ethos: a wholly calculable, measurable world is only possible on the basis of particular non-calculable, immeasurable values or vocations. Hence, efforts to replace politics with economics, judgement with measurement, confront a limit beyond which they themselves collapse. One of the critical questions, on which neoliberalism stands or falls, is why *economics* should be a better analytical basis for government than other political or scientific forms of authority. Further questions follow, including *which tradition* of economics, and *which conventions* of calculation, are to be applied in different spheres of government. At a certain point, neoliberal discourse encounters moral questions which, at least in its more positivist manifestations, it is unable to understand or answer.

THE CRISIS AND CRITIQUE OF ECONOMIC REASON

Where should one stand when confronted by contemporary pathologies of capitalism or individualism? This is not only a political and ethical question, but also a methodological one. To adopt a sociological perspective on the crises of neoliberalism is to assume that the causes and meanings of these events are to be found in socio-economic structures, institutions, inequalities and power dynamics. To a greater or lesser extent, it involves looking *behind* economic and psychological explanations, in search of a deeper reality. It is this which grants sociology its critical thrust: the narratives that liberalism provides about itself, focused upon individual reason, are found to be deficient at best or deluded at worst. Similarly, to adopt the stance of critical theory involves challenging the separation of ethics from instrumental reason, by re-describing technical rationality in the language of exploitation, domination and unhappiness. This is a more explicitly political stance, which seeks to use critique to catalyse crisis, to render the sustained no longer sustainable. The normative dimension of empirical judgement is brought to the fore, which assumes a certain normative authority on the part of the theorist.

These theoretical perspectives necessarily rest on certain presuppositions that vary between the technical (e.g. how to measure inequality) and the philosophical (e.g. an ideal of egalitarian community). One might go further and say that they also rest on certain epistemological and political assumptions about the role and responsibility of theory in public life. As admirable as these might be, they have the effect (often intentionally) of obscuring the alternative presuppositions and assumptions that are taken by *other* actors, experts, theorists and critics. In a rush to explain or to criticize, there is a risk that interpretation gets lost. Along the way, forces of rationalization, economization and individualism come to appear systemic or determined, rather than politically and rhetorically performed. With respect to our present predicament, the continued survival of certain neoliberal doctrines and presuppositions suggests that these may not simply be 'false' or 'exploitative' depictions of reality, but have become normative rituals in their own right, through which actors make sense of and criticize the world around them. This is what Philip Mirowski has termed 'everyday neoliberalism' (Mirowski, 2013).

A world in which politics has been heavily disenchanted by economics (of various styles and traditions, as we shall see) requires its own mode of enquiry, which is alert to the fact that political logic no longer provides the structures of collective experience and action for many people. Sociologists should recognize that the decline of socialism robbed modernity of one of its major sources of large-scale organization (Eyal et al., 2003). As Slavoj Zizek argued in response to the English riots of 2011:

The fact that the rioters have no programme is therefore itself a fact to be inter-preted: it tells us a great deal about our ideological-political predicament and about the kind of society we inhabit, a society which celebrates choice but in which the only available alternative to enforced democratic consensus is a blind acting out. Opposition to the system can no longer articulate itself in the form of a realistic alternative, or even as a utopian project, but can only take the shape of a meaningless outburst. (Zizek, 2011a)

Individuals find themselves in a paradoxical condition of sharing their renun-ciation of any shared narrative, denying themselves the use of social reason. For sure, sociology or critical theory might provide them with such a narrative, and thus reintroduce a form of political discourse where it appears absent. On the other hand, if we are to seek to understand the present, the performative and critical power of neoliberal discourse needs to be taken seriously, as a basis on which crypto-political and collective action does nevertheless take place. As Bruno Latour argues, political narrative seeks to bring a new collective entity into being through its performance, and cannot therefore also seek to represent reality entirely accurately (Latour, 2003). By seeking to render public life 'fac-tual' and 'explicit', neoliberalism seeks to constrain not only the ambiguity but also the inventiveness of politics, for better or for worse. Yet it nevertheless provides routines, rituals, shared experiences, government and forms of collec-tive representation; collectivity cannot disintegrate altogether. The question is how politics remains possible at all, and in particular, how the state remains authoritative, once heavily disenchanted by economic rationality. Simply replac-ing one set of 'economic' facts with another set of 'sociological' ones will not grasp the unwieldy way in which political-economic action takes place, once governed or authorized by a neoliberal logic.

Critique or interpretation?

To address this, I adopt the approach that has been variously known as 'conven-tion theory', 'pragmatic sociology' and the sociology of 'critical capacity' (henceforth as 'convention theory'), as developed by a number of Parisian schol-ars led by Luc Boltanski since the early 1980s. The premise of convention theory is that, for the most part, individuals are obliged and able to *justify* their own actions, and to *criticize* those of other actors around them (Boltanski & Thévenot, 1999, 2000, 2006). The coherence and the critique of socio-economic life are not only the work of social scientists, scholars or critical theorists operating as *post hoc* or external observers, but also by individuals themselves acting in social and eco-nomic situations, whose interpretations and judgements should be taken seriously. These include experts acting in firms, statistical agencies, public policy settings and professional services, who employ techniques, arguments and rhetorics that are not dissimilar to those employed by university social scientists. The codification of social scientific techniques and disciplines occurs only latterly, after certain forms of knowledge, measurement and evaluation have already arisen in society, beyond the academy. As Eve Chiapello has shown, for example, the rise of an economic science in the eighteenth century built directly upon conventions of valuation (including the categories of profit and capital) which accounting had already established for practical purposes within economic life (Chiapello, 2009). The appearance of *professional* social science at the close of the nineteenth century occurred only *after* its problems, objects and measuring devices had already arisen as practical concerns of modern institutions and government (Wagner et al., 1991; Wagner, 2001). The practical and political requirements of expert socio-economic knowledge are both historically and analytically prior to its methodological codification and professionalization. Precisely because modern liberalism potentially generates excessive uncertainty, expert disciplines, statistical frameworks and models have been introduced to make society manageable and predictable. But the problem of uncertainty is prior to political and expert responses, and is never entirely eradicated.

By this account, institutions, populations and situations 'hold together' as coherent, objective and meaningful for those who inhabit them, because they share certain critical and cognitive apparatuses, which are recognized internally as legitimate. These apparatuses operate at various scales: to speak of 'population', 'the economy' or 'society' as coherent empirical objects requires certain standards of measurement to be scaled up to the national level. Shared evaluative techniques allow actors to speak meaningfully and factually about what is 'going on'. *Principles of equivalence* emerge and are enforced, through which different people can be referred to as the same (for instance because they have the same 'IQ' score) or as different, enabling different varieties of inequality to become visible, which may or may not be considered legitimate. Distributions of goods and opportunities are underpinned by conventions that stipulate who is owed what, who deserves reward, what is to be shared and with whom. Even apparently amoral or *immoral* forms of economic distribution or organization can only persist in any stable or remotely predictable form, if they have codes and tacitly acknowledge norms through which to evaluate procedures. The task of convention theory is to identify and illuminate the normative, technical and critical resources that are employed, in the production of these coherent – or incoherent – situations. This implies that any critical analysis of neoliberalism as a historical period, composed of specific political and economic institutions, must also draw on an interpretation and genealogy of neoliberal ways of thinking, measuring, evaluating, criticizing, judging and knowing. Convention theory invites us to combine ethnographies of actors and institutions with hermeneutic and historical excavations of intellectual paradigms and political philosophies.

Not all action can be interpreted in terms of adherence to norms, and nor should all economic distributions be assumed as internally justifiable. While the sense of justice and injustice can be seen as an innate human capacity, which can arise in any situation, there are other capacities – or what Boltanski terms 'competences' – that otherwise condition action and relations. Boltanski notes that relations of love and violence are non-critical, in the sense that individuals immersed in them lose any distance from a situation, and make no appeal to any broader norm beyond the situation or person at hand (Boltanski, 2012). In that sense, what love and violence hold in common is a refusal of all principles of equivalence; they refuse to see a particular person or situation as an example of a larger class, or to compare them to anything else. Alternatively, individuals may go to great lengths to avoid or delay critical scrutiny or justification. Entrepreneurs might be seen as an example of individuals who operate between or outside of existing conventions (Stark, 2009). Rapid transformations of capitalist structures mean that individuals can avoid being held to account (Boltanski & Chiapello, 2007: 42). But for social relations to be organized into reasonably persistent, reliable and peaceful institutions, at some point there must be a shared sense of normativity, a shared basis on which to distinguish between people and between things and make evaluations of their relative worth. A common framework of valuation is needed if complex economic practices are to proceed without constantly breaking down into argument and negotiation.

The development and application of convention theory have been discussed at length elsewhere (Wagner, 1994, 1999; Wilkinson, 1997; Biggart & Beamish, 2003; Blokker, 2011). Here I want only to identify two of its central characteristics, and to explore how these might contribute to a critical analysis of neoliberalism. In particular, how might convention theory advance our understanding of neoliberalism as a form of 'disenchantment of politics by economics'? How might it help interpret the politics of the apparently apolitical – even anti-political – events that characterize contemporary socio-economic crises?

Pragmatism against empiricism

The first way in which convention theory will aid us is in highlighting the limits and conditions of empiricism (or objectivity) in the social, economic and political spheres, and hence the limits and conditions of disenchantment. It does this by excavating the normative and institutional underpinnings of technical and positivist forms of social scientific knowledge, including of economics. This is partly achieved through genealogies of the social sciences and associated measures and tools, for instance showing how particular forms of knowledge are pragmatically related to particular political problems. The ideal of positivist social science, especially prevalent in neo-classical economics and behaviourist social science, is to produce forms of socio-economic knowledge that are entirely value neutral and therefore objective. The Chicago School placed a particular emphasis on this. Quantitative and statistical analyses of social and economic activity supposedly exclude value judgements, regarding what is 'ultimately' or intrinsically valuable, replacing these with technical, extrinsic valuations. A single measure of value is substituted for multiple *values*. Facts replace judgements. In this respect, the birth of political economy and statistics in the late eighteenth century brought about a split between social theory and political philosophy, in which the former served as an empirical reflection on the direction and government of modern societies, while the latter continued to pose normative questions regarding the good or just society.

Convention theory questions the completeness of this separation, by highlighting the dependence of objective, empirical socio-economic analysis on critical and normative presuppositions. In Weberian terms, it unearths the private, silent 'vocation' of the modern social scientist, and articulates and publicizes it. It challenges the notion that political philosophy can ever be fully excluded from social theory, or indeed from social situations themselves. Economics and sociology are both attempts to create forms of *political physics*, separate from the *political metaphysics* that gave birth to them. They seek to replace moral rules (which people might obey, so long as they understand and recognize them) with scientific rules (which people obey unwittingly, as the natural world does) (Boltanski & Thévenot, 2006: 28–31). But in doing so, they simply shift questions of normativity elsewhere, into spheres of expert procedure and methodology, while often ignoring the irredeemably normative constitution of socio-economic life. For reasons explored by Wittgenstein, what governs individual action can never be fully explicated, not even by the individual concerned. The 'right' and the 'wrong' action (whether articulated in a moral sense or not) is something that is commonly understood by actors in the situation concerned, but cannot be entirely proved by referring to any explicit rule. No amount of 'evidence' can confirm what one ought to do in a given situation. There is always already a partly agreed-upon presumption, that a rule has validity and binds in certain ways, before the rule is actually invoked. In this sense, its 'physical' manifestation and application have a 'metaphysical' context, where these terms are taken to refer to that which can and cannot be expressed as a fact. Both the error and the political utility of the socio-economic empiricist are to forget the 'metaphysics' of what they're doing and of the people they are studying.

When we speak of a rule or individual possessing 'authority' we make a type of metaphysical claim regarding something that we are unable to entirely articulate or prove. There are necessarily silent and invisible qualities to authority which can be alluded to with explicitly moral language (this rule or individual is 'good' or 'fair'), but part of the function of such language is to leave something out. There are reasons to obey the law, for example, such as the fear of penalties, but if the law is solely authorized by such reasons it would cease to be the law (cf. Hart, 1961). As Wittgenstein remarked, 'if a man could write a book on Ethics which really was a book on Ethics, this book, would, with an explosion, destroy all the other books in the world' (Wittgenstein, 1965). The metaphysical discourses of moral and political philosophy do not, from a pragmatist perspective, actually succeed in grasping that which they refer to (such as authority, fairness, virtue), but they make sense in spite of this. By contrast, the empiricist discourses of the social sciences (and associated forms of management, statistics and governance of populations) seek to operate purely at the level of the sensible, the physical and the measurable. But they must also offer reasons how and why to do so, which draw them into moral appeals, which extend beyond the limits of the empirical. If, for example, a traditional institution such as a profession is to be replaced by a particular type of empiricist audit of merit, this substitution can only succeed if that audit can serve as an institution, with all of the procedures, rules and unspoken norms of obedience that go with that.

Consider the case of orthodox economics. Considerable moral and metaphysical presuppositions are at work in the assumption that the value of goods can be established via monetary exchange. Certain contingent *critical* presumptions structure the *technical* methods for evaluating efficiency in the language of price. Moral *values* contribute to any definition of economic *value* – which, taken as a unity, can be described as an 'order of worth'. Contrary to the positivist notion that economics has no *a priori* notion of the collective or the common good, Boltanski and Thévenot show that it rests on a particular philosophical anthropology, regarding the common humanity of individuals operating in the marketplace, recognizing one another as autonomous selves, separate from their property (Boltanski & Thévenot, 2006: 43–61). In the first instance, justifications for liberal markets must draw on moral claims about the nature of the common good, which must be more than merely utilitarian or calculative

(Hirschman, 1977; Fourcade & Healey, 2007). This must include the capacity to recognize and sympathize with the individual with whom one is exchanging goods, and respect their capacity to express preferences. Empirical techniques suited to the governance, measurement and audit of the market sphere emerged later, but remained implicitly indebted to a particular moral worldview. Markets, and subsequently the discipline of economics, appear to bring about a purely objective, neutral representation of value, both of humans (in the labour market) and of things. Yet this objective assessment only 'holds together' on the basis that certain moral, metaphysical assumptions about the nature of individuals have already been adopted. The normative substrate of empirical representations can be teased out by noting how technical terms such as 'price' are descended from moral terms such as 'price' and 'praise' (Beckert, 2011; Stark, 2011). Actors have to suspend various alternative possible interpretations, and ignore various discrepant events, in order to affirm to each other that they are in a market situation, to be analysed using market-based rhetoric and tools. It is their commonly understood context that makes certain types of socio-economic fact possible, and not vice versa.

From a convention-based perspective, what remains in constant need of explanation is how liberal modern societies are as coherent and predictable as they are. Once individuals are recognized as possessing their own powers of (more or less) autonomous critical judgement, against an uncertain ontological backdrop, the remarkable thing is not that crises or paradigm shifts occur periodically, but that they don't occur the whole time. At the root of 'normal' socio-economic order is the fact that individual actors are able to reach sustainable *agreements*, which they do so by producing various forms of justification for actions, including the provision of empirical evidence. The distinction between normative critique and empirical technique is a rhetorical rather than an ontological one. Both moral and empirical claims regarding the 'worth' of humans and things depend on being *tested*, if they are to win agreement from others. A law court and an accounting audit both have similar formal properties, even though only one of them is explicit about its concern with 'justice'. It is easier and quicker to reach agreement on the 'right' way to act by pointing to numbers, statistics and evidence than by appealing to 'ultimate' moral principles alone, which are less amenable to testing. Empirical claims are more persuasive, but their authority partly resides in their capacity to hide their metaphysical underpinnings. The positivist social sciences, along with various forms of 'governmentality' and statistics, seek to replace critique with technique, judgement with measurement, but they are constantly parasitical on higher order claims about *what* ought to be measured, and *how* it is legitimate to represent this objectively.

Pragmatism in pursuit of pluralism

Following on from this is a second crucial feature of convention theory. This is the recognition that there are always multiple and incommensurable moral spheres available to actors seeking to justify their actions and to criticize those of others. There are multiple 'ultimate' moral principles that can be appealed to, and no *truly* ultimate perspective from which to ascertain the validity of any single one of these, or from which to arbitrate when rival moral principles come into conflict with each other. Boltanski and Thévenot identify six different moral 'orders of worth', which they associate with respective political philosophies regarding the 'common good' of humanity. The very fact that there is more than one variety of political philosophy demonstrates an existential political problem of pluralism that political philosophy itself cannot solve, though can at least acknowledge (e.g. Walzer, 1983). The practice and experience of politics, unlike that of political philosophy, are of navigating between multiple accounts of the common good, striking compromises, reaching agreements, in spite of the inevitable disagreements regarding the worth of decisions, actions and things.

If there are multiple and incommensurable forms of 'political metaphysics', then there are also multiple and incommensurable forms of 'political physics'. Methodological disputes between economics and sociology, for example, cannot be resolved by appealing to 'higher' normative or empirical arguments: the two disciplines operate side by side, in parallel technical and critical spheres of evaluation. They possess different principles of equivalence, different presuppositions about what people hold in common, and therefore how they can justly be differentiated. The most that can be hoped for is some form of compromise and pragmatic translation between the two. When an economist defends a policy or activity in terms of its 'efficiency', or a sociologist explains an event in terms of 'class stratification', these are manifestations of rival expert conventions, which lack any established techniques of translation from one to the other. Individuals may be capable of mediating between the two – a rhetorical skill that Boltanski and Thévenot term 'prudence'– or they may be able to inhabit multiple critical and technical spheres simultaneously, facilitating what David Stark terms 'heterarchy' (Stark, 2009). But they cannot adopt a view from the 'outside' which will inform them of the best basis on which to evaluate a situation, either normatively or empirically. As Weber observed 'we are placed in various life orders, each of which is subject to different laws', and any hope for discovering a final, once and for all justification beyond these, will end in disappointment (quoted in Du Gay, 2000: 74).

The question of the *objective reality* of socio-economic events can be answered with scientific data, until a new situation of fundamental uncertainty arises. Uncertainty, as the first generation Chicago economist Frank Knight described it, is an existential fact of social and economic life, which underlies all apparently scientific calculations of the future (Knight, 1957). It can be hidden or dealt with in a number of ways, one of which is to represent it in terms of mathematical probability or risk. Another would be to allow markets to convert the uncertainty into a price.[2] The attempt to convert uncertainty into risk, which Knight viewed as the central purpose of economics, can succeed until a situation arises which is of sufficient novelty or ambiguity that established cognitive and calculative techniques are ill-adapted to measure or model it. Calculations of risk become defeated by uncertainty. Pragmatic sociologists focus on uncertain situations, where quantified objective reality breaks down, to examine the disputes that then break out over how and what to measure. It is precisely under conditions of uncertainty when the multiplicity and incommensurability of rival normative-empirical worldviews become visible, and when actors themselves become aware of the constructed nature of socio-economic reality (Boltanski, 2011). Economic crises exhibit precisely this condition, enabling multiple definitions and measures of socio-economic reality to emerge simultaneously, offering rival accounts of what is going on. Crises are only fully resolved once a single cognitive apparatus and narrative has become sufficiently dominant, as to provide a shared reality which various political, business and expert actors can all agree on and inhabit.

Via an examination of moral incommensurability, convention theorists hope to explain technical and empirical incommensurability as a basic problem of all institutions and organizations: they contain multiple ways of representing themselves, testing their performance and demonstrating their worth. Particular metaphysical accounts of the common good produce their own techniques for the testing and demonstration of value. Where a group of actors accepts both the metaphysical account and the associated techniques, then a shared socio-economic reality becomes possible. If, for example, Gross Domestic Product (GDP) is recognized as *both* a technically authoritative measure of economic activity, *and* a morally authoritative indicator of economic progress, then it successfully produces a reality which politicians, policy makers and public actors all inhabit and can be judged by (Perlman, 1987; Desrosieres, 1998). In the language of convention theorists, the situation 'holds together' for all concerned, even if dissenting voices challenge its technical and/or normative legitimacy. But incommensurable values and techniques of valuation may arise, to challenge the authority of such an indicator – for example, highlighting the fact that GDP fails to measure unpaid work by women in the home or the costs of environmental degradation. With multiple notions of the common good in play, and multiple techniques by which to assess it, the macro-economic reality might equally 'fall apart', and the positivist and technocratic ideal, of purely 'objective' socio-economic public discourse, no longer holds.

In these ways, convention theory rearranges the relationship between critique and its socio-economic object to recognize that modern society is replete with its own internal forms of justification, critique and evaluation, which inevitably come into conflict with each other. The semblance of coherence or incoherence of institutions is really an effect of agreements and disagreements that are constantly being renegotiated by the actors who inhabit them. One way in which capitalism reproduces itself is by maintaining its own internal varieties of anti-capitalism, thereby ensuring that the justification for capitalist activity is never reducible to its purely economic or monetary rationales (Boltanski & Chiapello, 2007). Confronted with contemporary neoliberal crises, apparently rooted in economistic, or even nihilistic worldviews, the task for the convention theorist is not simply to impose critique or sociological rationalization from without, but to interpret critical events (crises) via the critical capacities (critique) of the actors involved. Even anti-political events possess a residue of idealism, some normative account of justice and of political authority, which requires hermeneutic excavation.

One conclusion that *might* nevertheless be drawn, on the basis of such a pragmatist enquiry, is that neoliberalism's modes of evaluation and consensus-formation have ceased to perform adequately. Neoliberalism's paradoxical antipathy towards normative and political discourse means, inevitably, that it will struggle to maintain normative-political order, sooner or later. Problems particularly arise when the methodological presuppositions of policy-making elites (for instance, viewing crime in terms of cost-benefit analysis) become interpretive apparatuses that are available to non-expert actors 'in the wild' (such that the criminal *also* comes to view crime in cost-benefit terms). To recognize that actors possess justifications and critical capacities, even when they act destructively and egotistically, is not necessarily to assume that their arguments are accepted (or acceptable). If neoliberalism is now in crisis, which it may or may not be, a pragmatist perspective would highlight the ways in which chronic uncertainty has undermined the coherence and objectivity of its justifications. The technical and normative presuppositions of neoliberalism (which we shall investigate in due course) arguably no longer provide the basis of workable consensus. This may be partly because its own protagonists have failed to understand the normative, and therefore partly tacit and non-empirical, nature of the rules which it applies and the authority claims it seeks to make. To put that another way, perhaps policy makers and experts don't quite understand what they're doing.

But before we can consider that proposition further, we need to return to the institution which sits at the heart of neoliberal contradictions and its crises of authority, namely the state. How can convention theory be extended into governmental and sovereign domains? What changes when critical and technical evaluations are backed up by sovereign power and not simply by methodological authority?

CONVENTIONS OF SOVEREIGN ECONOMIZATION

The achievement of nineteenth-century liberalism was to produce a sense of economic activity as separate from and external to social or political activity (Polanyi, 1957). The 'social' realm arose as a set of identifiable policy problems or 'externalities', which were not fully calculated by market exchange, but nevertheless side-effects of it. The split between neo-classical economics and sociology, echoed in the concept of market 'externalities' that belongs to welfare economics, was a formalization of the interpretive and cognitive apparatuses that had emerged to deal with these parallel worlds of 'economy' and 'society' (Pigou, 1912). Meanwhile, the liberal state also sat outside of these two domains, with the effect of being separate and autonomous. Within the liberal imaginary, the science of economics is a mode of evaluation and measurement which belongs properly to the 'economic' realm, typically identified with market exchange.

Economic imperialism

A defining trait of neoliberalism is that it abandons this liberal conceit of separate economic, social and political spheres, evaluating all three according to a single economic logic. For Hayek, there was no 'separate economic motive'; enterprising, calculated, strategizing activity did not only begin when the individual entered the market (Hayek, 1944: 93). Despite wide variations in how agency is conceived, this basic assumption that all action is principally economic action is common to all neoliberal styles of theory (e.g. Friedman, 1962;

Becker, 1976). This effects a collapse of the separate logics of market, society and state, using the language and techniques of the former to enact a blanket economic audit of all three. In Foucault's words, neoliberalism:

> ... is not a question of freeing an empty space, but of taking the formal principles of a market economy and referring and relating them to, of projecting them on to a general art of government. (Foucault, 2008: 131)

Even when individuals or organizations are not acting in a market, the project of neoliberalism is to judge them and measure them *as if* they were acting in a market. If liberalism treated the 'economic', the 'social' and the 'political' as separate spheres, with their own discrete modes of evaluation, neoliberalism evaluates all institutions and spheres of conduct according to a single economic concept of value. In doing so, it has effectively collapsed the boundary around a distinct market sphere, and in doing so, abandons the notion of the social or public 'externality' that exists beyond the limits of commercial exchange (Coase, 1960).

Within the academy neoliberalism has been characterized by aggressive economic 'imperialism', whereby techniques that initially arose for the analysis of markets and commercial activity were applied to the study of social, domestic and political activity (Fine & Milonakis, 2009). Gary Becker's pioneering work since the 1950s on 'human capital' and the economics of crime, addiction and the family presaged a later popularization of such approaches, as manifest in the popular economics book *Freakonomics*. A pragmatic perspective would recognize economics as a set of techniques and normative presuppositions, that first emerged alongside liberal markets for practical purposes, and was only latterly codified and professionalized following the emergence of neo-classical economics in the 1870s. But once codified, and seemingly emptied of its normative content, these same techniques can travel beyond their initial sphere of application, namely the market, and evaluate *all* activity, as if it were oriented around price and exchange. Viewing the world 'like' a market, and governing it 'as if' it were a market, are hallmarks of neoliberalism.

Contrary to the view that neoliberalism represents a form of 'market fundamentalism' or simply a revival of nineteenth-century laissez-faire, in fact the key institution of neoliberalism is not a market as such, but particular market-based (or market-derived) forms of economization, calculation, measurement and valuation. A particular vision or nostalgic imagination of a free market may provide some political or normative orientation to neoliberal thinkers, but it is the scientific techniques, devices and measures that are more often used to drive market-like behaviour and performance evaluation further into a society and politics that are more distinctively *neoliberal*. Neo-classical economics, which rests on the assumption that value resides in the optimal satisfaction of stable and exogeneous individual preferences, has been one of the foremost techniques via which economization has proceeded, especially thanks to the work of the Chicago school of economics. Various other techniques of social and political audit, quantification and risk management have followed in its wake. Marion Fourcade has explored how even nature has become valued 'as if' it were a private, exchangeable good, using techniques such as 'willingness to pay' surveys (Fourcade, 2011). The British Treasury has codified various techniques for calculating the hypothetical price of non-market goods, published them in a single document, and now insists that all departments of government justify their spending decisions using these measurement devices (HMT, 2013). These produce what Caliskan terms 'prosthetic prices', which, in contrast to those generated at the moment of market exchange, are constructed through models and other calculative devices, as strategies to dictate how worth is constructed (Caliskan, 2010). In all cases, neoliberalism is typically less concerned with expanding markets per se, than in expanding the reach of *market-based principles and techniques of evaluation*.

Institutions which claim 'authority' or 'legitimacy', without any relationship to markets, calculation or individual choice, become the most crucial object of economic critique, for it is these whose rationale is least visible or explicit. Trade unions, guilds, cultural critics, families, artists, democratic procedures, law, traditions and professions all make claims to authority and justification, by appealing to tacit and/or incalculable notions of what counts as justice or the common good. They are, in a sense, 'enchanted' by virtue of their implicit appeal to particular varieties of political metaphysics, which exceeds or refuses measurement. They typically abstain from offering factual, quantitative justifications for their existence and activities, and employ language in ways that are self-consciously performative rather than positive. Neoliberal critique cannot simply abolish all of these institutions, or replace all of them with markets, but the targeted use of economics can seek to replace normative, critical evaluation with economic, technical evaluation. Economization represents a replacement of multiple varieties of 'political metaphysics' with a single economistic variety of 'political physics'. Incommensurable values and visions of 'the public', 'social justice', 'fairness' and 'right' are all calculated and evaluated, in terms of the quantitative language of efficiency, price and preference. Any source of intrinsic authority is emptied out, and replaced with extrinsic evaluation, yet this necessarily bestows intrinsic authority upon the economic techniques via which that evaluation is carried out.

The problem of sovereignty

Amongst all of this, neoliberalism's greatest dilemma concerns political *sovereignty*, in the sense of an *ultimate* source of political power or authority. Sovereignty represents a particular form of 'political metaphysics', but one which makes claims about the 'final' source of political power, rather than the 'final' measure of the common good. It is in the nature of sovereignty that its full physical potential is never quite revealed, which is how it succeeds in striking fear and establishing order. As in the classic Hobbesian definition, the sovereignty of the modern state exists as a form of invisible potentiality, which enables individuals in a free society to trust one another, seeing as each believes that this potentiality is real and capable of enforcing order. A state which revealed its full capacity for violence would have become merely physical (and thereby finite and measurable), and lost the sense of transcendence that gave it an aura of limitless power.

Sovereignty is metaphysical in the sense that it works through being largely withheld, and is exercised partly to provide proof that it exists. So long as everyone continues to believe in a source of sovereignty, then no further tests or visibility are required. Sovereignty can be performed, but it cannot be empirically proven or tested. A sovereign relies on particular rituals, texts, objects and bodies, which are presumed to mediate between the visible world of finite objects, and these unseen reserves of power. The clothing of sovereign actors or the words they recite in a certain order are a constant reminder of the state's unseen, unspoken capacity to enact violence, in excess of anything that can be calculated or rationalized. This isn't to say that different *varieties* of sovereignty can't also make claims about the common good. The notion of 'popular sovereignty' assumes that the ultimate source of power lies outside of the state in the populace, while 'legal sovereignty' depends on a tacit understanding that the law *should* be applied to everyone in the same way. These metaphysical entities get entangled with the potentiality of violence, to produce the sovereign political symbols and offices which sit at the heart of the modern state. In all cases, sovereignty depends on there being more to political institutions than meets the eye in terms of physical force. Political strategies which seek to render state and society entirely visible also, therefore, seek to empty them of sovereign authority.

As Foucault highlights, the typical neoliberal stance towards any claim to sovereign authority is to ridicule it. In a close parallel to the positivist critique of metaphysics, 'the economic critique the neoliberals try to apply to governmental policy is also a filtering of every action by the public authorities in terms of contradiction, lack of consistency and nonsense' (Foucault, 2008: 247). If sovereignty is to exist at all, then it cannot by definition be rendered calculable or measurable: it exceeds the limits of mere utilitarian policy. To be sure, Foucault himself was clear that immanent practices of expert, utilitarian governmentality must co-exist with sovereign institutions, such as law or parliament, rather than displace them.[3] Sovereignty and governmentality exist in parallel planes of political ontology, one exceeding any empirical manifestation of power, the other rooted entirely in tangible practices of measurement, construction and discipline. But the political riddle of neoliberalism has been that it seeks to criticize and reinvent sovereign bodies, using positivist and evaluative techniques that necessarily misrepresent what makes those bodies sovereign in the first place. It makes the modern state an *object* of economic rationalization, and not only an agent.

At the same time, as a practical political project, neoliberalism has been heavily dependent on sovereign institutions in order to carry out its reinvention of liberalism and transformation of society. The necessarily excessive, incalculable nature of sovereignty makes it an impossible object of complete economization, and for this reason it is an object that neoliberals have been drawn to like moths to a flame, as it represents constantly unfinished business. Neoliberalism seeks to place sovereignty on economically rational foundations, but then becomes entangled in questions regarding the authority – ultimately the sovereignty – of economic methodology as a basis for political critique, decision making and rule. The discourse and techniques of economics are not self-justifying: no formal rule can also indicate how, or whether, it should be obeyed. As a result, positivist techniques of rationalization will depend on silent, unseen sources of obligation, be they tacitly understood norms of cooperation or tacitly understood sources of political power.

Spheres of economization

The insight of convention theory, that 'political physics' is always derivative of 'political metaphysics', becomes a powerful basis on which to understand the limits, failures, varieties and crises of this sovereign economization. Positivist economic techniques, which are used with abandon across social, economic and political realms, must nevertheless be accompanied by some intrinsic justification for their use. Where the numerical, formal representations of economics lack some tacit, unspoken moral authority, they lose the capacity to produce a shared socio-economic world, recognized by multiple actors as 'real'. Where they are not tacitly backed up by sovereignty, they lack the power and legitimacy that are necessary to govern populations and economies. But seeing as how neoliberalism specifically seeks to rationalize, quantify and de-mystify sources of sovereign authority, such as law, executive power and democratic ritual, it inadvertently undermines its own capacity to govern with any form of metaphysical authority. The numbers and calculations it produces, by way of an alternative to notions of 'justice', 'common good' and 'public interest', potentially come to appear arbitrary and meaningless, in the absence of some higher claim regarding their political legitimacy. In this respect, in its entanglements with sovereignty, neoliberalism desperately saws at the branch it sits on. Exactly as Jamie Peck argues, 'neoliberalism's curse has been that it can live neither with, nor without, the state' (Peck, 2008: 39).

And yet neoliberalism *has* succeeded in constructing and sustaining forms of political authority, including legitimate forms of state sovereignty. It *has*, to some extent, found ways of coping with its own contradictions, for otherwise it would be incapable of governing as coherently as it does (or has done). Its market-based principles and techniques of evaluation do, in practice, succeed in being wedded to the state, and employed as a basis for authoritative political action. As will be explored in later chapters, this is only possible because economic techniques themselves become imbued with a quasi-sovereign form of authority – that is, they become ritualized and rhetorically powerful. They come to provide the procedures, constitutional frameworks and aesthetic flourishes which underpin modern political authority. Like the revolutionary pigs in George Orwell's *Animal Farm*, who eventually became indistinguishable from their former masters, economics enters the political realm with an ethic of cold, positivist rationalism, but gradually takes on the qualities of the 'non-sensical' sovereign powers that it was tasked with displacing. When economics is used as a substitute for law, eventually it becomes law-like. If economics is to provide a substitute for executive decision, it must somehow acquire the same form of charismatic authority as the decision maker. The financial crisis has rendered this fusion of sovereignty and economics far more explicit, as national states have had to draw on exceptional political resources in order to reinforce an otherwise collapsing market logic (Davies, 2013). The ontology of neoliberal power is therefore riven with a fundamental ambiguity (or even aporia), whereby it hovers between the measurable and the immeasurable, the empirical and the transcendent. Positivism becomes imbued with metaphysics, so as to maintain its epistemological and political authority, without ceasing to be positivist.

What we witness in the neoliberal disenchantment of politics by economics is therefore a series of movements, which can be described in the following sequence. Firstly, a set of economic techniques for measurement and evaluation arises in and around markets. These techniques are dependent on and derivative of various normative presuppositions about intrinsic value, which historically contributed to the justification and spread of free markets. Secondly, these techniques for measurement and evaluation became codified as the basis of a professional scientific discipline, from the 1870s onwards, following the birth of neo-classical economics. From this point forward, it was no longer inevitable that economics had any necessary relationship to economic institutions, although it remains implicitly derivative of a certain market-based moral philosophy. It became reinvented as the study of rational choice, which in its more behaviourist twentieth-century manifestation, was purely focused upon observable phenomena to be modelled mathematically.

Thirdly, these techniques became applied to evaluate and criticize the state (and various other social and political institutions) from the 1950s onwards. Debunking claims regarding the 'fairness' of law or the 'public ethos' of bureaucracy, and offering quantitative analyses in their place, was the major achievement of neoliberal critics during the Keynesian era. And fourthly, as these techniques infiltrated sovereign, political institutions from the 1970s onwards, they began to acquire forms of political legitimacy that they themselves are unable to explain. Under 'actually existing' neoliberalism, techniques of economic rationalization rarely colonize or invade the political, public and sovereign realms, as the metaphor of 'economic imperialism' would have it, without some justification of their own. Disenchantment is never quite as successful as that. Instead, they adapt to the particular rhetorical, normative and pragmatic purposes of the actors who use them. They borrow elements of the modern authority, which they are outwardly hostile to. The 'political physics' of economics adapts to co-exist with the 'political metaphysics' of modern political authority, and the normative presuppositions of the policy makers, lawyers, politicians and public actors who are the target of neoliberal rationalization.

It follows from this that the economic rationalization of politics and the state is a necessarily heterogeneous, multi-faceted project. Neoliberal economization encounters political and sovereign institutions shaped partly by a liberal logic of separation. Separation of powers, the cornerstone of liberal constitutionalism, leaves a hybrid sovereign political legacy that cannot simply be re-integrated via a blanket economic audit. The task of extending economics into political and sovereign realms is obstructed by the fact that there are multiple and incommensurable notions of authority at work in modern polities. Conventions of economization must adapt to their specific tasks and objects, meaning that they too develop in incommensurable ways. Viewed pragmatically, the economic 'imperialism' of neoliberalism comes to appear far less homogeneous and all-consuming than its critics might fear. Different political and sovereign objects require different conventions of evaluation in order to be rendered measurable and economically calculable. The judiciary represents a different challenge for neoliberalism than the executive, and the legislature represents a different challenge again. Arguably, neoliberalism overcomes the separation of sovereign powers by asserting the 'ultimate' (extra-juridical, undemocratic) authority of executive decision: this Schmittian proposition is explored in later chapters. The epistemological task is to eradicate 'separate' political and social realms, external to economic analysis, while the tools are a set of techniques and principles that have (in the past) been associated with the market sphere. But beyond that, there is ample scope for adaptation, flexibility and innovation. New techniques can be invented, and new interpretations of 'market' principles can be offered. Neoliberal appeals to 'the market' have often been used to defend monopolistic corporations; this is a flexible rhetorical project. The interplay of state, economic expertise and normative justifications is a fluid and contingent one. There is no single, ultimate doctrine of economic rationality which all public, political or sovereign actions can be measured against, although economic experts will speak and act as if their doctrine is 'neutral' and 'objective'.

Thanks to the plurality of sovereign domains and the plurality of conventions of economization, neoliberalism confronts the problem of incommensurability. There is more than one way of calculating the most 'efficient', 'competitive' or 'welfare-maximizing' policy. Different forms of political authority condition how different forms of economic calculation proceed, contributing to different normative stances towards the problem of economic uncertainty: some of these will be explored in later chapters. Economic technocracy encounters its limits, when rival varieties of measurement and calculation clash with one another. These draw their authority from different political sources, as they employ economics to provide different types of legitimacy. To do so, they assume different implicit accounts of economic agency, deriving from different implicit accounts of how 'free' markets ought, in principle, to work. The *realpolitik* of the neoliberal state means that economic calculations, moral justifications and political imperatives are constantly impacting upon one another. The image of a homogeneously economized political or public realm therefore remains an illusion, though one which serves various political interests. Following its disenchantment by economics and mantras of 'transparency' and 'evidence', politics mutates into something less visible.

STUDYING THE NEOLIBERAL EXPERT

The neoliberal state is an aggressively utilitarian state, in the sense that it seeks to make all political, legal and public action subject to quantitative empirical evaluation. Many Chicago law and economics scholars (the topic of Chapter 3) acknowledge their debt to Bentham, who they view as the pioneer of extending economic critique into the state (Kitch, 1983). Once rendered economically rational, the state is no threat to neoliberals, but instead their most important weapon. But the question then surely arises: how is this different from the rationalized, bureaucratic, welfare state? To what extent does this (heterogeneously) economized sovereign state defend the form of liberty (i.e. uncertainty) demanded by Hayek and his contemporaries? What is to prevent these expert, economized public institutions from themselves replacing 'the impersonal and anonymous mechanism of the market by collective and conscious direction of all social forces to deliberately chosen goals', just as the socialist planner had? The promotion of instrumental rationality, as a defence against political romanticism and/or socialism, is a concern that places many neoliberals close to Weber in their sociological orientation (Gamble, 1996). But to argue that neoliberalism merely seeks greater means-ends rationality in government is to miss the precise modes of authority that it seeks.

The planner is the first and primary enemy of neoliberal political thought (Hayek, 1944, 1945; Friedman, 1962). Producing a basis for modern, expert political authority *without* the potential to justify centralized economic planning was an over-arching goal of Hayek's intellectual career, and shaped the project of the Chicago economists who followed him (even while they departed from him in important epistemological and methodological ways). The spectre of the planner – imposing a single set of values upon the collective – haunts neoliberal thought and policy practice as the enemy of freedom. And yet under 'actually existing' neoliberalism, one could point to a great deal of evidence that Benthamite utilitarianism has indeed led to extended governmental interventions, and efforts to intervene in private choices: this was undoubtedly the experience of many public sector workers, professions and publicly-funded academics from the 1980s onwards. Hayekians might argue that the experience of 'applied' neoliberalism owed very little to Hayek's critique of centralised expertise, but neoliberalism is not only a particular form of bureaucratization, and not only distinguished by the fact that it uses economics (and other techniques associated with the market sphere) with which to carry out its evaluations and audits. Its authority claims, what knits its disparate adherents together, and the basis of its avowed liberalism, also derive from a particular value that is present in markets, but can be pushed into all other corners of society: competition.

The great appeal of market competition, especially for Austrian neoliberals, was that its outcome was unpredictable (Hayek,1963, 2002). The sense that it might, more importantly, be economically efficient was only taken up subsequently by the Chicago School (Bork, 1978). And yet as the world of sport testifies, vibrant competitions still create a need for experts and authorities, to create the rules, arenas, events, league tables and prizes for those who enter them, and to train, motivate, discipline and punish competitors. Once we are speaking of these deliberately constructed competitions, and not some existential or biological idea of emergent competition, we get a clearer view of the strange forms of authority which neoliberalism has generated and depended upon. We see new breeds of expert – coach, regulator, risk manager, strategist, guru – offering toolkits and advice on how to navigate and act upon a constantly changing and unpredictable environment. These technocrats do not fit tidily into categories of 'science' or 'politics', as they are neither 'objectively' disengaged like the scientist, nor goal-oriented like the politician. They are examples of what Mirowski has termed neoliberalism's 'anti-intellectual intellectuals': experts who declare that stable consensus is impossible, but nevertheless assert their capacity to rule over the unstable dissensus that results. What they offer are evaluative techniques through which to quantify different options, rank different candidates, give scores to different agencies. In a world organized around the pursuit of inequality, that is, by an ethic of competitiveness, these experts are able to represent the world in numerical hierarchies of relative worth. It is not just cold instrumental reason that underpins the authority of economics in the neoliberal state, but also its capacity to quantify, distinguish, measure and rank, so as to construct and help navigate a world of constant, overlapping competitions. The pragmatic utility of economic methodologies is to provide common *measures and tests* against which differences in value can be established. People do not 'naturally' appear as unequal (nor should we assume they 'naturally' appear equal). The very question of their sameness and their difference is one that only arises thanks to certain moral and technical claims, offered by various actors with varying levels of authority and expertise. The expert on which neoliberalism is most dependent is the one who is able to evaluate and score competitors, without bringing about some excessively peaceful resolution to the contest.

Experts of this nature have a paradoxical form of authority that is itself unstable. These experts produce a vision of society in which all differences are represented as comparative inequalities. But this also means that *inequalities in power* are also merely empirical and quantitative, meaning that they cannot possess any legitimacy. Those offering orders – bureaucrat, politician, manager – are to be obeyed simply because of asymmetries in empirical, physical power, not because of the reasons that might be given for obedience. In the build up to the financial crisis of 2007 onwards, it was commonly remarked that one problem was that financial regulators and credit raters could not compete with the vast salaries paid by the banks they were tasked with evaluating. This is the endgame of neoliberalism: normative authority collapses into empirical inequalities in economic power, and then the system itself becomes untenable, save for where new reserves of power can be found through which to enforce it.

Outline and approach of the book

The interpretive turn away from 'critical sociology' to the 'sociology of critique' invites the question of what is *added* to the critical and evaluative accounts provided by the actors being studied. Why read a pragmatist interpretation of neoliberal theory, and not simply read the neoliberal theory itself? Why perform social science at all, if not to impose a different yardstick of measurement or critique from the one that is already in use by the actors concerned? It needs to be stressed in response to these questions that the study of conventions remains *theoretical*: it still seeks to use the affordances available to the external observer, in order to produce a narrative that was not previously present (Boltanski, 2012: 31–32). Above all, there is the pragmatist assumption that, while individuals are possessed of a critical autonomy not accorded to them by critical theory, they nevertheless remain limited in the types of actions, decisions, statements and routines that are available to them. Conventions exist as sets of rules that condition and limit the forms of freedom that are available to people, although the ability to switch from one normative world-view to another means that freedom extends beyond the tramlines laid down by any single moral system. Discourse always presumes and communicates more than it explicitly expresses, and the task of hermeneutics is to bring this background context and presumed understanding into the foreground as a reminder of what can otherwise get forgotten.

But how to identify these conventions? How do they come to light, and what counts as evidence of them? In the first instance, they can be described via what Weber termed 'theoretical constructs' – artifices introduced by the sociologist, in order to make different forms of meaningful action distinguishable from one another. No amount of 'data' is adequate to prove that these are real or valid: actors themselves may not recognize them. These models or ideal types are hermeneutic devices, whose validity is to be judged in terms of how successfully they contribute to the understanding of others' actions. An interpretive model can only be constructed with a degree of speculation and imagination. As Boltanski argues:

> We are in a position to understand the actions of persons when, by putting this model to work, we have grasped the constraints that they have had to take into account, in the situation in which they found themselves, in order to make their critiques or their judgements acceptable to others. (Boltanski, 2012: 33)

The task is to describe what is presupposed when claims about socio-economic reality are being made. This is partly a question of identifying the methodologies and measurements that are being used in making these claims, but prior to that there are the assumptions of what is worth arguing over or measuring in the first place. Where experts seek to hide or forget such presuppositions, or deny normative or political dimensions of their actions, this type of excavation acquires a critical dimension in its own right, that, like genealogy, brings to light the fluidity, politics and contingency of taken-for-granted types of truth. This requires us to read positive economics 'as if' it were political theory, inverting the neoliberal project of measuring political actors 'as if' they were market actors.

Convention theory has often been put to empirical use in the study of the micro-dynamics of organizational life, so as to show how different notions of value are present in specifically situated disputes (e.g. Jagd, 2011). But it can be scaled up in order to understand the multiple and conflicting ways in which social and moral theory frames broader disputes over questions of justice and truth, organizing the very problem of modernity (Wagner, 2008). The focus in this book is on the multiple types of political authority that neoliberal critique makes available, specifically to the state. These types are never prescriptive as to exactly what the state should do. Rather, they are immanent moral-political philosophies that provide loose coherence to the techniques, methodologies, measurements and interventions of state actors, providing economic critiques *of* the state for use *by* state actors. Borrowing the approach of Boltanski and Thévenot's *On Justification*, I approach them through rhetorics of political philosophy, using conflicting philosophies of the common good to identify rival ways in which the state can pursue economically rational programmes. Three in particular are explored in later chapters: the liberal-juridical; the violent-executive (which tips into the exceptional); and the communitarian. These provide latent notions of authoritative political action that shape how economistic evaluation proceeds in and around the state. If a central task of neoliberalism is to make the state 'market-like', reducible to quantitative indicators and facts, there must be ways or styles in which this disenchantment is possible while still managing to appear legitimate.

The analysis in subsequent chapters is based on readings of texts and, in some instances, interviews with government officials and advisors in Washington DC,

London and the European Commission. Empirically, the focus is upon cases of expert discourse which bridge between economics and public administration in various ways and at various historical moments. The experts that interest me are critics of the state, though some also work for the state, be it as permanent officials, temporary advisors or consultants. They implement their techniques and measures in order to evaluate aspects of the state on the basis of various forms of economic rationality. Many of them move between academia, think tanks and government agencies, circulating ideas, evidence and methods as they go. This interpretive approach to policy elites is now an established tradition in political science (Yanow, 2000; Bevir & Rhodes, 2004; Fischer, 2009). The intriguing thing about policy experts and critics, from a convention theory perspective, is that in their individual statements and actions one can identify the justificatory resources that are available to the state more generally. If the distinction between the 'micro' and the 'macro' is a technological and rhetorical one rather than an ontological one, then there is 'macro-political' interest in studying statements likely to have large-scale rhetorical and performative power (Latour, 2005; Boltanski, 2012). The ontology of the state as such is not directly addressed here, instead the questions are those of how sovereignty can be rendered economically empirical while still retaining sufficient metaphysical and performative aura in order to hold together as legitimate and powerful. This is by its very nature a paradoxical venture.

The rest of the book is divided as follows. Chapter 2 addresses the idea of competition as a central organizing principle and ideal of neoliberal political authority. The neoliberal state acquires authority from generating and overseeing competitive activity, and this competitive activity then facilitates certain varieties of political authority. The chapter explores the paradoxical qualities of competition as a form of organization, in which actors are formally equal at the outset, and contingently unequal at the conclusion. Yet how that formal equality is defined, and how much contingent inequality is permitted, is open to various interpretations.

Chapter 3 explores the Chicago Law and Economics movement, which transformed legal and regulatory understanding of competition, in ways that shaped reforms in the USA during the 1980s and in the European Commission from the 1990s onwards. Law and Economics demonstrates the various properties and paradoxes of neoliberalism already explored in Chapter 1: it is a clear attempt to replace the substantive ethos and metaphysics of law with purely technical measures. Yet in doing so, it potentially undermines its own authority.

Chapter 4 carries out a similar analysis of 'national competitiveness' agendas from the 1980s onwards. Where Law and Economics saw neo-classical economics colonizing law, 'competitiveness' experts used the field of business strategy to colonize the executive branch of government. Nations, regions and cities are re-imagined as competitive actors – like firms – and the question of political decision making is posed as one of strategic navigation of economic uncertainty. Ultimately, the global economy comes to be treated as a competitive game in which nations are trying to win.

Chapter 5 looks at ways in which 'anti-critical' thought and evaluation are mobilized in order to avoid or delay a crisis. In recent years, and especially since 2007, various efforts have been made to reinforce existing modes of economic rationalization and defend them from critique. Two in particular stand out here. Firstly, there are various 'neo-communitarian' policy strategies through which 'normal' economic reasoning can be sustained, despite psychological or neurological or sociological pressures against calculation: these include behavioural interventions aimed at helping individuals to act in a rational economic fashion. Secondly, there are the exceptional sovereign measures which are taken to ensure that existing forms of economic rationality survive various forces (such as the global financial crisis) that might otherwise overwhelm them: these include the suspension of 'normal' market law.

The last chapter considers the fate of critique. Pragmatic sociology has been criticized for capitulating to expert governance and capitalist management, and abandoning the critique of exploitation and domination. This poses the question of whether there might be routes which move in the opposite direction, from the sociology of critique, back to a more orthodox critical theory (Boltanski, 2011). The book concludes by seeking the political routes beyond economism and/or sovereign domination, and what other sources of authority might be imaginable and viable.

NOTES

1 'To be neutral means to have no answer to certain questions' (Hayek, 1944: 80).
2 There is an important distinction here, which often gets elided, between treating *economics* as the calculative technology and treating *markets* as the calculative technology. Markets, especially from a Hayekian perspective, absolve the need for economic risk modelling, because various judgements about the future are channelled into the price. Conversely, economic models seek to quantify uncertainty, as an alternative to consulting

markets. However, models often play an important performative role in guiding market actors by providing 'prosthetic prices' to influence *actual* prices (Caliskan, 2010).

3 'We should not see things as the replacement of a society of sovereignty by a society of discipline, and then of a society of discipline by a society, say, of government. In fact we have a triangle: sovereignty, discipline and governmental management, which has population as its main target and apparatuses of security as its essential mechanism': M. Foucault (2007) *Territory, Security, Population: Lectures at the College de France, 1977-78*, Palgrave, pp. 107-108.

2

THE PROMISE AND PARADOX OF COMPETITION

Markets, competitive agency and authority

Since the banking crisis of 2007–09, public denunciations of 'inequality' have increased markedly. These draw on a diverse range of moral, critical, theoretical, methodological and empirical resources. Marxist analyses have highlighted growing inequalities as a symptom of class conflict, which neoliberal policies have greatly exacerbated (Harvey, 2011; Therborn, 2012). Statistical analyses have highlighted correlations between different spheres of inequality, demonstrating how economic inequality influences social and psychological wellbeing (Wilkinson & Pickett, 2009). Data showing extreme concentrations of wealth have led political scientists to examine the US political system, as a tool through which inequality is actively increased (Hacker & Pierson, 2010). Emergent social movements, such as Occupy, draw a political dividing line between the '99%' and the '1%' who exploit them. Political leaders and public intellectuals have adopted the language of 'fairness' in their efforts to justify and criticize the various policy interventions which influence the distribution of economic goods (e.g. Hutton, 2010).

It is important to recognize that these critiques have two quite separate targets, although the distinction is often blurred. Firstly, there is inequality that exists within reasonably delineated and separate spheres of society. This means that there are *multiple inequalities*, with multiple, potentially incommensurable measures. The inequality that occurs within the market sphere is separate from the inequality that occurs within the cultural sphere, which is separate from the inequality that occurs within the political sphere, and so on. Each sphere can potentially develop its own metrics and norms of evaluation (or even its own currencies) to rank and distinguish worth. For example, the education system is insulated from the market, but still produces inequalities of outcome, based on its own philosophy and tests of individual worth. Michael Walzer describes this form of inequality as 'monopoly' (Walzer, 1983). Secondly, there is inequality that erodes these distinctions and separations, enabling a single form of inequality to dictate the others, and one source of privilege to be converted into other sources. This is most obviously manifest where economic inequality dictates political and cultural advantages, and metrics based around market price end up dictating values beyond the limits of the market. For example, access to the media is heavily influenced by wealth. This is what Walzer describes as the problem of 'dominance'. Being fungible, money is often the facilitator of a shift from 'monopoly' to 'dominance'. Market power can be converted into other forms of power.

Since Rousseau, socialist critique has argued that economic inequality necessarily breeds political inequality because of the nature of private property; tolerating 'monopoly' within the economic sphere *must* eventually lead to 'dominance' of power across spheres (Rousseau, 1984). However, liberal critiques have focused more on maintaining separate and multiple spheres and measures of inequality. Unequal market outcomes are justified if they don't determine outcomes elsewhere. The critique of neoliberalism, as manifest in the rhetoric of the '99%', often moves between these two different critical registers. On the one hand economic inequality is deemed to be simply excessive *per se* (a critique of monopoly), on the other elites are accused of having translated their economic power into political or cultural power (a critique of dominance). Much contempory critique portrays neoliberalism as based on deception, whereby the rhetoric of opportunity was used strategically to hide the strategies of a very small interest group. And yet the policies and economic rationalities that facilitated this rising inequality were scarcely kept secret or developed behind people's backs.

Unless one subscribes to a notion of 'false consciousness', this raises an important question: why have so many critical denunciations arrived so late in the day? How did this extreme inequality develop, with so little opposition? One answer is that capitalism has drawn on anti-capitalist critique to constantly renew and justify itself (Thrift, 2005; Boltanski & Chiapello, 2007). Capitalism that privileges constant flux is more resistant to static modes of critique. Alternatively, one might suggest that, following 1989, the popular critique of inequality shifted from a socialist denunciation of economic 'monopoly' to a liberal denunciation of 'dominance': economic inequality was tolerated, but only on the basis that it was 'meritocratic', enabling 'social mobility', which required a separation of the market system from the political and educational systems. This was the moral-political economy that accompanied the *Belle Epoque* of the Blair and Clinton governments. It was this liberal promise of capitalism that has, arguably, been manifestly broken since 2007.

However, we need also to consider the role played by a more enthusiastic normative perspective on inequality. From this perspective, that of neoliberal theorists themselves, inequality is something to be actively generated, represented, tested, celebrated and enforced, as a mark of a dynamic and free society (Stedman-Jones, 2012). This is often concealed by the fact that the term 'inequality' has rarely been used in this affirmative sense, perhaps unsurprisingly since it refers only to an absence of something else (equality, however understood). Instead, rhetorics and theories of *competition and competitiveness* have been central to neoliberal critique and technical evaluations from the 1930s onwards. To argue in favour of competition and competitiveness is necessarily to argue in favour of inequality, given that competitive activity is defined partly by the fact that it pursues an unequal outcome. Processes and rules which facilitate (or aim to facilitate) competition can themselves be understood as offering a normative sanction for inequality in some way. A society that celebrates and encourages 'competitiveness' as an ethos, be it in sport, business, politics or education, cannot then be surprised if outcomes are then highly unequal. Critical denunciations of inequality as 'illegitimate' may miss the ways in which inequality *is* 'legitimate' because it is publicly and enthusiastically legitimated.

Yet competition isn't only defined by inequality of outcome. As this chapter will explore, 'competitors' must begin with something in common with one another if they are to 'compete'. In a marketplace the price system provides a common framework and language which all share and must recognize if competition is to take place. Paradoxically, competition also requires some sense of equality, at least at its outset, which may require political intervention to maintain or produce. Neoliberalism begins from a critique of socialist equality, but this does not mean that it operates without any philosophy of equivalence at all. It depends precisely on *constructing or imputing certain common institutional or psychological traits, as preconditions of the competitive process*. These serve as principles of equivalence, via which legitimate forms of non-equivalence can be quantified, constructed, represented and celebrated.

The great appeal of competition, from the neoliberal perspective, is that it enables activity to be rationalized and quantified, but in ways that purport to maintain uncertainty of outcome. The promise of competition is to provide a form of socio-economic objectivity that is empirically and mathematically knowable, but still possessed of its own internal dynamism and vitality. For Hayek, competition was a 'discovery process', and a 'process of the formation of opinion' (Hayek, 1963, 2002). The question which defines different styles and traditions of neoliberalism is this: *what is the technical instrument through which inequalities are to be produced, measured and legitimated?* What remains static, amidst the flux of uncertainty? With what device is constant flux to be rendered empirical? In some instances it will be the market price system itself (as favoured by Hayek), but in other instances it will be economic methods and theories which are used to gauge the 'efficiency' or 'competitiveness' of institutions, communities or individuals, without this being tested by any market as such. If the essential traits of a market can be identified, they can also be extracted and reinvented in non-market contexts. As the previous chapter argued, reconfiguring institutions to *resemble* markets is a hallmark of neoliberal government. The question addressed by this chapter is what principles, techniques and sources of authority are employed, in order to generate and govern competition, both inside and outside of the market.

The chapter is organized as follows. Firstly, I explore the justifications for competition that were made by a set of thinkers who I shall refer to as the 'early neoliberals'. These were primarily European economists and philosophers criticizing socialist and Keynesian planning between 1929–45, including Hayek and Mises, Henry Simons in Chicago, and the 'ordo-liberals' in Freiburg. These thinkers identified competition as the market's essential normative characteristic, and used this as a basis on which to advocate greater market freedoms, actively produced by the state. Secondly, I briefly review the theoretical innovations of two contemporaries of the neoliberal movement, who produced empirical justifications for and measures of non-market competitive activity. These are Ronald Coase and Joseph Schumpeter, both of whom offer theories of capitalist competition that extend beyond market institutions, which would prove crucial for subsequent neoliberal policy making. Thirdly, I address competitive activity in formal and pragmatist terms to try and understand what types of authority it requires and facilitates. By way of political ideal types, I describe two sources of authority afforded by competition: there is a quasi-liberal one, whereby *a priori* fairness is imposed upon the contest, and a quasi-violent one, whereby inequality is sought at all costs. Politically, competition is characterized by the confluence and tension between these two forms of authority. In conclusion I ask what it would even mean for neoliberalism to encounter a 'crisis', given that uncertainty and inequality are entirely in keeping with the neoliberal project.

THE JUSTICE OF MARKET COMPETITION

Markets are places or spaces in which competition takes place, between suppliers and between customers, such that there is choice regarding opportunities for exchange. Every empirical claim that liberal economics has made for markets, as welfare-producing institutions, dating back to Adam Smith, has depended on the recognition that competition is one of their defining characteristics (Smith, 1999: 159). It is the recognition that the same good has *more than one* potential producer, and *more than one* potential purchaser, that allows the market price mechanism to magically rise and fall until it has settled at a point where exchange can take place. Where there is only one available producer or only one available purchaser, that individual or institution has the power to fix the price at a level that suits them, constituting a monopoly. Welfare economists define this 'market power' – where one party can set the price unilaterally – as one particular class of 'market failure' (Pigou, 1912). Weber also adopted a classical liberal definition of a market, as existing wherever there is 'competition, even if only unilateral, for opportunities of exchange among a plurality of potential parties' (Weber, 1978: 635).

Competition, along with the institution of money, guarantees that markets are a 'positive sum game'. As long as two parties both act in their own interest and have multiple parties available to carry out exchanges with, the outcome will be an increase in the welfare of all. This utilitarian argument, with its assumptions about competition and the potential equivalence of money and goods, sits at the heart of the liberal defence of markets, as publicly beneficial institutions. It can even work in reverse, with market competition defined as the maximization of utility (e.g. Walras, 1954: 235). But surprisingly, it scarcely features at all in early neoliberal thinking. Competition is undoubtedly valued, but for its primarily moral, political and epistemological qualities, not its utilitarian or economic ones. As Hayek argued, the neoliberal:

> regards competition as superior not only because it is in most circumstances the most efficient method known but even more because it is the only method by which our activities can be adjusted to each other without coercive or arbitrary intervention of authority. Indeed, one of the main arguments in favour of competition is that it dispenses with the need for "conscious social control". (Hayek, 1944: 38)

Hayek's political pessimism stemmed from his belief that 'conscious', deliberate economic planning had come to replace faith in 'unconscious', unintended outcomes. Planning was what had usurped liberalism, with the most severe political consequences. And yet by proposing competition as the alternative to planning, Hayek and the early neoliberals were adamantly not proposing a straightforward return to Victorian laissez-faire or a 'small state' (Foucault, 2008). The crucial aspect of competition in general, and of market competition in particular, was that it offered a policy alternative to *both* planning (whether of the socialist, National Socialist or Keynesian variety) *and* traditional liberalism. In Hayek's view, the suppression of competition was the defining characteristic of all forms of totalitarianism, hence the claim that liberal and democratic societies which suppressed competition would not remain liberal or democratic for long. I want to suggest that what Hayek and his contemporaries seized on were certain crucial *paradoxes* of competition, through which they hoped to triangulate between traditional nineteenth-century liberalism and various forms of twentieth-century planning. Underlying this is a quest for a mode of instrumental rationality that preserves uncertainty, and a mode of scientific enquiry that does not result in stable authoritative truths. The paradoxes of competition can be mapped in various ways.

Firstly, promoting competition offers a role for the state that is crucially both active (in common with socialist states) and disengaged (in common with Victorian liberal states). The 1890s represent a crucial decade in the genealogy of neoliberalism, for it was then that the German, Austrian and US governments introduced the first pieces of modern competition law, starting with the American Sherman Act of 1890. Liberal political economists had argued that competition arose naturally and inevitably, thanks to the proximity of multiple producers and customers to one another and the use of money. However, the conglomerations, cartels and incorporations of the 'Second Industrial Revolution' of the 1880s and 1890s changed that, demonstrating that large, professionally-managed hierarchies could easily dominate markets, eradicating competitors through sheer force of will. This then created a new role for an active state in artificially and legally establishing the rules of the market: the state actively intervened via anti-trust, but without seeking to determine any particular outcome. Hayek was even prepared to describe competition policy as planning of a sort, but a unique form, which did not impose a 'conscious' objective or particular moral vision upon the collective.[1] Enforcing and promoting competition represent interventions in the form of the economy, but not its content (Foucault, 2008).

Secondly, competition represents a paradoxical combination of equality and inequality. The structure of an organized competition (including, in the liberal imaginary, a market) involves contestants being *formally equal at the outset and empirically unequal at the conclusion*. The neoliberal legal scholar, Wilhelm

Röpke, toyed with this enigma, proposing that 'inequality is the same for all' (quoted in Foucault, 2008: 143). The neoliberals of the 1930s and 1940s were adamant that competition possessed normativity of a sort that was not unlike the liberal normativity of justice. This similarity between a form of Kantian, juridical liberalism and technocratic, economic neoliberalism derives from the fact that both have an *a priori* view of individuals as equal. Hayek observed that 'although competition and justice may have little else in common, it is as much a commendation of competition as of justice that it is no respecter of persons', in the sense that it treats them all blindly and equally (Hayek, 1944: 105). Yet as a norm, competition is unlike any other: the most important rule of any competition is that the contestants may not cooperate or seek to act in an altruistic or moral fashion. It is an injunction to ignore all moral injunctions, and to act combatively in pursuit of inequality. So long as all the competitors obey this single norm, then the outcome will be unpredictable. So long as they recognize each other as equals at the beginning of the contest, then they have complete liberty to maximize relative inequality over the course of the contest.

Where Smith had viewed competition as something that emerged organically from markets, the early neoliberals viewed competition as something to be designed, legislated for and planned by a third party. Since the era of classical liberalism, management had appeared as a form of expertise specifically dedicated to controlling economic processes: the enforcement of competition was necessary to counterbalance this new power. Competition's quasi-normative legitimacy derived in part from the fact that it had rules, regulations and limits – that is, it had authorities who were available to enforce it, using sovereign law. The promise of anti-trust was absolutely crucial in this regard, offering a uniquely paradoxical route out of the Hobbesian choice between state power and anarchy. Anti-trust is a strange case of the state acting to *prevent* the outbreak of economic peace. Simons went as far as suggesting that the Federal Trade Commission (one of the two US anti-trust authorities) become the most powerful executive branch of government (Simons, 1937). The ordo-liberal school, that existed around Walter Eucken in Freiburg, identified cartels as a necessary precondition of Nazi political economy, and consequently advocated legislative attacks on economic power as a central component of any revitalized postwar liberalism. During this time, European and American neoliberals shared a worldview, in which a forceful rule of law would be required in order for the market to retain its competitive form. This had the benefit of defending the liberal properties of markets from monopoly and cartels, but it also had the benefit of restraining the state from imposing goals, plans or 'conscious' direction on society. As the next chapter will explore, from the early 1950s onwards the Chicago School became preoccupied with the dangers of state power, and increasingly downplayed the dangers of monopolies' economic power.

A critical question, which cuts to the heart of how neoliberalism is realized in practice, is this: is competition to be defined by the degree of formal equality guaranteed at its outset, or by the degree of contingent inequality that is produced as its outcome? Ultimately, competition must uphold a degree of each, one way or another, or else its perceived fairness or vitality will collapse. But we will see how neoliberals changed their emphasis on different aspects of competition, gradually relinquishing the priority of formal equality (which, in the USA, also underpinned the Jeffersonian ideal of small-scale producers in a marketplace) and increasingly focusing upon contingent inequality of outcome as the critical feature and test of a competitive system.

Following this, we might add a third way of understanding the paradoxical qualities of competition, as both an object of knowledge and policy: as a socio-economic practice or institution, it defies or transcends the disciplinary division between sociology and neo-classical economics that emerged following the marginalist revolution in economics during the 1870s (Fine & Milonakis, 2009). In simple terms this split had produced rival social sciences, one focused upon individual rationality, calculation and value, and the other focused upon institutions, norms and values. The challenge of socio-economics, ever since the demise of classical political economy, has been to find a path between an excessively 'under-socialized' view of the world, in which all outcomes are explicable in terms of individual calculation, and an excessively 'over-socialized' view of the world in which all action is explicable in terms of obedience to rules (Granovetter, 1985). The competitive process is not reducible to either neo-classical or sociological analysis alone, but defies the methodological assumptions of each. It involves adherence to norms, but the primary one being that cooperation between competitors is not permitted, and it involves individual calculation, but the presence and recognition of competitors cannot be excluded from any meaningful analysis of how the competition plays out. Economists had long struggled to conceptualize a process that seemed on the one hand like 'peace' and on the other like 'war' (Dos Santos Ferreira, 2012). The invention of game theory in the late 1940s partly accommodated the strategic element of competition within a neo-classical framework, but remained unable to explain the normativity of how competitive rituals are established. One way of understanding a 'neoliberal' is as an economist who wrestles tirelessly with sociological questions, though without ever resorting to sociological methods or evidence themselves. There is, as Foucault notes, a distinctly sociological concern with the structures of capitalism running through Austro-German neoliberal thought, but a deep fear of where an expressly social logic might lead politically (Foucault, 2008: 163). Clinging to the idea of competition is a way of coping with this dilemma.

Competitive markets or competitiveness?

The idea and formal characteristics of a market are more important to the initial neoliberal programme than any particular institutions or historical examples of markets. The early neo-liberals inherited a neo-Kantian worldview, which privileged *a priori* and epiphenomenal ideas in the construction and shape of social reality (Gerber, 1994, 1998; Gamble, 1996). Their question was how to render the market's formal characteristics tangible and enforceable. Following Foucault, I've argued that competition is the normative property of markets that appealed to the early neoliberals (Foucault, 2008: 119). Anti-trust policy, backed by the sovereign, legal power of the state, represented a type of active government that the early neoliberals were unanimous in their support for. However, a strange question then arises, of whether market institutions (legally mandated and enforced or not) are even necessarily the best means of realizing the market principle, and if the critical market principle is competition, might there be other, *non-market* institutions, policies and interventions which might just as easily deliver the specific virtues of competitive practices? For example, in the era of applied neoliberalism, sport very often served as a better manifestation of the market ethos than markets themselves, with politicians and business leaders defending economic inequality through analogies to sporting contests and 'talent'. League tables are another way of giving an empirical and technical form to the competitive market ideal. Is market competition necessary to deliver competitiveness?

The position taken by the early neoliberals was that open, decentralized markets, supported by a strong rule of law, *were* necessarily the best vehicle for delivering a free, competitive society. A spontaneously generated price therefore becomes the supreme form of socio-economic fact. Competitive norms would best be defended through defending markets and the price system, for *a priori*, liberal reasons. This was especially pronounced in the tradition of ordo-liberalism (which will be addressed further in the next chapter). The market would be the preserve of liberty, and law would be the preserve of the market. From the ordo-liberal perspective, certain behaviours and actions are ruled out by anti-trust, on the normative grounds that they contradict the principle of the competitive market order. There is necessarily a limit to how much inequality can be permitted from this perspective: the origins of modern anti-trust law, including in the

USA, stem from the need to protect weaker competitors from the threat of large corporations (Thorelli, 1954; Amato, 1997).

One consequence of this legalistic defence of the market system is that it also provides a basis on which to designate the limits to specific markets and to the market system in general. This normative defence of market competition is potentially compatible with a Walzerian justification of multiple spheres of inequality or rival modes of 'dominance'. Inequality in one market can be justified on the basis that it does not translate into inequality in another market (this is a problem that is addressed technically, where anti-trust agencies seek to carry out a 'market definition' when assessing the dominance of a firm). Furthermore, inequality in the economic sphere can be justified on the basis that it *does not* translate into inequality in the political or educational sphere. The German 'social market' economy is one manifestation of this tradition of neoliberalism, which asserts a strong commitment to market competition, but underpinned and defined by legal institutions which are set firmly by the state. Moreover, German neoliberal thought showed a strong awareness of the corrosive social effects of the market, which justified robust and separate social policies (Ptak, 2009). In Chicago, Simons had proposed that industries that could not be run on the basis of decentralized, competitive market principles (and therefore tended towards monopoly) should be taken into public ownership. Hayek was cognizant of the various public goods, such as transport infrastructure, that the price system was not suited to deliver (Hayek, 1944: 40). This recognition that the market had certain technical and moral limits was prominent in neoliberal debates up until the 1950s. While the Depression was still a recent memory, many neoliberals sought compromises between economic liberalism and elements of socialism that they accepted as necessary (Bergin, 2013). Some of them even understood their project as sharing a similarly progressive spirit as socialism, albeit with a desire to open up space for competitive forces. Foucault points to the French tradition of neoliberalism, which (anticipating the active labour market policies of the Anglo-American 'Third Way' in the 1990s) suggested a role for the state in helping people back into the economic game, on occasions when they have been excluded from it (Foucault, 2008: 202). These various attempts to delineate and regulate the normative limits to market were at odds with the Chicago School of the 1950s and onwards, and especially with the American conservative tradition to which American neoliberalism became loosely allied.

The early neoliberal programme was preoccupied with such constitutional, or at least institutional, questions. There is remarkably little concern with economic or utilitarian questions or efficiency during this period, and the writing retains an explicitly normative and critical character. This can be interpreted in two ways. Firstly, the terms of much public intellectual debate at this time were being set by socialists, and subsequently, Keynesians. Hayek was notoriously paranoid about the extent to which socialist opinions had permeated the public sphere, which inspired him to establish the Mont Pelerin Society as an effort to resist this intellectual tide (Plehwe, 2009). Providing non-socialist answers to sociological questions was the priority. Focusing the state upon competition, rather than upon plans and outcomes, appeared to do precisely this. Secondly, there was a strong sense that the economics profession and neo-classical economics had done very little to defend economic liberty. Lawyers, philosophers and public intellectuals offered greater hope for the defeat of socialism and reform of society than technical experts. The split between economics and sociology, that had followed the demise of classical political economy, was a symptom of the neutering of economics as a weapon of liberalism (Schumpeter, 1954: 756).

However, as the neoliberal intellectual movement became increasingly dominated by economists and business interests, its emphasis began to switch from a concern with the normative conditions of legitimate inequality (such as law and the price system) to one with the contingent capacity for inequality. Cases of this transition will be explored in greater detail in the next two chapters.[2] The question is how it remains possible to speak of 'competition', without there being clearly visible institutional rules and limits to that competition. As we shall now explore, particular theories of competitive agency came to the fore, while the emphasis on regulated markets as quasi-egalitarian arenas of competition faded from view. These theories developed in parallel to the early neoliberal movement, though largely outside of it.

JUSTIFYING CAPITALIST POWER

Where 'competition' is a term that can only be applied to the institutional *form* taken by markets, there can be no basis on which to know, justify and evaluate the practices and outputs that accompany enterprising, entrepreneurial and profit-seeking behaviour in and of itself. By this standard a 'competitive' action can only be defined negatively, as one which does not disrupt or distort the price system or one whose outcome cannot be predicted, but this does not enable the value of different types of competitive behaviour to be judged. For Hayek, this was precisely the point. Competition is a dynamic process which facilitates the attainment of new knowledge: it cannot itself be subjected to objective empirical analysis. We know when it is absent, but there can be no scientific view of it when it is present (Hayek, 1963, 2002). In Fernand Braudel's sense of the distinction, the early neo-liberals were committed to 'markets', but risked ignoring or even opposing 'capitalism', where the former implies transparency and *a priori* equality, and the latter implies hierarchy and inequality (Braudel, 1979). There is a lack of empirical economic nuance in this defence of market competition.

How else could economic competition be conceived, in ways that weren't simply deduced from the formal institutional character of markets and the price system itself? How might the justification of inequality be detached from a normative commitment to particular legal or sociological principles? Or to pose these questions another way, with what justification might power, hierarchy and con-trol be admitted into the competitive economic game? Unless the capacity to plan and monopolize is admitted as a legitimate feature of the competitive pro-cess, then any vision of competition remains abstracted from the realities of corporate capitalism. In many ways, the story of post-1945 neoliberal critique is of its mutation from a *justification for markets* to a *justification for business*, where the former represents a check on public economic planning, but the latter produces freedoms for private economic planning (Crouch, 2011).

Given the complexity and flux of modern capitalism, the pragmatic question is *at what moments* and *with what technical devices and measures* is socio-economic life to be rendered empirical and numerical? Given that uncertainty must be reduced occasionally or to some extent, what is a legitimate means of doing so? From a Hayekian perspective, the price system is the supreme instrument for rendering dynamic situations empirical, but one whose representations are themselves in constant flux. But economics is itself a practical instrument for rendering uncertain situations empirical: alternatively, uncertainty is actively reduced, through the force of entrepreneurial or managerial will (Knight, 1957). Less dogmatic theories of competition are those which recognize the role of managerial and entrepreneurial power within the process, and employ economic methods to represent what is going on.

I want to explore two ways in which economic competition is rendered knowable and testable, so as to still privilege inequality of outcome, but without a norma-tive commitment to the market price mechanism or any other institutional *a priori*. In a spirit of capitalist realism, which would prove crucial for the theo-retical and practical development of neoliberalism in the second half of the twentieth century, each of these seeks to abandon the abstract faith in liberal markets. Yet as I will seek to show, in place of that normative commitment to market institutions, they inadvertently inject an alternative commitment to a particular vision of individual agency – one whose validity is primarily testable by expert economic analysis, rather than markets. The first, belonging to Ronald Coase, provides a justification for capitalist power through presuming an ideal vision of the rational, maximizing individual, borrowed from neo-classical economics. The second, belonging to Joseph Schumpeter, does the same through presuming an ideal vision of the heroic, creative entrepreneur. By switching from a formal-structural emphasis on *competition as an essential property of markets*, to a psychological emphasis on *competitiveness as an essential trait of individuals*, these economists occasioned a key shift in how competition (and competitiveness) would later be conceived. At the same time, they implicitly offered justifications and empirical measures of monopoly that could dissolve any normative boundary around the market sphere. 'Freedom' is recast as the freedom to exploit, rather than to exchange. The mere *possibility* of future competition, as judged by the expert eye, becomes more important than the reality of existing competition as manifest in a market. These justifications and measures began to be taken up by states and policy makers from the late 1970s onwards, providing the expert governmental infrastructure that would constitute applied neoliberalism (examined in Chapters 3 and 4).

Ronald Coase and the efficiency of power

Ronald Coase was a British economist, taught and influenced by Hayek at the LSE in the 1930s, but rarely associated with neoliberalism until much later in his career. He emigrated to the United States in 1951, taking a position at the University of Virginia, before joining the Chicago Law School in 1964. His lasting contribution to neo-classical economics lay in his theory of transaction costs. This started out from the intuition that capitalist industrial structures only rarely con-form to the vision of a competitive, liberal market as imagined in the abstract formulations of neo-classical economics. Yet rather than abandon neo-classical economics in favour of a more institutionally-nuanced theory, his innovation was to reinvent it for empirical use, in such a way that it could interrogate market *and non-market* structures side by side. Evaluation by economics replaces evaluation by markets. The rational choice presuppositions of neo-classical method serve as the principle of equivalence, against which behaviour can then be judged.

In a seminal essay, 'The Nature of the Firm', Coase addressed the question of why firms exist at all, if markets are as efficient as classical and neo-classical economics had maintained (Coase, 1937). Retaining a methodological presup-position of individual, rational choice on the part of individuals, Coase suggested that all economic activity – including market exchange – produces costs of coordination and communication amongst individual actors, given the manifold uncertainties that they all face. Even competitive markets possess their own 'transaction costs', in the creation of contracts, enforcement of property rights, regulation, discovering reputations and so on. In many cases, these costs may be sufficiently low that exchange mediated by price is still the most efficient form of coordination. But in some circumstances, markets may be more costly than other types of institution, rooted in non-market norms of cooperation and hierarchy. Firms exist, Coase reasoned, to the extent that organizing in hierarchies, with wages and job security accepted in exchange for obedience to managers, is more efficient than trading in markets. Given that cooperation between humans carries far greater uncertainties than property rights, between humans and things, hierarchical organization plays a crucial role in delivering efficient economic outcomes. By the same token, markets exist to the extent that price-based exchange is more efficient than hierarchical organization or some other mode of cooperation. There are multiple institutional means of handling uncertainty, which need to be judged through empirical evaluation.

The critical move made by Coase was to separate neo-classical price *theory* from the market price *mechanism* (Davies, 2010). He assumed, in the neo-classical tradition, that all individuals are constantly engaged in calculating the net cost or benefit to themselves of different courses of action, as rational maximizers. But he also abandoned the assumption that markets are the principle arena in which this type of psychological calculation does or should occur. Exhibiting an implicitly neoliberal trait, transaction cost economics is instrumental in extending a market-based principle and technique of evaluation beyond the limits of market institutions. All institutions – markets, firms, social networks, states – come to appear as equally amenable to a neo-classical analysis, with the crucial proviso that the costs of coordination and communication are included in the overall audit of their efficiency. For Coase, it was no longer a question of what counted as efficiency in an abstract sense (a question which invariably produced the answer that markets are efficient), but one of how to gauge the relative levels of efficiency of different empirical industrial structures, including real people, with real problems of trust and commitment. Remarkably, *even the price mechanism of the market* becomes subject to the efficiency audit of price theory. 'Efficiency' becomes an always relative and measurable term.

In another paper, which later became one of the most-cited articles in the history of economics, 'The Problem of Social Cost', Coase addressed the question of how regulators should respond to the problem of 'externalities' – that is, when the actions of one agent (for example, a firm) impose costs on another, the classic example being pollution (Coase, 1960). The British tradition of welfare economics defined 'externalities' as another form of 'market failure', like monopoly, which typically required intervention by a third party (such as a regulator) in order to redress this inefficiency and get the market functioning correctly again. Yet Coase argued that this approach had crucially neglected to include the full costs associated with different ways of resolving the problem. It included the cost of the 'externality' to the injured party, but forgot to include the costs associated with regulation, including those imposed upon the regulated actor. It failed to account for the fact that pollution, say, has clear benefits *to the polluter*. In many cases, Coase reasoned, it may be more efficient (in the aggregate) to let one agent impose 'social costs' upon a rival, and leave them to work out the damages or redress between themselves, than to employ law and regulation as a means of restoring some vision of a 'perfect' competitive market. As long as their property rights were sufficiently well defined, they could discover the most efficient resolution between themselves.

There is no normative or *a priori* notion of an efficient or perfectly competitive market in Coase's work, instead there are tools for evaluating particular industrial structures on a case-by-case basis using empirical data. Nor is there any sense of moral responsibility in Coase's worldview, only a question of optimal aggregate welfare. Where one party is dominating or exploiting another, observers should not automatically prioritize the interest of the latter, but assess the situation empirically. Coase's unspoken normative implication is that monopolists and dominators have rights too. As one student of Coase explained, 'in economic terms, both the injurer and the injured may be said to have caused an accident' (Priest, 2005). The ultimate arbiter of value is no longer the institution of market price or the perspectives of the competitors involved, but the objective methodological perspective provided by neo-classical economics, which assesses utility in the aggregate.

From the Coasian perspective, legitimate 'competitive' activity is any activity that is efficiency maximizing (in the precise neo-classical sense of consumer welfare), but the institutional structure of that activity becomes an open empirical question. It may in theory include monopolistic or predatory activity. By abandoning any ideal vision of a free, competitive order (such as the one held by the early neoliberals), Coase pointed towards a starkly realistic vision of how free competition occurs, in which large corporations asserted their interests, expanded their property entitlements and mobilized their legal muscle as part of the competitive game. But he also provided a source of justification for this:

that it could be calculated as efficient in the aggregate. If the early neoliberals had hoped to use law to make the economy conform to a particular liberal ideal, Coase demonstrated that contingent, capitalist activity, by profit-seeking actors *already was* typically ideal. Certainly, it could not necessarily be improved upon through the intervention of regulators or law-makers. Admitted into regulatory practice, this theory serves as a major filip to large corporations (Crouch, 2011).

Joseph Schumpeter and the creativity of power

Coase demonstrated that non-market institutional arrangements could, by neo-classical evaluation, be more efficient than markets. The exercise of power, hierarchy and cooperation could reduce transaction costs, improve consumer welfare and thereby be deemed competitive. The arena of competition was far broader than any individual market. Joseph Schumpeter effectively produced a similar justification for non-market, monopolistic modes of competitiveness, but from entirely different methodological premises. Both the *agent* at the heart of Schumpeter's method and the *style* of economic reasoning were radically unlike those of neo-classical economics, and far closer to those of his compatriot Hayek. In their relationships with the neoliberal 'thought collective', Schumpeter and Coase's careers followed opposing trajectories. While Coase became increasingly integral to the neoliberal critique of the state thanks to his growing proximity to the Chicago School, Schumpeter began as a contemporary of Hayek and Mises in Vienna, but later poured scorn on Hayek's Mont Pelerin Society and distinguished himself at Harvard, the centre of the US economics establishment at the time and notoriously snooty towards Chicago. What Schumpeterian economics provides for the re-theorization of competition is an appreciation of the radical *differences* in the psychological properties of the competitors. These are not a basis for objective evaluation, but simply emerge contingently and unpredictably. In pragmatist terms, what Schumpeter offers is therefore not so much a normative principle of equivalence between competitors, but an awareness of the *facticity of difference* between them. Some actors are simply more powerful and capable than others.

Schumpeter's great work, *Capitalism, Socialism and Democracy*, was published in 1942, two years before Hayek's *Road to Serfdom* and offering a similarly pessimistic view of capitalism's future, as being gradually stultified by bureaucracy and a rationalist desire to control the future. But unlike Hayek, he understood that this ethos was as powerful within private enterprises as within government bureaucracies and planning agencies. The competitive practices of large corporations often created little wealth, but allowed a narrow definition of efficiency to stifle creativity and radical productivity improvements. Bureaucrats and professional managers acted efficiently in the short term, while undermining the long-term viability of capitalism. Eventually, Schumpeter believed, a deadening rationality of hierarchy and routine would destroy capitalism altogether (Schumpeter, 1976).

The capacity to inject uncertainty back into the capitalist system came not from markets, but from the psychology of unusual individuals willing to defy existing institutional logics, namely entrepreneurs. The entrepreneur enacts 'new combinations' of technologies and practices, so as to inject novelty into circuits of capitalism (Schumpeter, 1934). A great deal hangs on the psychology of the entrepreneur, which is to refuse ordinary routines and boundaries. The entrepreneurial mentality does not seek success within a given set of institutional rules, but through the invention of new institutional rules, which others will later have to play by. For this reason, entrepreneurs cannot be easily classified or theorized, because by their nature, they move between existing codes, norms and institutions (Schumpeter, 1934: 77–78; Stark, 2009). Nor do they reside in any particular institutional domain of society. In his later life, Schumpeter was even prepared to accept that entrepreneurship may be most likely 'within the shell of existing corporations', where routinization could be disrupted from within (quoted in McCraw, 2007: 496). What is clear in Schumpeter's analysis is that the entrepreneurial personality is *uncommon*. It acts against existing conventions, which structure socio-economic reality for the majority of people, rather than within them. Entrepreneurship operates through counter-acting norms, and for this reason can never be stabilized into any norm of its own.

According to Schumpeter, the competitive spirit of entrepreneurship cannot be reduced to the quest for economic gains. The mentality of entrepreneurship is such that it looks beyond the specific rewards currently on offer, towards a far greater form of competitive success in the future, in which the very landscape of capitalism has been re-shaped by the entrepreneur's will. It is more like 'the will to conquer: the impulse to fight, to prove oneself superior to others, to succeed for the sake, not of the fruits of success, but of success itself' (Schumpeter, 1934: 93). In the process of inventing a new productive landscape, existing ones are made redundant – the process famously described as 'creative destruction'. This process cannot be framed by any existing set of rules or market institutions, because rules and institutions are internal to the process itself. The entrepreneur's gambit is to forego a positive valuation in the present, to be able to dictate the very terms of valuation in the future. All that remains 'outside' of the process of creative destruction is the principle – or rather the psychological possibility – of entrepreneurship itself. Capitalism must offer an outlet for mili-taristic instincts, or else it will subside into bureaucratized socialism.

Schumpeter's work expands the field of competition in two ways, accommodating power and strategy within the competitive process as it does so. Firstly, the relevant *time-scale* of competition is greatly expanded, so as to include strategies and investments that only reap dividends over the long term. The entrepreneur looks beyond markets as they exist in the present towards markets that could exist in the future. It spots types of human need or desire that are not presently served and which consumers may not even be aware of. Given the lengthy time horizons of such competitive strategy there are necessarily far greater uncertainties involved, meaning that a rationalist risk assessment or calculation of future return on investment becomes unhelpful. But the reward for successful entre-preneurship is a monopoly, bringing very great profits indeed. This monopoly is justified in view of the uncertainties that have been confronted, and also because it – like everything else within capitalism – will eventually be super-seded by the arrival of new competitors and new monopolists. In certain cases entrepreneurs and inventors will need government support to ensure that they will reap adequate monopolistic rewards from their innovations, hence the case for many intellectual property rights.

Secondly, this expands the arena of competition to include a greater variety of cultural, political, technological and sociological factors. The orthodox classical and neo-classical view of a competitive market witnesses firms all producing similar or substitutable goods, striving to reduce the costs of production in order to cut prices and grow market share. Technology and culture are treated as 'exogeneous', external to the calculations of producers and consumers. The entrepreneur, by contrast, strategically draws on social networks, scientific research, technological insight and imagination to make their 'new combinations'. They necessarily employ forms of 'restrictive practices' to ensure that their competitive advantages (when they arrive) aren't immediately replicated by competitors.

In Schumpeter's analysis, neo-classical economics only exacerbates the crisis of capitalism, by offering excessively rationalized, short-term evaluations of eco-nomic practices. This serves the needs of a professionalized bureaucracy and management class, who seek to govern economy and society using numbers, but it excludes (or misrepresents) the power of the entrepreneur, who acts on the basis of vision and desire rather than scientific calculation. The game of capitalism 'is not like roulette, it is more like poker' (Schumpeter, 1976: 73). The most important forces within capitalism, from this perspective, are those which cannot be calculated or modelled, but require strategic navigation and inspiration. The outcome of the competitive process is determined by 'non-economic' virtues and assets, such as the cultural and psychological propensity to innovate and cooperate.

Competitive psychologies

It is meaningless to speak of 'competition' unless there is not only some sense of equivalence amongst those deemed to be the competitors, but also some outlet for contingent differences to be represented. The very notion of 'inequality' as an outcome assumes that there must be *something* equal about those whose difference is being measured, proven, justified or criticized. The appeal of markets, to the early neoliberals, was that they could potentially provide this common world, within which all forms of difference and plurality could then be expressed, in quantitative (i.e. price) terms. The importance of Coase and Schumpeter, to my analysis, is that they replace this *institutional format* for competition (namely the market) with psychological formats of competition. What ultimately facilitates, drives and justifies competition and competitiveness is found in individual psychological capacities. A crucial difference between them is that the Coasian psychological capacities are deemed common to all, whereas Schumpeterian psychological capacities belong only to a strange minority. Coase's neo-classical methodology presumes that human beings are all possessed of the capacity to negotiate agreements; Schumpeter's romantic belief in entrepreneurship assumes that only a rare minority are able to act towards long-term triumphs. Coase offers a principle of equivalence while Schumpeter affirms the facticity of difference. Applied neoliberalism is arguably based on some entanglement of these two anthropological worldviews, whereby certain powerful actors are able to *purchase and acquire* a greater calculative and strategic capacity than others, thanks to consultants and professional advisors.

In style of reasoning and in their policy implications, Coase and Schumpeter's theories are strongly divergent. But what each provides, in very different ways, is a theoretical and methodological basis on which to judge and criticize institutions that challenges the finality of the price system. These theories have a number of common features. Firstly, they recognize the legitimate role of *power and restraint* in the economy, as a means of reducing uncertainty on the part of economic actors. Laws, intellectual property restrictions, contracts, hierarchies, leaders and social networks all become positively valuable. Monopoly becomes potentially legitimate, albeit with different sources of justification (Coase because it is 'efficient', Schumpeter because of the long-term vision that achieved it).

Economic planning, the *bête noire* of the early neoliberals, is sanctioned by these economists, though the planners in question are running businesses, not public administrations. The uncertainty of the future is reduced thanks to management and leadership within the private economy.

Secondly, they implicitly bestow a new authority upon economics as a source of critique, justification and affirmation. For Hayek markets are themselves information processors, generating quasi-objective representations of what is going on in the economy that no expert or government can rival. The market could not be 'wrong' because there was no independent standard by which to prove this: competitive activity could only be 'wrong' if it sought to subvert the authority of the price system. Coase and Schumpeter offer theories which can themselves be used as a standard of critical and objective evaluation. Coase's economics can be used to evaluate whether industries, rules and contracts are organized to maximize utilitarian output. Schumpeter's economics can be used to judge whether they are organized in a way that is open to being transformed. Economic theory and methodology then provide a critical measure against which capitalism can be judged. There is no need for *actual* market competition to challenge a monopoly if economic analysis can demonstrate that the potential for competition still exists. This in turn facilitates the growing political authority of economic experts in the governance of a wide variety of institutions and processes. Chapters 3 and 4 will explore how Coasian and Schumpeterian economics provide the neoliberal state with the technical instruments with which to judge the rationality of sovereign institutions.

In the language of convention theory, Coase and Schumpeter provide rival 'critical capacities' by which the world can be criticized, measured and tested. These rest on certain assumed metaphysical propositions about what is common and uncommon to human beings. For Coase, it is assumed (as a property of neoclassical methodology) that all human beings are engaged in the rational pursuit of preference satisfaction, whether inside or outside of the market, and can negotiate (or dominate) in pursuit of it. Value is to be found in maximizing this satisfaction, and we will see in the next chapter how regulators have imported the Coasian measure by applying a 'consumer welfare standard' as a basis on which to evaluate industrial organization. For Schumpeter, it is assumed that some human beings have a capacity to impose themselves on others through more or less peaceful means. This is an *anti-equivalance* principle, which sees the stabilization of conventions as a potential inhibitor of capitalist potency, and therefore the disruption of normality as a good in its own right. These assumptions become the unspoken 'metaphysical' presuppositions upon which certain types of empirical statements will depend. The empiricist reduction of the social and political world to economic facts depends on methodologies and theories, but these in turn depend on presumptions about agency and the character of shared (and unshared) humanity. If, in whatever way, these philosophical anthropologies come to appear untenable, then methodological and expert edifices will collapse.

Without a fixed arena, within which legitimate competitive activity is to take place, it becomes harder to distinguish illegitimate competitive activity. Attempts to subvert, bypass or control the market are no longer *a priori* bad. Both theories are cognizant of the destructive aspects of capitalist competition, which they make justifiable on the basis that they are beneficial in the aggregate and/or in the long term. On the basis that individuals are assumed to be acting in their own interests, and will employ various forms of domination in order to do so, it becomes difficult to state when precisely monopolistic and predatory activity ceases to be beneficial. If an individual signs a highly restrictive employment contract, but does so in a calculated way, must this therefore be deemed efficient? How long should a patent last, before beneficial restriction becomes harmful restriction? These are the sorts of problems which would later bedevil neoliberal policy makers.

METAPHYSICS OF NEOLIBERAL AUTHORITY

The rhetoric and performance of neoliberal authority involve appeals to 'evidence' and economic evaluation as the test of legitimate competitive activity. A great deal of expert and institutional work goes in to making these appeals publicly viable, as we shall see. However, empirical evidence always arises from institutional and pragmatic concerns, and on the basis of certain vocations and perspectives. Value neutrality and scientific objectivism have their own ethical and institutional preconditions. What counts as a valid empirical representation of a dynamic, competitive situation will depend heavily on one's own position in relation to it. Consider the various perspectives surrounding a game of professional tennis, and the different matters of 'fact' that are at work as a result: each player strives to focus their minds on winning the next point; their coach needs to form an expert view on how their performance can be improved; the umpire needs to make sure that the rules are being enforced correctly and fairly; the audience keep looking at the scoreboard; and the gambler in the betting shop is only interested in the final score. In dynamic situations, with multiple perspectives at play, there is rarely an 'ultimate' empirical representation that is valid for all. On the other hand, the neoliberal promise of competitive forms of organization is that they will periodically produce clearly distinguishable 'winners' and 'losers' that all will agree on.

Before we can look at how empirical economic claims can act as a source of neoliberal political authority, we first need to consider the pragmatics of competitive activity in order to better understand the different forms of judgement and discourse that such activity facilitates and requires. Prior to any empirical question as to the qualities or quantities of a given competition (or competitive act) are certain presuppositions about what it even means to be involved in a competitive situation. If we can bring some of these presuppositions to light, we can also begin to understand the forms of authority that hover in and around competitive situations. To do this, I adopt a pragmatist approach to the performance of competitions, as found in the work of Goffman (Goffman, 1997). The conventions which underpin empirical evaluations and proofs derive in part from the practical circumstances that give rise to them. Commonalities in these circumstances need bringing to light, such that conventions of empirical representation can be identified and interpreted.

The starting point for this interpretation, and the reason why this leads us towards questions of authority, is the recognition that all competitions have rules. To favour competition is never to favour anarchy. There must be a very minimal sense of *a priori* equality, or some element of fairness, in a competition, if it is to be recognized as 'real' and not 'rigged'. A principle of equivalence must be logically prior to the facticity of difference, if it is 'competition' that is going on, and not brute violence. However, as already discussed, the rules of competition are very unlike the rules of virtually any other type of institution, in that they must debar peaceful or cooperative activity. This produces the further curiosity, that (unlike, say, a play or ritual or other type of performance) the outcome of a competition cannot be known in advance: this was precisely its appeal to Hayek. If one competitor were too obviously superior to another, then the outcome would cease to be unexpected. Competition would thereby lose its exploratory epistemological quality. The initial sense of fairness and the uncertainty of outcome are therefore co-dependent. The need for contestants to begin as formal equals (in some however weak sense of the term), and conclude as empirical unequals, points towards certain minimal constraints on what it means to conduct competitive activity.

This tension between 'equality' and 'inequality' sits at the heart of any competitive event or activity. Wittgenstein observed that any game 'has not only rules but also a *point*' (Wittgenstein, 2001: 564) but in fact a competitive game has two 'points': one is to ensure that competitors remain constrained by some norms of equality, playing by the same rules, the other is to ensure that they resist these norms at all costs, in search of inequality. If either of these 'points' were lacking, it would be impossible to describe what was going on as 'competition'. It would tip either into a form of completely peaceful, normative fairness or into violent, existential combat. The appeal of a competition lies in the tension that is maintained between these two outer-lying political teleologies or ideal types. One way of defining competition, and the forms of authority that it creates, is that it is never quite as fair as 'justice', and nor is it ever quite as brutal as 'violence'. The *ideal types* of 'justice' and 'violence' must somehow be at work within a competition if it is to be attractive to contestants and audience, but they must also remain in an irresolvable tension with one another.

The enigma of any game, as Wittgenstein saw it, is that its rules cannot fully express its point. There is a gap separating what is written down as rules and the actions of a person who is obeying them. What one *understands* by rules always exceeds their linguistic expression: interpretation bridges the gap between statements and actions. The 'authority' of a rule-giver or commander lies in a shared and largely unspoken understanding that certain statements, institutions, decisions or individuals should be obeyed. It is also necessary that there is a shared and unspoken understanding about what obedience might practically involve. This consists of a particular relationship between what is made explicit and what remains tacit. The same is true of state sovereignty: in order for a sovereign to demonstrate their immeasurable power, it is necessary that viewers can interpret this demonstration as such, rather than require the state's full physical capacity to be put on display (which, in exhausting itself, would be to contradict what it sought to demonstrate).

Different modes or ideal types of authority rest on different ways of understanding the relationship between the manifest statements of rules or orders, and the unseen or unspoken ethos or potentiality which accompanies them. What we are grasping towards here is not particular empirical policies, regulations or decisions, but the types of immanent political philosophy that accompany them. For example, Weber's famous three forms of authority – the bureaucratic, the traditional and the charismatic – refer not to actions or visible demonstrations of power, but to shared presuppositions on the part of those who willingly obey power. Authority consists in not having to physically compel obedience, but to rely on a common sense of what is legitimate and who deserves to be obeyed. The justice (or empirical value) of a given course of action can only be proved in any ultimate sense, if there is already a shared sense that the judge is viewing the situation from the right position, in the right way. The silent pragmatics of authority necessarily precede their spoken statements and empirical proofs. Following the hermeneutic approach of Boltanski and Thévenot, the task here is to unearth the latent forms of political philosophy that render power legitimate, but in the particular circumstances of competitive situations (Boltanski & Thévenot, 2006).

The liberal spirit of competitiveness

Even in the classical, liberal vision of competition, as a natural and emergent occurrence, there is an implication of norms constraining how competition takes place and guaranteeing a sense of fairness. Any social competition has practices which are deemed 'anti-competitive' in some sense, even if these are determined by the competitors themselves (as in a friendly game of football) rather than by third party authorities with the power to enforce the rules. Forms of combat which lack any norms or limits – for example, where an individual attacks another in the street unexpectedly – cannot be described as 'competition', even though they may clearly thrive off and generate inequality: we would hesitate to describe a successful attacker as the 'winner' in such a scenario. There are of course borderline cases. A brawl may acquire an audience which start to comment on who is 'winning'. And modern warfare has been conducted with some very weak sense of normativity, for instance regarding the wearing of combat uniforms and official 'declarations' of war, but without ever being described as a 'competition'. Human competition is never entirely existential.

To put this another way, competition facilitates and requires *judgement* or critique. While competitors may get so immersed in their situation that they lose the capacity to distance themselves from it, and take a critical or objective view of what is going on, this is liable to be interrupted when they feel that something 'illegal' or 'unfair' has occurred, or else when others take that view. Critical moments punctuate competitive processes, when activity is evaluated, not simply for its value but for whether it is compatible with the rules. This makes some form of intervention or interruption necessary. The French neo-liberal, Louis Rougier, argued that the state needed to perceive the economic 'game' *'not [with] the indifference of a spectator, but the neutrality of an arbitrator'* (quoted in Bergin, 2013: 76). The Hayekian view of the market sought to make the price system the only ultimate judge or critic of behaviour, and yet it would remain necessary that certain authorities (anti-trust regulators) were present to prevent competitors seeking to undermine the price system itself.

A standard of judgement, such as 'consumer welfare', is needed against which competitive behaviour is to be criticized and periodically stopped.

The rules of any competition must do two things. Firstly, they must uphold the central norm of all competitions, which is that the contestants may not cooperate. In the market realm, this is manifest as anti-cartel legislation. In many other realms, such as educational tests, cooperation would constitute 'cheating' or 'fixing'. Secondly, they must define the limit to acceptable inequality, as it occurs within the temporal and spatial limits of the contest. Competitors may not cooperate, but nor may they use *any* contingent power available to them. They will inevitably seek to twist the interpretation of the rules in their favour, but they cannot seek to rewrite the rules altogether or suspend them without undermining the residual sense of fairness that distinguishes any competition from brute combat or corruption. Equally, competitors cannot seek to force rivals out of the game permanently, which in the language of anti-trust would be classed as 'abuse of dominance'.

We might therefore say that a competition must be imbued with a liberal *spirit*, inasmuch as the abstract idea of equality before the rules must exert some influence over how the contest is performed and its rules interpreted. 'Spirit' is used here in the same sense of Weber's 'spirit of capitalism', as referring to *a philosophical idea that justifies practical engagement on a moral and psychological level* (Weber, 2002). In pragmatic terms, the 'spirit' always exceeds what can be articulated or stated as a rule. The liberal spirit of competition can best be identified with the hypothetical 'original position' proposed by John Rawls, in which individuals are imagined creating the rules of society, but behind a 'veil of ignorance' regarding how the contingent inequalities in wealth, ability and power are likely to be distributed (Rawls, 1972). This theoretical device was invented by Rawls as a philosophical artifice to 'nullify the effects of specific contingencies which put men at odds and tempt them to exploit social and natural circumstances to their own advantage' (Rawls, 1972: 136). The original position is a form of game, in which no contingent empirical identities, skills or traits are allowed to influence the outcome (in that sense, it is a competitive game which never gets started). This method for defining justice still accommodates inequality, but only on the basis that nobody would reasonably choose to live in a society of complete equality of outcome (it is here that Rawlsian liberalism borders on Hayekian neoliberalism). Rawls argues that 'injustice, then, is simply inequalities that are not to the benefit of all' (1972: 62): it is from an ideal notion of equality that a justifiable model of competition can be deduced, by Rawls's logic. This chain of reasoning somewhat inverts that of the neoliberals, for whom the common good can be guaranteed by particular empirical visions and techniques of competition.

A competition must in some way perform this abstract idea of equality. Inevitably, contestants will bring varying levels of skill, power and enthusiasm to any competition, which ought (ideally) to influence what type of unequal outcome results. The contestants will seek to ensure that the competition is conducted in ways that maximize their own contingent advantages, but the rules must be applied such that, to some minimal extent, those contestants are restricted to an equal extent. So how then does a competition's spirit of *a priori* equality differ from that imposed by liberal law? In what precise sense does the fairness of a competition differ from the fairness of justice? The crucial distinction lies in the question of universality. While law only becomes tangible or visible when it is imposed on specific persons, in specific times and places, it is accompanied by a metaphysical sense that it nevertheless applies to *everybody*. This is its partly unspoken metaphysical component, which distinguishes sovereign rule from just governmental rules. It is not just a rule of a game or a particular institution, it is also *the law*. If it fails to maintain its universalistic aura of applying to *all people equally all the time*, then it ceases to be recognized as 'justice', and becomes a set of technical and disciplinary instruments. The performance of justice strives for finality. Unlike, say, the Schumpeterian entrepreneur, the victor in the courtroom is not simply enjoying a few years of dominance, but has in principle settled a dispute forever.

By contrast, the rules of a competition are limited in time and space. They apply equally to all contestants, but not to those who exist outside of the limits of the competitive arena. Like a theatrical play a competition is a managed event, in which a *sense or spirit* of fairness is on display, but it is understood by competitors and non-competitors alike that this is more or less bracketed from the broader fairness or unfairness of 'society' at large. Where a legal trial seeks to be once and for all, performances such as audit or sports seasons come round periodically – they lack an 'ultimate' quality. One way of understanding this bracketing is to recognize that competitions can rest on empirical evaluations ('has the student answered the question correctly?', 'did the ball cross the line?') or on aesthetic evaluations ('which figure skater deserves the gold medal?', 'which novel deserves the prize?') but never on moral evaluations. The question of what competitors *intended* to do is largely irrelevant, whereas in the courtroom it is crucial. A game in which the winner was the 'best' or 'most virtuous' person would not be a game at all, but the ideal political society. The very act of circumscribing activities within a competitive arena, subject to specific rules of competition, is an invitation to abandon ethical questions of how one 'ought' to behave or how society 'ought' to be, in favour of strategic efforts to defeat opponents and maximize one's score. 'Fair play' may still be recognized, but only in a secondary sense, as implied by the term 'moral victory', which is anything but an *actual* victory. If the pursuit of fairness came to predominate over the pursuit of victory, the competition would have ended. The capacity of competition to keep ethics at bay ('values over which men can only fight', as Friedman put it) is another way of understanding the enthusiasm that neoliberals have always expressed for competitive forms of interaction. But this also means that 'gaming' (in which the competitors focus on the explicit statement and implementation techniques of rules, and not their spirit or 'point') is one of the constant threats to neoliberal authority.

A central defining question, common to both liberal theories of justice and to the design and theory of competitions, is 'what do people have in common?'. While liberal theories of justice pose this question in relation to all human beings and essential human capacities, competitions pose it in relation to a *limited* set of contestants and to *empirical* or *aesthetic* human traits. For liberal philosophers such as Rawls, common humanity consists in the capacity to reason: the original position is populated by a set of human beings who are stripped of all their capacities and identities, other than their shared powers of reasoning. In an analogous fashion, arranging a competition involves identifying a particular common human trait (enterprise, speed, beauty, efficiency) and then formulating a set of rules, techniques and measurement devices whereby different people can be judged and compared according to that trait. This can otherwise be referred to as 'commensuration', in which a single measure of value is used to render multiple, diverse phenomena comparable and rankable (Espeland & Stevens, 1998). In competitions humans are not all equal before the law, but *a designated set of humans are equal before the measure.*

The appeal of any competitive game depends partly on how much it is sealed off from broader political questions of justice and injustice, and the intrinsic notions of human worth which they relate to. If it is entirely sealed off (and it appears to reward arbitrary, meaningless human traits) then it looks irrelevant and futile (Goffman, 1997: 131). One way of resisting the imposition of competitive rules is to argue that they have nothing to do with what is *really* valuable in society, as people might argue of intelligence tests for example. But if it is insufficiently sealed off (and it appears to be governed by external political and economic forces) it loses its integrity, as a separate sphere, in which universal critical and moral questions are suspended. Another way of resisting the imposition of competitive rules is to argue that the game is *excessively* penetrated by external politics, for example in the claim that a firm has been protected from competition by the state or that nepotism has determined a labour market outcome. A competitive game that remains 'interesting' (both for participants and observers) is one that strikes a balance between being overwhelmed by 'external' influences and seeming excessively divorced from them. The same can be said of economic competition (Knight, 1935).

In the absence of some rule-giver or referee, competitors themselves have to uphold the 'liberal spirit' of competition. Smith's moral vision of the marketplace was of just such a competition, overseen by an imaginary 'invisible hand', but ultimately dependent on the moral 'sympathy' of traders with one another (Boltanski & Thévenot, 2006). Yet with a third party, the question of *how liberal, how fair* to make the contest is taken out of the competitors' hands. An authority is introduced, who takes the rules as they exist, and enforces them with a quasi-judicial spirit. The rules themselves cannot insist that they are interpreted and imposed fairly. But by appealing to an unspoken idea of justice, which transcends any particular competition or written rules, the figure of a referee attains some authority over the contest, by virtue of acting in a liberal spirit, even if no competition can be entirely liberal in nature. This figure only gains their liberal spirit by virtue of their practical position, as the independent outsider. If they lose this position (if, for example, a football referee is seen socializing excessively with one of the teams before the game) then no degree of fidelity to the rules can restore the sense of injustice that may surround their judgements. There is an unavoidable gap between the rules and the 'spirit of the rules' (or what Wittgenstein terms the 'game' and its 'point'), but the task of the liberal competitive authority is to minimize how this gap is exploited by the competitors. Keeping the application and interpretation of the rules as close to the spirit of *a priori* formal equality, as if imbued with Rawls's original position, ensures that the rule-enforcer retains authority and that the competition continues to seem sufficiently fair, if never utterly fair.

The violent threat of competitiveness

If a competition were only imbued by a liberal 'spirit' of fairness, then it would lack any vitality or surprise. It would not put competitors to the test or generate empirical inequality. The competitors would seek to ensure that the outcomes were the fairest reflection of their respective inequalities – but in doing so, they would be cooperating and therefore breaking the first norm of any competitive situation. Just as it must be assumed that competitors have some abstract sense of equality before the rules, and are equal at least until the contest has started, so it must be assumed that they desire victory or relative supremacy, almost regardless of how it is achieved. The rules and referee can be relied upon to impose minimal constraints of equality; the task of the competitors themselves is to maximize inequality in ways that benefit themselves.

To do this, they need a *strategy*. The strategic mindset does not look at the rules in terms of how they formally define victory, but looks at *other competitors* and asks how they would least like the game to be played. It is purely focused upon finding the sources of inequality most likely to result in victory, and which won't be immediately debarred by the rules (or rather, by a quasi-judicial interpretation of the rules). For sure, it may be that victory can be achieved through strategic forms of cheating, and that the competitor can get away with this. While no rule can ever stipulate that cheating is permitted, it is implicit in any competitive situation that it can and will occur. For example, there are sports such as ice hockey, in which illegal, violent activity is a constant and relatively 'normal' occurrence, which players, spectators and umpires are generally tolerant of, or even excited by. Cheating even has a legitimacy of a sort, if it is motivated by a desire to win. To be 'competitive' is to ignore how a game 'should' be played, or what human traits the rules are aiming to reward, and to focus on how one's own contingent traits can be employed against those of the opponents (Massumi, 2002: 77). This is most acute in 'zero sum' competitions, such as sports, in which one side wins and the other loses, but they cannot both win. But it is also present in 'positive sum' competitions, such as school exams (in which there is no limit to how many people succeed), in that individuals might train for the tests by focusing on the particular character of the test, rather than on the 'ability' it is supposed to measure. Performance audits always invite this form of 'gaming' and unintended consequences – in fact an effective audit or test is not one which successfully measures 'real' worth, but one that produces incentives for the right kind of gaming or minimizes destructive gaming.

An effective competitive strategy is therefore radically anti-normative. While the rules (and any external enforcer of them) seek to uphold the 'spirit' of fairness in how the competition is conducted, the strategic competitor not only ignores this spirit, it also seeks to subvert the interpretation of the rules in ways that are advantageous to themselves. If the 'point' of the game, from the liberal perspective, is to maintain some minimal level of equality in the face of measurement, the 'point' of the game from the strategic perspective is to do the opposite. What justifies such hostility to fairness and equality? Perhaps 'justify' is the wrong word here, implying as it does that there is a higher normative principle at work. The competitive commitment towards winning and defeating is really an entirely immanent and existential one. It rests on no idea of how the contest ought to be conducted, but purely on the contingent situation at hand. It stems from no higher principle, but from the existential fact of radical difference. This is what Carl Schmitt termed 'the political', which is hostile to all forms of moral constraint: 'The specific political distinction to which political actions and motives can be reduced is that between friend and enemy', Schmitt argued, but this is offered as an anthropological truth, and not a moral principle (Schmitt, 1996: 26). Within Schmitt's existential sense of the political, the pursuit of radical inequality attains a logic and motivating power all of its own, independent of any principle of justification, which is ultimately manifest in mortal combat. The question of why or with what justification 'we' should triumph over 'them' becomes meaningless where warfare is concerned, which 'has no normative meaning, but an existential meaning only, particularly in real combat with a real enemy' (Schmitt, 1996: 49). Brute, unreasoning violence in defence of friends, and against enemies, is described by Schmitt as a basic fact of being human. It is also this ontological definition of politics-as-difference which liberals blindly deny or suppress, with their appeal to justice-as-commonality.

Competitive strategy is imbued with the motivating power of the 'friend-enemy' distinction. Indeed, there is a genealogy connecting the analysis of military strategy and the academic field of business strategy. In Schmitt's account, the existential fact of the 'friend-enemy' distinction underpins politics as a radically contingent form of decision making which resists the imposition of rules or laws. The true character of 'the political' becomes manifest in the decision to try and destroy the enemy using violence. There is no *a priori* limit to what is politically possible or permissible, only contingent limits of power, which have to be strategically factored in to decision making. The critical defining decision available to the politician is whether to wage war or not.

A wholly strategic competitor acts according to political necessity, in response to the contingent inequalities and threats within the contest, rather than out of any sense of *a priori* fairness or common humanity. 'The political', in Schmitt's specific existential sense of the term, is a necessary animating force in a competition, for otherwise the abstract normative questions of *why* victory is desirable, or *why* the rules are as they are, will undermine the vitality of the contest. The event of political violence closes down the space of judgement, which the liberal spirit of competition opens up: it generates instinctive and unreasonable behaviour, without objectivity or critical distance. In situations of violence – or the near-violence of 'the political' – all notions of equivalence, measure or justification are refused (Boltanski, 2012). The essential *difference and inequality* between the competitors are what matter at such moments, and not their essential commonality and equality.

Violence cannot properly be described as a competitive 'spirit', in the sense used by Weber, for that term implies a moral justification or regulatory principle, which in turn implies an appeal to the common interest. Instead we should speak of the *violent threat* that underpins vigorous competitive strategy, the lurking sense that material force could possibly be used in order to achieve victory. This is metaphysics of a sort, though certainly not in any deontological sense. Rather, it is metaphysics as existential possibility, as future actions that do not yet exist, and are undetermined by anything other than sheer will. The violent threat of competition commands competitors to interpret the rules in a purely self-interested fashion, to see how the game might be played in ways that maximize advantage over the 'enemy', ultimately so as to survive. The rules' normative, liberal nature – of being the same for all – is resisted, and they are interpreted in ways that are as unfair as possible.

But a competition is still a reduced, delimited version of violence, just as it is a reduced, delimited version of liberalism. It is not universalistic enough to be identifiable with 'justice', but nor does it ever attain the contingency of sheer combat: it hovers in a governed space between the two. Schmitt complained that when liberals sought to pacify 'the political' with rules, they reduced it to mere 'competition', which lacked any existential, violent quality (Schmitt, 1996: 72). Economic combat or sport may involve inequality, but never the radical inequality sought in warfare (which is precisely why liberals value them). A strategic competitor thus pushes as hard as possible against the rules, seeking to define the competition and interpret its rules in ways that make victory most likely. In viewing inequality as the 'point' of a competitive game, and not equality, they strain beyond the limits of what is legal, using extraneous tactics, gaming and subtle forms of cheating, none of which are (or can be) codified in the rules. But they are inevitably still limited by the rules and the authority that enforces them: measure or judgement still has the final word, and not brute force. Intuitively speaking, they are also likely to maintain their own sense of 'right' and 'wrong' in the conduct of the competition, which even the most strategic political combatant may struggle to throw off psychologically.

Just as competitors can delegate responsibility for upholding the 'liberal spirit' of competitiveness to an independent third party, so they can also delegate responsibility for the 'violent threat' to a heavily partial coach of some kind. Sports coaches, business gurus, life coaches, 'leaders', business lobbyists, motivational speakers and national business representatives are all examples of authorities whose task is to boost the competitive performance of those they represent or lead. They take the strategic decisions on how to 'win', and develop psychological and cultural approaches to enhance the competitive desire and teamwork of their 'friends'. This is an immanent view of competition, in which the rules are only ever constraints to be got around. Fuelled by the 'violent threat' of competitiveness, this authority commands obedience for no justifiable reason, but purely on the basis that they have the ability and will to succeed. Their decisions are obeyed purely because they are in the position of deciders.

The strategic view from 'within' competitive situations may still employ empirical evidence and tests, in order to achieve agreements amongst 'friends' or to motivate them against 'enemies'. It is no coincidence that world wars have been times of great innovation in economic and psychological measurement and statistics, as these are useful tools when seeking to plan for more existential contests. But pragmatically speaking, the character and purpose of such empirical claims are very different from those made by those seeking to adjudicate *over* competitions. Those whose authority derives from the 'violent threat' of competition will use evidence and numbers in ways likely to be divisive in order to demonstrate how and why 'we' need to triumph over 'them' and how we might do it. The pragmatic power of facts and figures, in such situations, is to energize, orientate and disrupt, rather than to achieve peaceful agreement. Often, the perceived objectivity or neutrality of this empirical data is less important than its aesthetic impact. Numbers which incite paranoia regarding falling competitiveness, or triumph regarding victories, perform effectively. Those which offer cold, impartial judgements on the situation may be quite useless for those striving to navigate uncertain situations (Knight, 1957).

THE AUTHORITY OF ECONOMICS

To understand what drives inequality under neoliberalism, we first need to understand how neoliberals conceive of equality (or, perhaps more helpfully, equivalence) and how it is manifest in practical terms. What will be the common framework, measure or test through which shared differences will become apparent? What is assumed about human beings, in order that valid quantitative representations of difference can become possible? For the 'early neoliberals' such as Hayek, the market itself would become the common evaluative device, which was capable of converting all differences into a common language of price. As long as they were constructed and run competitively, there would be no need for any 'external' or additional evaluation of how the competitors were performing. This nevertheless assumes that competition is limited to specific institutional arenas and leaves open ample scope to impose alternative institutional arrangements, where markets are either unwelcome politically, or impractical (Davies, 2013). Hayek's support for the welfare state, Simons' commitment to the nationalization of key industries, the ordo-liberal enthusiasm for the 'social market' demonstrate that the early neoliberals were offering a justification for what Walzer terms 'monopoly' (separate inequalities in separate spheres) and not 'dominance' (the power of one sphere over all others).

As the next chapter explores, it was Coasian economics (in tandem with the Chicago School) that altered this profoundly. The objective perspective of the economist – implicitly working for a university or state regulator – would provide the common standard against which activity could be judged. Of course economics does not *replace* the price system, indeed economics is very often entangled with the price system (Callon, 1998; Caliskan, 2010), but the *a priori* equality of competitors becomes presumed, as a matter of economic methodology, which stipulates that all agents are endowed with equal psychological capacities of calculation. It is because this assumption is maintained when *evaluating* all institutions and actions that it massively broadens the terrain of legitimate competition, and opens up vast, new possibilities for legitimate inequality and legitimate restraint. Walzerian dominance is sanctioned, and not simply monopoly. The Coasian vision of fair competition rests on an entirely unrealistic premise, namely that individuals share a common capacity to calculate and negotiate, rendering intervention by public authorities typically unnecessary: the social reality of lawyers' fees is alone enough to undermine this fantasy. Yet in one sense, this is a mode of economic critique that is imbued with the 'liberal spirit' described earlier. It seeks to evaluate the efficiency of activities, on the basis of the assumed equal rationality of all, and the neutrality of the empirical observer.

Like Coase, Schumpeter facilitates a great expansion of the space – and time – in which the competitive process takes place. Various 'social' and 'cultural' resources become drawn into the domain of competition, with the goal being to define the rules that all others must play by. Monopoly is undoubtedly the goal of competitiveness. But unlike Coase's economics, Schumpeter's makes no methodological assumption regarding the common rationality of all actors. Instead, it makes a *romantic* assumption regarding the inventive power of some actors (entrepreneurs), and the restrictive routines of most others. Any objective judgements regarding valid or invalid actions will be rooted in static methodologies or rules. Entrepreneurs have no rules, and respect no restraint. They seek no authority or validation for what they do, but are driven by a pure desire to dominate. In this sense their own immanent authority comes with a 'violent threat', which is endorsed by the neoliberal state as Chapter 4 discusses.

These theories of competition are not 'ideological' and nor are they secretive. They are not ideological because they do not seek to disguise how reality is actually constituted or to distract people from their objective conditions. They have contributed to the construction and constitution of economic reality, inasmuch as they provide objective and acceptable reports on what is going on, that succeed in coordinating various actors. Moreover, they are sometimes performative, not least because of how they inform and format modes of policy, regulation and governance. Inequality has not arisen by accident or due to the chaos of capitalism or 'globalization'. Theories and methodologies, which validate certain types of dominating and monopolistic activity, have provided the conventions within which large numbers of academics, business people and policy makers have operated. They make a shared world possible in the first place. But nor are any of these theories secret either. They have been published in peer-reviewed journals, spread via policy papers and universities. Without shared, public rationalities and methodologies, neoliberalism would have remained a private conspiracy. Inequality can be denounced by critics of neoliberalism, but it cannot be argued that – in an era that privileges not only market competition but *competitiveness in general* – inequality is not publicly acceptable.

NOTES

1 'Planning and competition can be combined only by planning for competition, but not by planning against competition' (Hayek, 1944: 43).
2 Bergin offers a compelling account of the transition that occurred within the Mont Pelerin Society, as Milton Friedman became an increasingly dominant figure in the Society from 1961 onwards, alienating many of the elder European members, such as Ropke, in the process (Bergin, 2013). The rising number of American economists in the Mont Pelerin Society was one symptom of its gradual relinquishing of its initial philosophical and social ambitions, and corresponded to its increasingly laissez-faire, capitalist outlook, in contrast to the early concern with designing a new liberal order.

3

THE LIBERAL SPIRIT OF ECONOMICS

Competition, anti-trust and the Chicago critique of law

enry Simons is a central figure in the development of the American tradition of neoliberalism, which developed at the University of Chicago between the 1930s and the 1970s. Yet Simons was never highly revered as an economist and he was generally considered a maverick, with personal difficulties which led to his suicide in 1946. His 1934 programmatic text, *A Positive Programme for Laissez-Faire*, was viewed as far-fetched in its ambitions to recreate a liberal economic order, against the backdrop of the New Deal (Simons, 1937). While the book was greatly admired by Hayek (a close friend), Coase later described Simons as a 'utopian'. But it was Simons' awkward quality which led Jacob Viner, then head of the Chicago economics department, to seek an appointment for him in an alternative department. The University of Chicago had recently established a law programme which needed someone to run it. Viner proposed Simons for the position (hoping to make him the Law School's problem) to which he was appointed in 1939, making him the first economist to ever run a US law school. By subsequently transferring and attracting more economists to the Law School – most importantly, Aaron Director – Simons gave birth to the 'Law and Economics' movement and discipline.

Over the subsequent forty years, Chicago Law and Economics would grow from these accidental origins to widespread prominence within American legal thinking. Over the course of this journey, various transformations would occur, as this chapter will explore, with profound implications for the understanding of law, regulation and the definition of 'competition'. The authority of economics and economists within many state agencies would grow, to some extent at the expense of traditional legal expertise. Judges would learn to reason like neo-classical economists, leading *The Washington Post* to raise the alarm in 1980 that federal judges were being 'brain-washed' by Chicago ideas. A radically empiricist view of law would emerge, which understood its sole function to be the alteration of economic incentives for the promotion of efficient outcomes. In an archetypically neoliberal fashion, the sovereign and normative dimensions of law were treated as metaphysical nonsense, which were only used by judges and other public actors to conceal their own interests and objectives (Davies, 2010). The question of 'just or unjust' became replaced by one of 'efficient or inefficient'. This critical and technical programme registered its greatest successes in the field of anti-trust, where it greatly reduced the remit and authority of competition agencies, beginning in the USA in the late 1970s, before permeating the European Commission from the early 1990s onwards (Pitofsky, 2008; Buch-Hansen & Wigger, 2010).

Chicago Law and Economics exemplifies the key aspects of neoliberalism examined in the previous two chapters. Firstly, it attempts to reduce political metaphysics to political physics, disenchanting politics (or in this case law and judicial authority) by economics. It explicitly seeks to empty out the ethical, performative and *a priori* components of law, and leave only its positive, measurable, empirical elements. In this respect, it is radically utilitarian in the manner of Jeremy Bentham, as many of its pioneers and adherents recognize (Posner, 1981; Kitch, 1983). It does this thanks to audacious acts of disciplinary and professional imperialism on the part of neo-classical economists, who not only taught and trained lawyers (following Simons' appointment) but also provided an entirely new basis on which to think about the authority of law and of judges, namely the measured *efficiency* of rules and rulings. Empirical outcomes are the barometer of justice, and not conscious intentions, actions or processes. This represents a major departure from the legal epistemology of the early neoliberals.

Secondly, and consequently, this gives rise to a rapid inflation in the authority and power of neo-classical economics, from a positive academic science of rational choice, to a quasi-constitutional process for public decision making. The case of anti-trust exhibits this, and will be addressed in detail here, but efforts to replace norms with economic *tests* extend across the neoliberal state. To hold such authority, neo-classical economics and economists cannot simply offer up their techniques and measuring devices for use by the state, they must also operate with justifications and critical bases on which to employ *these* techniques and devices as opposed to others. Within anti-trust and regulatory agencies, economists must become embedded in a set of institutional conditions, which will allow their methods to be conducted in a neutral, independent academic fashion, while also being professionally subservient to the legal experts who put anti-trust cases together. The authority of the neo-classical method requires constant affirmation and institutional support. It must be projected in implicitly normative terms, despite its claims to be free of any normativity. And upon arrival in the state, this style of reasoning is projected in implicitly *sovereign* terms, despite its claims to be hostile to all nonsensical talk of sovereignty.

Thirdly, Law and Economics makes a particular *Coasian* definition of 'competition' the empirical test of valid action on the part of firms and states. To be sure, this definition of 'competition' comes to be equated with that of 'efficiency', in the narrow neo-classical sense of the term, usually understood as 'consumer welfare'. But the idea of competition, as an uncertain and unequalizing dynamic, continues to do crucial work in how the neo-classical critique of law and of the state is conducted. If Law and Economics was *merely* utilitarian in a Benthamite sense, there would be no clear reason to distinguish this paradigm from social-ist planning. It is because Law and Economics combines Benthamite empiricism with a particular (Coasian) idea of free competition that it preserves a central feature of neoliberalism, and remains hostile to state interventions. It strives to square the circle between liberalism and utilitarianism, through an idiosyn-cratic appeal to the rationality of individual decision making. At work here is the latent metaphysics of the neo-classical method itself: the presupposition of calculating, individual rationality serves as a regulative liberal principle in the way in which outcomes are evaluated. It is this method that is responsible for producing empirical, numerical facts out of an uncertain process, and thereby also producing a shared sense of what is going on.

Finally, we can see that this tradition of neo-classical economics acquires and requires a 'liberal spirit' of authority, once it is embedded in anti-trust agencies, law courts and regulators. The neo-classical economist becomes an adjudicator, external to the contest, tasked with upholding some minimal idea of *a priori* freedom and the equality of competitors. Economists become *quasi-judicial* in their authority. They ensure that all combatants are equal before the measure of efficiency, in the same way that judges ensure that all citizens are equal before the law. They perform crucial work in regulatory agencies in delineating pre-cisely what counts as evidence of competition, while actively excluding a great deal of information that lawyers might otherwise have considered. From a pragmatist perspective, the neo-classical economist oversees the procedures through which efficiency and inefficiency can be spoken about in empirical terms in legal settings. They perform an active role in the *commensuration* of evidence, taking heterogeneous situations and institutions and processing them in ways that make them numerically comparable in a court of law. Chicago Law and Economics scholars would dispute such a normative characterization. But by examining how neo-classical economics is applied and justified empirically in particular legal situations, we get a glimpse of its 'liberal spirit' – that is, its purported fairness and blindness.

This chapter details the genealogy of law and economics, as a strategic and highly effective process of economization, first of legal thinking and then of legal and regulatory institutions. It demonstrates how this attempt to strip the state of its metaphysical 'liberal' authority must eventually bestow a quasi-judicial authority upon economists, and a normative status upon the procedures of Chicago price theory if it is to function effectively. The psychological assumptions of that theory become implicitly regulatory principles for how the state comes to understand justice, at least in the 'economic' sphere, but increasingly beyond. Neo-classical methodology becomes a form of authoritative procedure, which must be performed in a credible fashion, before an audience which recognizes its authority, if its findings are to be accepted. This pragmatist analysis requires us to pay close attention to the forms of rhetoric and persuasion that have characterized Law and Economics, and how lawyers have gradually ceded authority to economists, or rather, learnt to speak and think like economists (just as economists have instinctively come to act in a 'lawyerly' fashion in law schools and state agencies).

The most significant outcome of these processes was a wholesale reappraisal of monopoly, resulting in a model of applied neoliberal policy and law in which large concentrations of corporate power and high profitability were typically justified on efficiency grounds. The mere *possibility* that a dominant firm might be challenged in the future came to be viewed as a sufficient means of constraining their power. Whether or not such a possibility existed was deemed testable through abstract economic modelling, rather than any actual market events. While the Chicago School retained a dogmatic faith in price *theory*, as a methodological basis on which to judge individual behaviour and institutional efficiency, this involved a declining commitment to the price *mechanism* as a feature of decentralized, competitive markets. As the authority of economists came to condition that of lawyers, 'price' went from being a visible phenomenon at work in a liberal market society, to being a metaphor through which experts would analyse different forms of industrial organization. In the

Chicago School epistemology, the core tenets of economic liberalism (choice, competition, price, freedom) are converted into methodological premises, which are not necessarily institutionally manifest or apparent to the actors themselves. Equally, institutional forms which *appear* entirely illiberal to the actors themselves, and indeed to lawyers, may actually be deemed efficient and competitive by the Chicago price theorist. The liberal spirit of competition becomes increasingly overshadowed by the violent threat of competition. This then sows the seeds of legitimacy crises.

The chapter is in three parts. In the next section, I examine the development of Law and Economics at the University of Chicago, between Simons' appointment to the Law School and the first Law and Economics texts of the early 1970s. The influence of Coase is crucial in this regard, in enabling the Chicago School to lose its final vestiges of European neoliberalism, which had involved a degree of *a priori* commitment to the form of markets, the institution of price and the rights of market actors. Secondly, I examine how Law and Economics transformed the legal and policy thinking regarding competition, in ways that led to rapid growth in the neo-classical economic capacities of states from the 1980s onwards. Thirdly, I look at what this means for how competition is defined and enforced in practice in the USA and EU. This chapter draws partly on interviews with economists and lawyers working in anti-trust agencies, quotes from whom are included in the footnotes.

THE FUSION OF LAW AND ECONOMICS

The fusion of law and economics was an abiding preoccupation for neoliberal thinkers from the 1930s onwards. The paradoxes of competition reappear at the interface of legal and economic analysis. Law is concerned with generalities, whose legitimacy is potentially independent of economic incentives or outcomes. Economics (at least in its neo-classical variety) is concerned with utilitarian questions of efficiency and effects. Enacting anti-trust policy necessarily involves a degree of conflict or compromise between these two epistemological and professional worldviews, which will determine the extent to which anti-trust is viewed in the procedural terms of market fairness or the utilitarian terms of optimizing output. Prior to the emergence of neoliberalism, there were a number of efforts made to bring law and social science together through pragmatism and compromise, as manifest in American legal realism (Fuller, 1934; Pearson, 1997). But from the mid-1930s onwards, neoliberals renewed these efforts with greater critical urgency and inter-disciplinary assertiveness. This was manifest in two traditions, which are in some respects inverses of one another: in an *ordo-liberal project of extending legal analysis into economics*, and then in a *Chicago School project of extending economic analysis into law*. If the synthetic objective was the same for both, the styles and policy implications differed markedly.

Ordo-liberalism: law as market order

The ordo-liberal tradition achieved one distinctive fusion between law and economics. The ordo-liberal Freiburg School was led by Walter Eucken from the early 1930s onwards, successfully avoiding interference from the Nazi government. It was influential in advising the allies on the reconstruction of the German economy following the war, in particular in highlighting the importance of cartels in facilitating the Nazi takeover of the economy, and hence of anti-cartel legislation in a postwar liberal Germany. The school had been planning for postwar economic reconstruction over the course of 1942–43 and was instrumental in adding strong anti-trust provisions to Germany's 1948 constitution and creating the conditions of a European competition framework (including the prevention of State Aid) in the 1957 Treaty of Rome (Gerber, 1998; Ptak, 2009). This tradition shaped the European Commission's style of competition enforcement right up until the 1980s (Buch-Hansen & Wigger, 2010).

Ordo-liberalism privileged an explicitly moral-philosophical idea of a competitive market, in which no individual firm or other actor could exert power over others. Eucken's idea of 'complete' competition was one in which the price system directed all economic processes, and no individual competitor could unilaterally influence price. Empirically speaking, economic agents were recognized to be motivated by the creation and pursuit of plans so as to reduce the uncertainty of the future. As Eucken wrote, 'At all times and places man's economic life consists of forming and carrying out economic plans' (quoted in Labrouse & Wiesz, 2001). However, this posed the threat of certain firms acquiring dominance over others, and ultimately over society. The type of economic equilibrium sought by the ordo-liberals was an institutional one, whereby an essential economic *order* would be established through law in which no single interest was in power. Nobody, neither state nor firm, should be able to plan with great confidence. Monopolies and cartels needed breaking up, regardless of the benefits they might produce (Bonefeld, 2012). Policy makers should be limited to 'indirect regulation' – that is, interventions aimed at the formal structure of the economy and its relation to society – and not to specific outcomes. In this regard, Hayek and Simons were highly sympathetic.

The ordo-liberals were keen sceptics of neo-classical economics, which they believed had abandoned any critique of industrial capitalism, or any normative concern with the design and construction of a liberal market. The task for the ordo-liberals was to translate liberal economic concepts into a legal language, which could then be used as the basis for economic and political governance, not simply in particular institutions or markets but across society. As the ordo-liberal Franz Böhm imagined, liberal capitalism would need an 'economic constitution' – a set of sovereign laws which made the competitive market order the template for society at large (Gerber, 1994). Liberal political principles would become fused with and preserved by neoliberal economic institutions:

> Civil rights and liberties have no value in themselves; they only acquire their significance through the institution of competition ... These rights and liberties are the prerogatives of combatants and they forfeit their raison d'être when the combat ceases. (Quoted in Grossekettler, 1996)

The 'liberal spirit' of economic competition shines through this sort of claim, suggesting that liberal metaphysical notions of right can be rendered tangible or physical via the particular institution of a market. The fusion of a liberal phi-losophy of justice with the socio-economic institution of a market would occur through a reorientation of the judiciary, towards the upholding of economic competition. Economic competition becomes a substitute for and guarantee of political liberty. As Foucault explores in his detailed exposition of ordo-liberalism, in the postwar period, the German market was historically and logically prior to the state, being put in place under American reconstruction and rule (Foucault, 2008: 102–105). This precedence means that, for German neoliberals, the market can coherently be treated as the constitutional principle on which the state's authority depends.

Ordo-liberalism was inspired by a sense that economics had failed to defend economic liberty, and consequently political liberty. Neo-classical economics was deemed sociologically ignorant regarding the importance of power, regulation, industrial concentration, technology and norms within twentieth-century capital-ism. But rather than divert economics towards norms and institutions (as Coase and the later Chicago School of Law and Economics would do), ordo-liberalism diverted legal attention towards the sanctity and vitality of the price system. This therefore represents one particular strategy for the fusion of law and economics. In practice, it would mean an active role for the judiciary in shaping the institu-tions of capitalism, upholding a degree of *a priori* freedom on the part of competitors, and blocking monopolistic practices on principle. The role of the state in the ordo-liberal worldview was to defend the liberal spirit of competition at all costs, maintaining a sense of fairness in the market and placing unambiguous regulatory limits around the 'violent threat' of combative economic practices. The executive branch of government was treated with suspicion, but an active judicial branch was central to how an 'economic constitution' would be upheld. From the ordoliberal perspective, the decline of the Weimar Republic into National Socialism was explicable in terms of a weak state permitting the gradual pollution of market mechanisms with social and political agendas (Bonefeld, 2012, 2013). A strong state would be needed to prevent this in future.

Ordo-liberalism won its greatest political achievements in the wake of World War Two, but its influence has waned ever since. This particular fusion of law and economics granted the state the right to intervene economically without concern for the empirical consequences, offering justifications based on the ideal 'order' and structure of free market capitalism. Legalism remained prior to economism: while law was applied to the economy, law itself was not subjected to an economic critique. If anything, neo-classical economics was subjected to a legalistic critique. Hence, from many neoliberal perspectives, ordo-liberalism remains mired in the metaphysical nonsense of universal rights, freedom and *a priori* equality, even if this nonsense becomes channelled into the marketplace via the political establishment of an 'economic constitution'. Certainly for Eucken, the order of a competitive market was a metaphysical essence and not an empirical or measurable phenomenon (Ptak, 2009). Under ordo-liberalism, *price* acquires a magical, metaphysical quality akin to sovereignty, acting as the technical guarantor of liberty and consensual interaction. The dynamism of the market would counteract the quantitative rationalism of economic calculation, which threatened to strip modernity of its vitality (Bonefeld, 2013). It is the absence of this strongly liberal form of neoliberalism that characterizes the 'actually existing' neoliberalism that was implemented from the 1970s onwards. The neoliberal state lost its judicial right to intervene in the competitive game, purely on principle, and was instead restricted to justifications based in empirical considerations of efficiency. This was thanks to the Chicago School's own distinctive fusion of law and economics.

Chicago: economics as legal audit

Both Hayek and Simons were socially and intellectually close to the Freiburg ordo-liberals during the 1930s and early 1940s. They too were entranced by the magic of the price system, which facilitated coordination without any 'conscious' collective will. Simons viewed monopoly as the greatest obstacle to renewing liberalism and repeatedly tried to hire Hayek during the early 1940s, though without success. Following the publication of *The Road to Serfdom*, the conservative Volcker Fund offered to fund a project which would take Hayek to Chicago, and produce a US version of the book. This was belatedly established as the Free Market Study, which was led by Director between 1946–52, although Hayek was only able to finally move to Chicago in 1950 (Van Horn & Mirowski, 2009). Notably, the Free Market Study was also conducted in the Law School, and not the economics department, which was partly a mark of how ideological it appeared to mainstream economists.

Influenced by Simons and Hayek, the 'second generation' Chicago School (dominated by Milton Friedman, George Stigler and Director) had also worked around the assumption that the strong rule of economic law would be a crucial ingredient for any future neoliberal system. The assumption, which held at least until the early 1950s, was that economic freedom would require a vigilant state (especially in the realm of anti-trust) to prevent monopolistic and cooperative practices from subverting or circumventing the price system. As late as 1968, Stigler was a contributor to the Nixon administration's Neal report on anti-trust, which recommended the active deconcentration of industries by government agencies. Yet by the mid-1970s, this was very far from the position of the Chicago School or its Law and Economics movement. Contrary to visions of American neoliberalism as 'market fundamentalism', the Chicago position swung away from the ordo-liberal and early neoliberal one, towards an idiosyncratic view of competition with scant *intrinsic* respect for the price system and far greater sympathy for monopolies. Within this view, the competitiveness of individual firms could be evaluated by economists (using hypotheses and models), and not necessarily by the presence of competitors.

The genesis of Chicago Law and Economics contains two critical paradigm-shifting moments. The first arose when Director (appointed head of the Law School, following Simons' death) was invited by the legal scholar Edward Levi to assist him in teaching the school's anti-trust class. There is evidence that from 1950 onwards Director had been growing increasingly suspicious of his colleagues' faith in anti-trust as the guarantor of liberty and/or efficiency (Van Horn, 2009, 2011). It seemed to presume too much certainty on the part of government lawyers, and not enough common sense on the part of firms or their managers. The economic rationale for anti-trust law (that is, its measured effects on price and efficiency) had not been subjected to a truly economic analysis. In the classroom, Levi would offer legalistic explanations of why active anti-trust was a necessary precondition of a competitive market, which otherwise tended towards inefficient monopoly. Director would then respond, dismantling the argument using neo-classical economics, showing how legal interventions might conceivably undermine the efficiency of the market. He was particularly scornful of the use of merger law to prevent vertical integration (between firms and suppliers), which would become a major focus for the Chicago critique of anti-trust. As one attendee of the class later reminisced, 'for four days Ed would do this, and for one day each week Aaron Director would tell us that everything that Levi had told us the preceding four days was non-sense' (Kitch, 1983). The class also included Robert Bork, the conservative lawyer who would later do more than anyone to push Chicago Law and Economics into public policy circles.

An irony of this situation was that the lawyer – in this case, Levi – was more wedded to the market price mechanism than the economist. In common with the ordo-liberals and the American anti-trust authorities at the time, Levi assumed that any business strategy that disrupted the *a priori* form of a com-petitive, decentralized market was anti-competitive. Director's insight was that in empirical industrial situations there were plenty of conditions under which monopolistic practices could be efficient in terms of measured output: for example, the monopoly might simply be an outcome of a firm innovating or cutting costs more effectively than their competitors. Consumer welfare might be higher with one or two efficient producers, than with a choice of ten compet-ing and inefficient producers. Director was edging towards the same institutional insights that Schumpeter and Coase had already arrived at (Director had in fact met Coase more than once at the LSE in the 1930s).

The second critical event was a seminar hosted at Director's home in Chicago in 1960, when Coase presented his paper, 'The Problem of Social Cost', to 20 senior Chicago economists, including Friedman and Stigler. Stigler later described it as 'one of the most exciting intellectual events of my life' (Kitch, 1983). As explored in the previous chapter, Coase's theory of transaction costs meant radically abandoning any ideal or *a priori* vision of an optimal institu-tional arrangement, making the efficiency of decentralized markets (and all industrial structures) an open empirical question, to be gauged through careful empirical application of price theory. As a critique of Pigou's theory of exter-nalities, Coase had argued that industrial strategies which undermine competition could potentially be efficient, relative to the alternatives (especially when those alternatives included costly regulatory interventions). Given that he was, to all intents and purposes, offering a critique of the liberal commitment to decentralized open markets, it was little surprise that he had an initially unsym-pathetic audience in Chicago economists. A vote taken at the beginning of the evening revealed that there was unanimous opposition to Coase's argument. In his acute scepticism towards regulation, he had, in the words of one observer, 'out-Chicago'ed Chicago' (Priest, 2005: 356).

Yet this paper succeeded in creating a new framework for the economic analysis of law, which would become the distinguishing feature of Chicago Law and Economics. Coase's paper suggested that most neo-classical economists suffered from an idealistic vision of economic processes as occurring without transaction costs, but occasionally encountering problems of 'externality' which could be resolved through regulatory intervention. What this missed was that, in reality, all economic activity, both regulated and unregulated, carries costs. The task for the economist should be to evaluate the legal arrangements which are the least costly *in the aggregate*, relative to other viable courses of action, as opposed to unrealistic visions of a 'perfect' or transaction costless market. A clarification of property rights (such that two parties could settle damages between themselves) might often serve as a more efficient alternative to regulatory intervention. Coase offered a new paradigm of analysis, one that was far more sceptical of the state than the early neoliberals and chimed with the laissez-faire or 'anarcho-capitalist' sympathies of Friedman, who circa 1960 was becoming the dominant figure, not only within the Chicago School, but also the Mont Pelerin Society (Foucault, 2008; Bergin, 2013). The seminar at Director's house was a turning point in itself, as Coase gradually won over the assembled group. A vote at the end of the evening showed unanimous support for his position. Members of the Chicago Law and Economics movement later joked that law and economics could be divided into 'BC' and 'AC' – before Coase and after Coase (Stigler, 1992).

The Levi/Director anti-trust class and Coase's seminar presentation both high-light certain characteristic features of how the Chicago Law and Economics operated rhetorically and culturally. Firstly, as has been widely remarked on (and celebrated by its protagonists), there was a macho ethos of intellectual combat (Van Overtveldt, 2006): an argument or idea could only survive in this climate if it could withstand a combination of rationalist attack and audit by common sense – where common sense meant the basic psychological assumptions of neo-classical price theory. Legal arguments about what a market or economy 'ought' to look like were revealed as a form of metaphysical 'nonsense' before the tribunal of economic rationalism. Levi's argument about the normative necessity of anti-trust was revealed by Director to be just such nonsense; Coase, on the other hand, turned the tables on Chicago, and was even more immune to normative claims than they were. In this respect, Chicago economists were already behaving like lawyers in a courtroom, marshalling evidence and counter-evidence, seeking holes in opponents' arguments and attempting to demolish one another with their rhetoric.

The ethos which unites the style of Chicago School argument with its content is a valorization of *contestability*. From the Chicagoan neoliberal perspective, this holds as much in intellectual life as in economic life. There is no limit to how much influence and power a good argument or a good business should be allowed to have, so long as there remains the possibility that others may contest it. This corresponds closely to Popper's idea of the 'open society'. Accepted arguments must be falsifiable *in principle* and monopolies must be challengeable *in principle*. To compete (intellectually or economically) becomes far tougher under these conditions, as it potentially involves defying the entire status quo – as Friedman and his colleagues were self-consciously doing. What this philosophy typically exaggerates is how contestable monopolistic powers are in practice.

Secondly, through a series of accidents and disciplinary experimentation, neo-classical economists arrived in positions of teaching and training lawyers. Simons' move to the Law School precipitated this, with Director's appointment cementing it, resulting in a number of Chicago economists (including Stigler and Gary Becker) spending some or all of their time teaching law. The crucial thing about Director's intervention in Levi's anti-trust class was not that it altered how economists thought about regulation and law, but how *lawyers* thought about them. In fact the economic establishment (then dominated by Harvard) was largely impervious to the Chicago way of thinking until the 1980s, which was viewed as obsessively libertarian. And yet by privileging clarity of thinking and simplicity of reasoning (derived from neo-classical economics), the Chicago approach appealed to lawyers in the traditions of pragmatism and positivism, especially those with conservative sympathies such as Bork and Posner. The legal realist tradition of the 1920s and 1930s had attempted to provide a social scientific explanation and justification for law, but never using neo-classical economics, and never with quite such hostility to moral reasoning.

The Chicago fusion of law and economics occurred through persuading lawyers to abandon their concern with metaphysical notions such as 'justice' and 'right', in favour of empirical questions of measurable output, but this required certain rhetorical skills on the part of the economists who spread this message. Richard Posner, who would become the leading figure of Chicago Law and Economics, was a lawyer who had never studied economics, but stumbled upon it in the

1960s, discovering that price theory simply made greater 'sense' than what his legal colleagues were arguing (Teles, 2008). Its resolutely simple premise – that the best action is the one which maximizes welfare – coupled with the assumption that each individual knows what welfare means for them, could devastate far more philosophically sophisticated notions of justice. The ability of economists, such as Director and Coase, to communicate this style of reasoning beyond the economics profession was fundamental, as Posner recognized:

> [Coase] has what to a lawyer is quite important, an unusually lucid and simple style of writing … When I read it, having no knowledge of economics at all, it seemed to me to make perfectly good sense. The fact that it was very well and clearly written enabled him to communicate with me in a way that most economists could not. (Kitch, 1983: 226)

Where the ordo-liberals sought to impress upon the judiciary the importance of particular economic institutions and structures (competitive markets, the price mechanism etc.), the Chicago Law and Economics movement sought to impress upon lawyers a particular utilitarian style of thinking and reasoning. In her analysis of Coase's rhetoric, Deirdre McLoskey points out that his style is a 'lawyerly' one, peppered with terms such as 'in fact', disparaging of abstract 'blackboard economics', and constructed around a careful building up of an argument based on stories and metaphors (McCloskey, 1985). The Law and Economics project was (often explicitly) one of replacing the political metaphysics of justice with the political physics of neo-classical economics. The challenge was always viewed as a rhetorical and pragmatic one, as Stigler indicated:

> The difference between a discipline that seeks to explain economic life (and, indeed, all rational behaviour) and a discipline that seeks to achieve justice in regulating all aspects of human behaviour is profound. This difference means that, basically, the economist and the lawyer live in different worlds and speak different languages. (Stigler, 1992: 463)

This betrays the lingering influence of Hayekian constructivism, the notion that expert discourses and disciplines are responsible for shaping how the world appears to us. The task of Chicago Law and Economics was to fuse legal and economic professional discourse, such that 'efficiency' became a proxy for 'justice'. This disciplinary and professional imperialism would yield inevitable consequences, both for regulation and politics, although few expected the scale of transformation that Law and Economics would effect (especially in the field of anti-trust) from the late 1970s onwards.

Chicago Law and Economics has two core dimensions. The first uses neo-classical economics to analyse the empirical economic effects of law. 'The Problem of Social Cost' provided an analytical framework with which to do this, building on an earlier paper of Coase's, which had critically analysed telecommunications regulation in the United States. What distinguished the Chicago (and Coasian) view of law was its complete disregard for its sovereign or normative character. Law becomes reduced to its technical and empirical elements, such that its 'basic function ... is to alter incentives' (Posner, 1981: 75). Anything that was tacit, invisible or deontological was assumed to be a form of metaphysical nonsense. The concern of lawyers should be the same as that of economists: costs, incentives and utility. Following Bentham, utility is to be evaluated in the aggregate (not on the margins), with no cost left out of the assessment, such as that of legal or other public action. This has some uncomfortable ethical implications, primarily that if one party can gain sufficiently from a particular action at the expense of other parties, this is potentially justifiable in terms of aggregate welfare. Freedom is recast as the freedom to exploit – the social relation of capital, not the social relation of the market. Rights, norms or conscious intentions do not come into it. Justifiable regulation is therefore utility maximizing (according to economic analysis) but not necessarily 'fair' in any vernacular sense of the term. The very basis for legal authority shifts from a liberal language of universality to an economic language of efficiency.

This aspect of Law and Economics was used to transformative effect as a critique of regulation and anti-trust. Director's scepticism towards the claims made by anti-trust authorities, which he developed over the course of the School's Anti-trust Project of 1953–57, inspired micro-economists to start questioning the empirical effects of various other state activities. During the 1960s, Stigler's work on regulation and Becker's work on crime heralded a radically anti-normative vision of rules and law, in terms of the behavioural incentives they created. In the 1970s this approach produced the books that would bring about a revolution in anti-trust policy, Posner's 1976 *Antitrust Law* and Bork's 1978 *The Antitrust Paradox*, which systematically dismantled the claims that were being made by Harvard economists, liberals and government officials in favour of aggressive anti-trust interventions.

The second dimension of Chicago Law and Economics used neo-classical economics to *explain* how law was created and enacted, with Posner the leading exponent of this. Once again, the single presupposition adopted by Law and Economics scholars in this regard is that individuals act rationally to maximize their own interests, whether inside or outside of markets. Neo-classical economics can just as easily be applied to explain the behaviour of lawyers or bureaucrats as firms or consumers: as Coase put it 'economists have no subject matter' (Coase, 1988: 3). Rather than treat public servants and judges as exceptions to the standard neo-classical psychological model, Chicago neoliberals assume that they are equally self-interested. In tandem with the 'public choice' school of political science, which emerged in the 1950s at the University of Virginia, Chicago economists analysed legal and bureaucratic decisions in terms of the private interests that they served, and assessed their impact on aggregate efficiency. In Hayekian style, Chicago scholars demonstrated how actions made in the name of the public were, paradoxically, usually less efficient than those made in an unplanned, contingent fashion. Posner's famous argument – that common law is efficient because it grows organically from particular private cases, ruled without regard for the 'public interest' – highlights the conservative bias of this methodology (Posner, 1981). Self-interested and instinctive decisions are, almost by default, efficient, for why else would they have been selected? But decisions made on behalf of others (or the public in general) are very often inefficient, resting on erroneous views of what individuals privately value. Yet these inefficiencies are too often concealed, due to a lack of measurement and explication in the public realm. The vocation of the Law and Economics scholar is to bring the underlying psychological incentives, benefits and costs of the legal system to light.

Price as sovereign or as metaphor?

The divergence between ordo-liberalism and the Chicago School is profound, most importantly for how we are to understand the phenomenon of a *price*. This has major implications for the particular form of neoliberal authority, in particular for how its liberal spirit is interpreted. Where the fusion of law and economics is conducted from a legal vantage point, as was the case for ordo-liberalism, prices attain a constitutional quality in mediating social and economic relations. The hope of the ordo-liberals (and to a great extent Simons and Hayek) was that the price system could acquire a form of political sovereignty that would maintain all political forces in a state of finely balanced equilibrium as a guarantor of liberty. Price thereby attains a moral and political aura, which makes it the final arbiter of value across society. From Hayek's more conservative perspective, one great quality of market prices is that they are explicit. The public appearance of price – just like the public appearance of sovereignty via flags or palaces – is therefore crucial to its value.

By employing constitutional law in the service of market competition, ordo-liberalism makes the price system the guarantee of freedom. Price is not simply one technical instrument amongst many, but becomes symbolic of the overall order of society. To abuse the price system in any particular instance would be to offend the essential order of a free society. Thus when upholding competition and attacking dominant firms states are safeguarding a normative ideal, and not promoting any empirical outcome. The ordo-liberal critique of monopoly implicitly revives an early modern belief, that there is such a thing as a 'just price' for something, which arises through a fair process. It follows that other political solutions must be found for those goods which the price system cannot be trusted to deliver.

A number of Chicago School economists retained aspects of this classically liberal respect for prices, as a system of public symbols, until the 1960s. But in much of their work, 'price' mutates from an institutional phenomenon to a metaphorical category. Where ordo-liberals maintained a dogmatic allegiance to the price mechanism of the market, Chicago neoliberals diverted this towards the price theory of neo-classical economics. Price theory simply states that, faced with a range of options (be they in a market or not), individuals will select the one which delivers the greatest welfare to themselves, however understood. For economists such as Gary Becker, this is simply one particular 'approach' to explaining human behaviour, even when individuals themselves are not 'conscious' that they are acting in this way (Becker, 1976). Any situation can therefore be analysed *as if* it were a market, even when it *appears* that choice-making behaviour is neither free nor calculated. In a pragmatist and constructivist fashion, Chicago Law and Economics abandons the analysis of markets and prices as legally and publicly understood, and picks up an analysis of *market-like* behaviour, analysed according to a *psychology of price*, which may not be apparent to the agent being analysed (Foucault, 2008: 223).

In contrast to the ordo-liberal position, in which prices have an explicitness and public aura about them, Chicago epistemology privileges the economist's analytical insights over the intuitions of market actors themselves. More importantly, the two are operating in entirely parallel perspectival realms, with the latter not really 'knowing' what is going on. Friedman's 1953 statement of methodological principles affirms this very point: in his well-known analogy, a billiard player may be able to direct balls expertly round the table without knowing the laws of geometry, and a businessman can achieve profits without understanding the laws of economics (Friedman, 1953). The Hayekian faith in 'unconscious' processes is converted from a sociological level, whereby competition accidentally produces the best outcome, to a psychological level, in which pragmatically engaged individuals are not really conscious of what they are doing or why it works. When I interviewed one prominent Law and Economics scholar, he informed me:

> I never teach law and economics as a tool saying why I'm smarter than you are. I try to teach it as a tool that says 'a lot of things that you've done are really clever, and you don't even know why, and let me explain to you what I think is driving you, and tell me if it resonates with you once we make it explicit'.

Economics acquires a quasi-therapeutic role, in bringing unconscious causality and rationality to the fore. 'Price' becomes a methodological tool, through which otherwise random, uncritical and complex behaviours are rendered empirical, quantifiable and judgeable.

Once price becomes a metaphorical category, the institutional and historical specificity of the actual marketplace is lost, and economics becomes a basis on which to interpret psychological processes across all social, economic and political spheres. Divorced from any liberal normative commitment to open competitive markets, the Chicago price theorist is a resolutely sceptical and empiricist technician, who is free to apply an efficiency audit to all institutions – public and private – equally, regardless of whether they appear 'economic' in character. Yet by subjecting them to economic analysis, they are effectively rendered economic after all, by being reduced to quantified and measured effects. This humility conceals a deep hostility towards political metaphysics and the elitism of legal liberalism. At the same time, it undermines whatever vestiges of moral authority remained in the neoliberal vision of society. If metaphysics remains at all, it is in the form of neo-classical methodology, which presumes a certain transcendental idea of individual agency, in a crypto-liberal fashion. But expert methodology is a far weaker guarantor of the 'liberal spirit' of competition than robust legal rules of market conduct, as the early neoliberals and ordo-liberals had pursued.

NEO-CLASSICAL ECONOMICS ASCENDANT

A long-standing mantra of anti-trust authorities is that their function is to 'defend competition not competitors'. Being small and vulnerable should not automatically grant a firm the right to legal protection. In the USA, the anti-trust agencies and the courts paid lip service to this idea during the 1950s and 1960s, but in practice they regularly penalized firms for growing excessively large and profitable (Amato, 1997). The era of the 'Warren Court' propagated great political confidence in the capacity and necessity of the state to defend the public from corporate power. Three pieces of legislation underpin US anti-trust enforcement: the 1890 Sherman Act; the 1914 Clayton Act (which had created the Federal Trade Commission); and the 1936 Robinson-Patman Act. Drawing on these legislative resources, the Federal Trade Commission (FTC) and the Department of Justice (DOJ) anti-trust division intervened to block a wide range of industrial strategies on the part of US firms. These included: blocking horizontal mergers (between competitors) and vertical mergers (between suppliers and customers); busting cartels and price-fixing; breaking up monopolies and excessively concentrated industries; blocking product bundling (the sale of multiple products as a package) and tying (where a product in one market is sold in combination with a product in another market); preventing exclusionary practices (seeking to keep competitors out of a market); and defending small businesses from aggressive competition, such as predatory pricing.

During this period, the FTC and the DOJ were heavily dominated by lawyers, whose professional vocation was to bring cases against firms to court and then win them (Muris, 2003; Schmalensee, 2007). The entire thrust of these agencies, at least until the late 1960s, was towards punishing firms who appeared to be disrupting the pattern of normal competition, as understood by lawyers. Accompanying the legal interventionism of the anti-trust agencies in the postwar period was a dominant paradigm of competition economics, emanating from the work of Harvard economist Joseph Bain, known as the Structure Conduct Performance (SCP) approach. Drawing on empirical cases, Bain's theory paid great attention to the particular technological and institutional characteristics of industries, in an effort to understand how firms sought to raise the barriers to new market entrants. Markets that were effectively competitive could still be criticized on the basis that they possessed latent structural potential to reduce future competition. In common with both ordo-liberalism and welfare economics, this rested on an idealist epistemology in which the market possessed an essential form which was efficient and also needed protecting by the state. One decisive claim made by economists working within the SCP paradigm was that high profits signified the presence of monopoly or excessive concentration, meaning that firms faced an incentive to keep their profits down or else risk an anti-trust intervention. Economists who worked in the FTC during the 1970s recall firms seeking to deny that they were successful, for fear that this would attract anti-trust investigations.[1] Economists entering the FTC and the DOJ during the 1950s were steeped in SCP thinking, which bred suspicion about large and successful firms, and meshed well with the liberal-legal vocation of competition lawyers.

The Chicago critique of anti-trust

The Chicago School was resolutely hostile both to the zealous interventionism of government lawyers and to the apparent idealism of Bain's SCP approach. Both of these were charged with the error highlighted by Director and Coase, of exaggerating the potential inefficiencies of private action by large firms, while ignoring the costs, errors and imperfections of public policy and law. Bain viewed high profit and industrial concentration as the consequences of anti-competitive behaviour: Chicago saw them as positive side-effects of efficiency (Pitofsky, 2008). By the late 1960s, with the anti-trust agencies pursuing firms in an increasingly erratic fashion, and the courts endorsing them, Chicago economists were becoming exasperated with the legal hostility towards business. The blocking of vertical mergers (between suppliers and customers) was viewed as especially illogical within the Chicago School, a critique that Bork had first developed during the anti-trust project in 1954 (Bork, 1954). Coase joked that he was sick of teaching anti-trust because 'when the prices went up the judges said it was monopoly, when the prices went down, they said it was predatory pricing, and when they stayed the same, they said it was tacit collusion' (Kitch, 1983: 193). Chicago Law and Economics scholars were convinced that the situation was hopeless.

And yet by the late 1970s this had changed quite dramatically, thanks to a series of intellectual, political and institutional paradigm shifts, all of which contributed to the growing authority of Chicago-style neo-classical economics in the legal regulation of markets. These all depended on the rhetorical power of economists to shape legal thinking, which produced a new economic rationalization of anti-trust, and greatly reduced the scope of regulatory intervention. Thanks to the influence of Chicago Law and Economics, the liberal authority of the state to correct, delimit or discipline the decision making of businesses was weakened significantly. From the early 1990s onwards, this same influence slowly permeated the European Commission with similar consequences. These events and processes were crucial factors in shaping the character of 'actually existing neoliberalism' (in contrast to the proposed, more normative neoliberalism of the early neoliberals) that swept across the USA and Europe from the 1970s onwards.

Thanks to the inspiration of Director and the influence of Coase, the Chicago School had shifted strongly away from the ordo-liberal definition of competition as a formal property of markets towards an empiricist definition as the maximization of utility. In true Coasian fashion, this standard was only ever a relative one, in the sense that a 'competitive' outcome was the best available one, and not a perfectly efficient (i.e. transaction costless) one. This was a deeply agnostic definition of competition, which dispensed with preconceptions (both legal and economic) about how markets ought to be structured or regulated. It is this that underpinned Posner and Bork's programmatic critiques of anti-trust, both of which effectively turn the gaze of economic critique away from private industry and towards public agencies and legal institutions. Posner and Bork had both worked as government lawyers, Posner in the FTC in the mid-1960s and Bork in the DOJ in the early 1970s, and been influenced by Chicago price theory. They had therefore seen the apparently illogical way in which anti-trust was interpreted and enforced at first hand, and set out to refound it on rationalist, neo-classical principles. Not being trained economists, they were also entirely untouched by the influence of Bain and the Harvard SCP paradigm.

Their books both start with the assumption that the sole goal of an anti-trust intervention should be to increase efficiency, typically understood in the neo-classical sense of 'consumer welfare'. It was this core founding principle that they suggested had got lost in amongst the legalese and liberal idealism of American anti-trust enforcement over the 1950s and 1960s. But in a classically Chicagoan fashion, they stress the importance of costing in the implementation of law and the threat of regulators undermining efficiency through the pursuit of some ideal market structure. Lawyers had typically ignored the costs that regulation imposed upon the actors being regulated. As Director had first argued in Levi's anti-trust class, monopoly could result in efficiencies that government lawyers were blind to. Posner argued:

> To the extent that efficiency is the goal of antitrust enforcement, there is no justification for carrying enforcement into areas where competition is less efficient than monopoly because the costs of monopoly pricing are outweighed by the economies of centralising production in one or a very few firms. (Posner, 2002: 2)

Bork in turn offered a brilliantly simple basis on which to re-found anti-trust policy: "'competition" for purposes of anti-trust analysis, must be understood as a term of art signifying any state of affairs in which consumer welfare cannot be increased by judicial decree' (Bork, 1978: 51). In practice, this represents a significant increase in the freedom and discretion of managers and capital. In true Chicagoan style, what businessmen think or say they are doing is deemed insignificant in comparison to what economists can prove is 'actually' going on at an 'unconscious' level (Bork, 1978: 121). What may appear to be anti-competitive or irrational behaviour can still be critically evaluated *as if* it were driven by competitive, rational instincts.

The particular differences between industries or specific firms are downplayed by the critical apparatus of Chicago price theory. Qualitative insights into technology or case studies (as the Harvard tradition had privileged) become usurped by a quantitative analysis of market data. This is the precise sense in which economics becomes judicial. It is no longer simply furnishing legal analysis with additional empirical data, rather its formalistic methodological premise enables all firms, in all sectors, to be judged according to the single test of economic efficiency. Economics serves judgement over capitalism – 'a unified framework for understanding all human behaviour' – and is blind to other types of moral appeal or the heterogeneity of institutional logics (Becker, 1976: 14). The fact that anti-trust then becomes much simpler in its aims is viewed, even by critics of Chicago, as a welcome achievement of Law and Economics (Rubinfeld, 2008).

As a rhetorical project, Chicago Law and Economics sought to highlight the epistemological and metaphysical nonsense at work within liberal legalism, and to replace both with a utilitarian calculus of efficiency. As Chicago-influenced lawyers, Bork and Posner were the fruits of this rhetorical strategy. But for the legal mainstream of the 1960s and 1970s, Law and Economics represented a radical affront to legal epistemology. Most of all, the implication of Law and Economics (and of Coase's epistemology in particular) was a transformation in what should count as 'evidence' in a legal setting. FTC and DOJ lawyers had traditionally fought cases by hunting down 'hot documents' from firms – that is, pieces of evidence that proved an intention to distort competition, reduce choice, crowd out competitors or interfere with the price-setting function of the market. This legal epistemology assumed that actors knew what they were doing, and that guilt resided in a deliberate departure from the norms of a competitive market.

By contrast, the neo-classical epistemology that ran through Law and Economics, as manifest in Bork and Posner's books, ignored intentions, practice and norms in favour of measured effects as calculated by economists. Moral responsibility for the outcome was virtually irrelevant in most instances. From this perspective an industrial strategy that *appeared* competitive to a lawyer (because, for instance, it consciously avoided market dominance) could be *effectively* inefficient, and hence uncompetitive, from a neo-classical perspective. More typically, actions which *appeared* anti-competitive to a lawyer (such as vertical mergers and various other routes to conglomeration or price manipulation) could be calculated as *effectively* efficient, and hence competitive. Lawyers and liberal regulators had assumed some sort of zero-sum game between the public

interest and the private interest, which SCP economics endorsed by highlighting the problem of high profitability. However, for Bork this missed 'the obvious
fact that more efficient methods of doing business are as valuable to the public
as they are to businessmen' (Bork, 1978: 4). An efficient monopoly was more
competitive, by Bork and Posner's standard, than an inefficient market. Yet this
flew in the face of legal orthodoxy.

The Chicago anti-trust revolution

How then did the Chicago definition of competition come to oust the formal
legal definition, and the SCP economics that accompanied it? The power and
authority of government anti-trust lawyers were effectively challenged on two
fronts simultaneously – by Chicago-influenced judges and economists in the
courtroom, and by economists within anti-trust agencies themselves.

The dissemination of Law and Economics ideas within the American legal
establishment was actively engineered by Chicago scholars during the early
1970s. Henry Manne began running a series of summer schools in 1971 to train
lawyers in the basic principles of neo-classical price theory, and was funded to
do so by a group of corporations concerned by the growing reach of the anti-
trust agencies (Manne, 2005). From 1975 onwards a second camp was
established for law professors, and the following year a summer camp was
offered to federal judges. The consulting firm Lexecon was established by
Chicago economists to provide economic analysis to firms engaged in competition battles, thereby enabling those firms to marshal Law and Economics
reasoning in the courtroom. A watershed occurred with the Supreme Court's
General Dynamics ruling in 1974, where the FTC was defeated, having brought
a case claiming that the coal-mining industry was becoming excessively concentrated. The Supreme Court overturned the FTC's ruling, on the basis that
industrial concentration was not inefficient *per se* – a utilitarian rebuke to the
FTC's critical assumption that actions were to be judged in terms of their impact
on the overall structure of the market. While FTC and DOJ lawyers continued
to operate in the paradigm that had accompanied aggressive anti-trust interventions for the previous three decades (with little resistance from their in-house
economists), justices were becoming swayed by the Chicago critique of public
law. In 1978, the Supreme Court cited both the Bork and Posner books for the
first time, in its *GTE Sylvania* ruling, indicating the growing status of utilitarian
reasoning (Miller, 1989; Amato, 1997). By the late 1970s, firms being prosecuted
by the US anti-trust agencies discovered that more than half of the cases could be
overturned on appeal (Miller, 1989). The Posner and Bork books were regularly

cited in arguments in favour of vertical integration, and the FTC and DOJ had begun to abandon investigating such merger cases by the end of the 1970s (FTC, 2003).

While the courts exerted an influence from without, economists within the FTC and DOJ could not put up great resistance to the interventionist instincts of lawyers until the 1980s, following Ronald Reagan's appointment of William Baxter to run the DOJ. One reason for this was that the economic orthodoxy of Bain and the SCP paradigm was more sympathetic to active anti-trust than the Chicago approach which would succeed it. As Kuhn noted of scientific revolutions, there is a generational dimension to paradigm shifts: an entire cohort of Harvard-influenced economists needed to retire before the Chicago worldview could become properly entrenched. But the diminished authority of economics *in general* was also a factor in interventionist ethos of the FTC and DOJ until the late 1970s. From a Chicagoan perspective, it wasn't simply that anti-trust authorities were employing the wrong economic rationality (although that was one complaint), but that they were operating without any economic rationality at all.

The FTC's economic expertise has always been contained in a single Bureau of Economics, which operates with a quasi-academic ethos of pursuing economic analysis in a politically and legally disinterested fashion. For instance, the Bureau publishes economic studies of particular industries, unconnected to any particular legal cases, to produce insights into their specific characteristics. In the early years of the FTC, economists had actually outnumbered lawyers, but this was reversed during the 1920s. During the 1950s, the authority of the Bureau of Economics was progressively undermined, with economists being transferred into legal teams where they were unable to pursue their analyses independent of legal requirements to prosecute, and the production of economic studies declined markedly. The status of economic evidence (framed in terms of SCP) in the courtroom was at an all-time low during the late 1950s and early 1960s, with a flippant FTC maxim being that 'one incriminating letter in the files is worth the testimony of ten economists' (FTC, 2003). 'Hot documents' counted for more in the courtroom than calculations of price effects. Yet these trends began to reverse in the mid-1960s, with a new Director of the Bureau of Economics recruiting heavily and economic studies being revived. Economic studies, that were scarcely conducted at all in the early 1960s, made a revival from the late 1960s onwards (FTC, 2003). Economists that had been transferred into legal teams were transferred back into the Bureau of Economics. The voice of economists was thus becoming louder by the end of the decade.

These various institutional changes created the conditions for a form of disinterested empirical analysis which was antagonistic to liberal interventionism, and especially so once economists had begun to internalize the Chicago critique of anti-trust laid out in Bork and Posner's books. Following Baxter's appointment to the DOJ economists were encouraged to speak out against anti-trust cases, if they believed that these rested on erroneous economic foundations. In 1982 new merger guidelines were published by the DOJ, based upon clear Chicago principles, including a recognition – thirty years after Director had made the case – that vertical integration was rarely anti-competitive. In the DOJ, the ratio of economists to lawyers shifted from one in twelve in 1980 to one in eight in 2000 (Posner, 2002). Professional antagonisms developed between economists and lawyers in the early 1980s, as the former became increasingly sceptical towards the arguments of their legal colleagues and confident about criticizing them. A Chicagoan epistemology held sway, and as an FTC economist recalled,: 'The Bureau of Economics went from being "loved" by the lawyers and supporting litigation to being the unpopular quality control enforcers who would say in a very vigorous way, wait a minute, here are the reasons why this may not make sense' (FTC, 2003: 97). Aside from the professional tensions, the Chicago revolution was rapid. The entire scope of anti-trust enforcement was drastically reduced, and the status of economists in the courtroom and inside the agencies grew markedly. The legal presuppositions of the 1950s and 1960s, which chimed with SCP economics in their suspicion of large highly profitable businesses, were abandoned. By the time of the 1988 *Sharp* ruling, it was simply assumed that measured efficiency was the sole test of legitimate competitive activity or anti-trust intervention (Amato, 1997). US corporations, and nominally consumers, were the immediate beneficiaries, while small businesses were the potential losers. Whether the pursuit of 'efficiency' (defined as 'consumer welfare') does in practice benefit consumers is a moot point (Fox, 2008; Crouch, 2011).

A similar series of shifts took place in the European Commission's competition authority, DG Competition, approximately twenty years later. DG Competition had maintained a strongly legalistic, ordo-liberal approach to competition enforcement, from its origins in the 1950s, through to the 1986 legislation which created a single market. As we have seen, ordo-liberalism prioritized dismantling dominant firms, purely on the principle that this disrupted the order of the competitive market. Ordo-liberal influences were weaker by the early 1990s, and the 1990 merger guidelines betrayed signs of Chicago influence. In 1991 the US government and European Commission signed a bilateral agreement on anti-trust, which aimed to prevent mercantilist attacks on one another's firms.

Yet DG Competition was not equipped to carry out sophisticated neo-classical analysis to the same extent that the FTC and DOJ were, and was accused of continuing to target US firms for the benefit of European competitors. Political pressure was applied on the European Commission to import Chicago principles, via the professional networks of the FTC and US law firms, and the intellectual reach of economic journals and seminars (Dezalay & Sugarman, 1995). The creation of the International Competition Network in 2001 might be seen as an effort by the USA to use 'soft power' and intellectual influence to disseminate Chicago School-thinking amongst European competition experts. High profile cases, particularly against GE Honeywell, raised severe alarms in Washington that DG Competition was still acting without the appropriate form of authority.

As with the FTC and DOJ in the late 1970s, the crucial turning point came in 2002, when two major cases were overturned on appeal, on account of DG Competition's inadequate economic analysis. This signalled the type of legitimacy crisis that the US authorities and firms had been waiting for. In response, DG Competition hired a Chief Competition Economist in 2003, who set about establishing a Chief Economist's Team, modelled on the FTC's Bureau of Economics, though substantially smaller (not least due to the smaller supply of European economists working in the Chicago, Coasian tradition) (Roeller & Buigues, 2005). Where economists had previously been distributed around DG Competition, and tasked with supporting lawyers in their cases, now the agency had its own, quasi-academic empirical research capacity to keep its lawyers in check. This empiricist, Chicagoan paradigm is referred to as the 'effects-based approach' in Brussels.

THE JUDICIAL ECONOMIST AT WORK

The liberal spirit of neoliberal authority infuses how the empirical representation of competitive processes is performed. Objective judgements must be imposed from a position of exteriority and neutrality, if they are to succeed in establishing legitimate inequalities. The authority of a given critique depends partly on the pragmatic situation of the critic: it also depends on critique being performed with an appropriate ethos, style or vocation.

The application of Chicago School ideas in a legal context, such as an anti-trust authority, requires highly sophisticated institutional arrangements. It also requires particular professional norms on the part of economists, who are expected to act as dispassionate academic analysts *and* as legal assistants simultaneously. As Posner foresaw in his landmark statement on Law and Economics, 'the economic theory of law presupposes machinery for ascertaining the facts necessary to correct application of law' (Posner, 1981: 7). This machinery is complex and requires constant maintenance. The Chicago School critique of law in general, and of anti-trust law in particular, began with Simons' unlikely move to the Chicago Law School – but it could only be completed with particular institutions and practices which would allow government legal experts to confront a constant economic audit of their reasoning, by economists capable of communicating their logic across professional boundaries.

This particular dimension of neoliberal authority is dependent on two professional disciplines discovering a shared language. Lawyers must listen to and understand economists, and economists must adopt a lawyerly style of reasoning. The courtroom and the seminar room come to support similar forms of exchange: intellectual combat, attempts to falsify knowledge claims, the testing of 'sense'. Within the anti-trust agency the lawyer retains nominal authority over the economist, inasmuch as the economist works for the lawyer on putting legal cases together. Yet, pragmatically speaking, the economist attains the rhetorical power to shape definitions of evidence and uphold certain norms of methodological and epistemological reason. They come to act as the state's in-house auditors, remaining constantly watchful of their legal colleagues, in order to ensure that metaphysical and substantive notions of 'justice' and 'fairness' are not creeping back into the application of economic law. The reality of measured effects must trump that of presumed intentions and agency. Following the various rhetorical victories of the Chicago Law and Economics movement, this tradition of neoliberalism finally depends upon various institutional and vocational arrangements within regulatory agencies, to ensure that the fusion of legal and economic thinking succeeds in the day-to-day application of law.

There is a paradox at the heart of the Coasian framework, which plays out in the application of Chicago-style neoliberal policy, and it concerns the possibility of attaining an independent, objective view upon economic reality. On the one hand, Coase suggests that an optimal outcome is a subjective matter, to be gauged only from the perspective of those parties affected by it. This is a sceptical, Hayekian epistemological position, which would require only that the state creates the right *a priori* conditions for decentralized interactions, such as protection for the price system and property rights. Competition, from the Hayekian perspective, is itself a 'discovery process' which generates knowledge, but cannot be an object of knowledge (Hayek, 2002). But on the other side, Coase argues that the empirical use of neo-classical economics (what is often referred to as industrial organization economics) can be employed to assess the relative efficiency of different institutional arrangements, drawing on price data and 'revealed preferences' (i.e. behaviour) (Buchanan, 2005). It is this that allows Coasian economics to become a useful tool for regulators and state lawyers. The 'objectivism' or 'scientism', which Hayek deplored, creeps back in to the neoliberal tradition, elevating neo-classical economic analysis to an unprecedented authority in determining the optimal institutional and legal arrangements (Hayek, 1942). An epistemology which originally doubted the possibility of any impartial view of the world, save for a blindly liberal commitment to price and competition, mutates into one which credits neo-classical economics with an objective perspective. Ironically, where every other actor is considered by Chicago scholars to be driven by rational self-interest – the bureaucrat, the judge, the parent, the trade unionist, the politician – the neo-classical economist is elevated to a quasi-judicial status, from where he can evaluate socio-economic behaviour and data in an entirely disinterested manner. As Mirowski has argued, the single political choice offered by neoliberalism is either to credit the policy analyses of economists or to have no government policy at all (Mirowski, 2013). Perversely, by having no concern with concepts of 'justice' or 'right', the neo-classical economist is alleged to be even more judicially independent than the lawyer or the judge, who labour under certain metaphysical prejudices. The economist's vocational and epistemological distance from moral reasoning is the crucial ingredient in neoliberal legal authority.

The dominant Chicagoan epistemology is one of Popperian scepticism – that objective knowledge is whatever has not (yet) been falsified, but could be. By this standard, a valid anti-trust intervention is one in which economists cannot find a flaw: it is considered to make 'sense'. Since the Chicago critique of anti-trust triumphed, this sceptical yet objectivist epistemology has been imported into anti-trust agencies themselves. The effect of this has been to heighten concern regarding 'false positives' (erroneous anti-trust interventions) and reduce concern with 'false negatives' (erroneous non-interventions). An authoritative anti-trust intervention is first and foremost one which passes the test of making economic sense, that is, its empirical rationality cannot be falsified. Within the dominant Chicago paradigm cartels are the sole exception, which remain illegal regardless of their economic impact, and are therefore subject to criminal investigations: legal epistemology survives in these cases. Yet in other matters – mergers, market dominance, tacit collusion, preventative and predatory practices – lawyers are dependent on neo-classical analysis, demonstrating that the behaviour of firms is producing an outcome that is less efficient than the alternative of regulatory intervention. The authority of such economic evidence depends on its apparent objective, quasi-academic quality, which enables it to subject legal reasoning to a constant dispassionate critique. How is this independent empirical view from the 'outside' institutionally facilitated, and how is it channelled into the legal community? Let's take these two questions in turn.

Institutional conditions of economic objectivism

Kant argued that the political injunction of an Enlightened leader should be 'argue as much as you like and about whatever you like, but obey!' (Kant, 1970: 59). Anti-trust agency economists have a similar obligation to their legal superiors, meaning that they must somehow combine intellectual curiosity and public critique with a professional dedication to serving the state. In Weberian terms, they combine a scientific vocation towards the pursuit of economic objectivity with a political vocation to their public office (Davies, 2011b). The testing of efficiency in a value neutral way becomes a scholarly-lawyerly vocation in its own right.

Economics teams in the FTC, DOJ and DG Competition consist of PhD-level industrial organization economists, many of whom might otherwise have pursued careers as academics. Each team is led by a Chief Economist, who is typically a senior and highly reputed academic on a fixed term contract (2–3 years) such that they do not become influenced by any government career ambitions, but retain a vocation primarily to academic research. These economics teams remain quasi-independent from the legal teams working on particular cases, and observe a number of academic rituals and norms, that owe nothing to the requirements of lawyers or public office. Economists are encouraged to engage with a larger public of academic economists, via journal publishing, conference attendance and 'brown bag lunches' in which noted industrial organization economists are invited to present at seminars. Economists in the FTC and DOJ publish memoranda on particular cases, with their names attached to them. Some FTC economists might spend as much as 30% of their time conducting and publishing research, unconnected with any immediate legal cases of the agency. Specific industrial sectors are researched and written about, using empirical neo-classical economics, regardless of whether anti-trust suits are being considered for the sector concerned.

In response to previous doubts about its impartiality, DG Competition introduced additional institutional mechanisms to try and anchor its economic expertise outside of the legal community. Along with the creation of a Chief Economist's Team, the DG has an Economic Advisory Group on Competition Policy of 20 senior academics, which can be commissioned by European Commissioners, the Competition Director General or the Chief Competition Economist to offer an 'opinion' on matters related to competition in the European Community. Most dramatically, DG Competition's own Chief Competition Economist is formally entitled to publish a critical 'opinion' on competition enforcement, if he believes that economic logic is not being applied or followed adequately (Roeller & Buigues, 2005). This extraordinary measure effectively offers an in-house economist on a fixed-term contract the authority to trigger a constitutional crisis in DG Competition: it would necessarily be accompanied by his own resignation and most likely force the Director General's as well, throwing the entire authority of the agency into doubt. Notionally, at least, the authority of DG Competition stands or falls on the judgement of a single academic, whose judgements depend upon a particular set of methodological principles of evaluation.

Competition agency economists are therefore surprisingly active members of academic and policy public spheres. There are two justifications for this. The first is that the academic public sphere will provide anti-trust economists with access to latest theoretical and empirical analysis, which could at some point become crucial in the implementation of anti-trust rules. Academic journals and conferences address highly esoteric matters, which lawyers would be typically unable to understand. New theoretical approaches to the analysis of industrial organization are introduced without any regard for their practical implications for anti-trust or empirical efficiency. Anti-trust agency economists may discuss these matters in internal seminars and brown bag lunches, with equally little concern for their potential practical usefulness. However, at some point – perhaps several years later – these theoretical innovations and methods might become crucial in how an anti-trust case is put together.[2] They will need to be rendered sufficiently simple that agency lawyers, and ultimately judges, can understand their implications. But if government economists do not stay close to the forefront of academic research on industrial organization, and remain focused only on assisting legal teams with cases at hand (as occurred during the 1950s and early 1960s), then there is a risk that anti-trust agencies will encounter new economic ideas for the first time in the hands of opposing legal teams in the courtroom. This is precisely what happened with Chicago School theories in the 1970s, which were used successfully by private economics consultants to defend firms in court, before they had exerted any influence over the FTC or DOJ. The vanguard of academic economic research is therefore a crucial legal resource, for cases five or ten years down the line.

A second justification for economists' engagement with these public spheres is that critique heightens their epistemological authority, and by proxy the authority of the anti-trust agency. Just as Coase successfully transformed the Chicago School's definition of competition in Director's home in 1960, by subjecting himself to a barrage of intellectual attacks, public spheres are instrumentally harnessed by anti-trust agencies, as potential tests of theoretical coherence.[3] Anti-trust economists speak of presenting at academic conferences in order to be kept 'on their toes'. Chief economists are hired, with strong academic reputations which, it is assumed, they would not be willing to risk, to act as canaries in the mineshafts of anti-trust law enforcement. There is at least the *potential* for elected politicians to challenge the actions of anti-trust agencies, drawing on the opinions and publications of the agencies' own economists. DG Competition's Chief Competition Economist has exceptional powers of veto over the agencies' decisions that have already been noted. Creating the professional conditions for economists to speak and act independent of their legal and bureaucratic superiors, without fear for their careers, is a critical ingredient in establishing at least a veneer of neutral empiricism on the part of the anti-trust agency overall. The manufacturing of transparency around an agency's economic reasoning is a crucial ingredient in its normative authority.

These economists are therefore in a peculiar position of authority, in which they hold government offices with secure terms of employment (save for chief economists), in the classic manner of Weberian bureaucrats. But entirely unlike Weber's definition of a bureaucrat (who foregoes the pursuit of status or honour in exchange for permanence of office), government anti-trust economists also publish opinions and analyses in their own names, beyond the limits of their bureau. Debate is open and uncensored, while it goes on in seminar rooms, conferences and the offering of published 'opinions'. They have a mandate to scrutinize and test the state's legal activities, from a rationalist neoliberal perspective. Yet they are also in the pay of the state, and must obey lawyers when they are drafted in to individual legal teams to work on specific cases.

Economizing legal reason

The rhetorical and interpretive work in fusing legal and economic reason occurs when economists are drafted into legal teams to work on specific cases. A legal team may consist of five or six lawyers, and one or two economists to assist in putting evidence together, and advising on what types of claims are likely to stand up in court. One of the most significant consequences of the rise of Chicago Law and Economics in anti-trust policy has been for economists to be consulted much *earlier* in the development of cases. In the era when lawyers were more autonomous in the interpretation and application of anti-trust law, economists were only brought in to work on cases when it was already established that these would be pushed through to conclusion. The economist's task was to furnish a legal team with evidence that competition was being impeded in some way, it was not to advise on whether the case was economically rational or not. But the rising authority of neo-classical economics in defining competition, with its own idiosyncratic epistemology focused upon 'effects' rather than actions, has meant consulting economists at the *outset* of case formation.[4] In an economized legal world, the lawyer can no longer believe his own eyes: certain behaviours which look anti-competitive may in fact be deemed competitive, in terms of its aggregate effects.[5] As a result, the economist must be consulted far earlier in the process, to discover whether or not there is even a problem in the first place. This way, economic advice can save lawyers from pursuing cases which later fall apart in court, due to inadequate economic reasoning. Scepticism and falsification at the outset act as safeguards against falsification at the conclusion.

Assuming that the economist deems a case to be worth pursuing, what then does their role consist of? While they remain members of the economics team, interacting with their peers in that community, they contribute to cases as instructed by lawyers.[6] During the transition to a Chicago School view of anti-trust, frictions between economists and lawyers were frequent, as lawyers gradually came to recognize that they needed to take advice from economists that could be seen as obstructive. During the early 1980s in the FTC and DOJ, and the early 2000s in the European Commission, economists developed reputations as 'case killers', offering various reasons why the lawyers' argument was faulty – just as Director had done with regard to Levi in the Chicago Law School classroom of the early 1950s. More successful forms of inter-professional cooperation witness economists advising lawyers on how to think about a particular case, what sorts of questions to ask, what type of 'second request' (where a firm being investigated is asked to provide particular forms of evidence) to put in, what might be the right way of structuring a particular problem.

In this regard, the authority of the economist in the legal process involves delineating what is *relevant* to an anti-trust case. Before any evaluation of whether competition is or isn't being impeded, there is an *a priori* question of what would even count as evidence of this. What would such evidence look like, and where might it be found? Equally importantly, legalistic presuppositions regarding how competition 'should' be instituted need to be dismantled and excluded from the empirical investigation. A precise grammar is introduced and policed by economists, which establishes the limits within which lawyers are free to act. The replacement of political 'metaphysics' (language of freedom, rights, conscious intentions, justice, agency) by political 'physics' (language of effects, price, unconscious intentions, efficiency and consumer welfare) is achieved through designating that only the latter is relevant to an enquiry. Where once the economist provided economic evidence, within the limits and requirements of a legal procedure, now the economist employs the presuppositions of neoclassical economic methodology in order to shape what those limits consist of. The lawyer works within the rhetorical and procedural limits as defined by a particular Chicago definition of competition, and pursues their own vocation and professional goals from within these limits.

The methodological presuppositions of neo-classical economics come to serve as the legitimate procedure for legal reasoning and decision making. For Law and Economics scholars such as Posner, the advantage of these presuppositions is that they lack substantive concepts of fairness: their metaphysical emptiness is their prime virtue. But methodologies are nevertheless norms, which govern the actions and rhetoric of those who abide by them. From a wholly pragmatist perspective, the political virtue of neo-classical methodology is that it imposes very tight restrictions upon government lawyers, in terms of how they are able to define a breach of competition.[7] While government economists might engage in scientific public spheres to debate the 'facts' of certain industrial scenarios, once the economist engages with a legal case or enters the courtroom, their authority consists in how successfully they can carry out certain methodological rituals, prove certain propositions to a legal audience, and demonstrate the irrelevance of counter-claims made by defendants. The difference made by the Chicago School is that, before any voice can be legitimately heard with respect to a competition case, the speaker must first have assumed certain presuppositions about the nature of agency and what counts as a test of competitiveness (namely measured efficiency output).

CONCLUSION: THE JUSTICE OF EFFICIENCY

The authority of economics, in juridical and regulatory settings, does not depend on economists establishing certain objective facts with complete agreement. The sheer complexity of much Chicago School modelling mitigates against empirical proofs being provided in a very widely acceptable fashion. The capacity of economics to bring disputes to an end, as is the function of any judgement, is dependent on procedures being adequately followed, which are a combination of the methodological, the legal and the institutional. Publics must be permitted to witness this happening, in order that judgements can be cast over capitalist competition in ways that are recognized as liberal in *spirit*, that is, with some *a priori* assumption that the competitors are to be evaluated equally. What this chapter has sought to highlight are the various ways in which law and economics become meshed, epistemologically, methodologically, normatively and institutionally.

The most obvious historical consequence of the Chicago revolution in anti-trust (and in regulation more broadly) was far greater freedom for dominant competitors within the overall contest of capitalism. The new assumption, that efficiency is the goal of anti-trust and that monopolistic and exploitative practices are often efficient, led to a mode of regulation that was far more sympathetic to the interests of large businesses than during the 1950s and 1960s. This created the regulatory climate that would permit the rise of 'shareholder value' as the legitimate goal of corporate governance during the 1980s and 1990s. Necessary corroboration to this is provided by the claim that the 'barriers to entry' are far lower than they may appear: new competitors *could* arrive to challenge the monopolist, if only they have the strength and belief. The self-mythology of the Chicago School as bringing precisely such a challenge to Harvard and the liberal establishment meshes with this understanding of capitalism.

Through fusions of law and economics, the neoliberal state discovers the *liberal spirit* of its authority, in the sense explored in the previous chapter. As a replacement for the pursuit of justice itself, neoliberalism offers the goal of competition as a form of quasi-justice, which lacks a substantive concept of the common good. Ordo-liberals, and to some extent Hayek, found the liberal spirit in the machinations of the price system and the market order itself. There was a sense of fairness about how choice, exchange and price fluctuations occurred, that was honest regarding its metaphysical nature. Certain aspects of competition couldn't be entirely articulated – as Eucken argued, 'it not only includes traditions, laws and customs, but the spirit in which men live and keep to "rules of the game"' (quoted in Labrouse & Wiesz, 2001: 100). To put that another way, prices were not simply particular empirical instruments amongst many, as numbers on a particular screen or shop counter, they carried a higher form of authority and sovereignty, that derived from the overall socio-economic order that regulated them. They were the *ultimate* empirical representation of otherwise uncertain processes. Behind the ordo-liberal defence of prices was a quasi-Durkheimian faith in the society that legislated for them and defended them from planning.

For ordo-liberals, the sanctity of the market order itself, as perceived by lawyers, is the test of 'fair' and 'unfair' play. Inequality has a limit, which is reached when a single player attains *power* over others, via the power to dictate prices. Chicago Law and Economics has no truck with such metaphysical concepts of fairness, offering neo-classical economics as the sole authoritative principle by which legitimate behaviour should be evaluated. What Chicago economists rarely reflected on is *why* this should be so, other than the positivist belief that economic reasoning makes more 'sense' than legal reasoning. It is simply assumed that the neo-classical method possesses a form of neutrality, that makes it suitable for the reinvention of legal process. The method itself is therefore credited with possessing a liberal spirit. It is price theory, not the price mechanism, which is the test of fairness.

This has two final implications which are relevant to neoliberalism's subsequent legitimacy crises. Firstly, Chicago School epistemology renders the phenomenology of economic activity almost irrelevant. What individual businessmen or consumers or the public think is going on is merely their 'conscious' perception: what is really going on is to be assessed by expert neo-classical analysis, focused only on a *presupposed* or *unconscious* rationality of the actors and the measurable effects on outcomes. This means that the authoritative facts of economic activity are entirely invisible to those who conduct it. If something seems 'unfair' or mispriced or exploitative, this is irrelevant. Price loses any form of moral authority over people, and becomes purely a metaphor or methodological trope. There is a right and a wrong way to conduct neo-classical economics, but there is no right or wrong way for businesses to behave. This effectively legitimates any type of industrial behaviour, no matter how apparently unreasonable, but so long as it meets the expert test of being objectively efficient.

The seeds of the market's moral crisis are sown, once prices lose any relationship to an intrinsic notion of fairness. Budget airlines that advertise at one price, and then sell at another, share a similar disdain for the moral authority of the price system as teenage looters, for whom theft is simply more efficient than shopping. Visible, institutionalized prices become just one more empirical phenomena, within the shifting sands of capitalist evolution, rather than legitimate arbiters of worth, as Hayek had once hoped. As a result, the entire system of exchange and production comes to look like an opportunity for exploitation, without any sense of how things ought to be done – not even when it comes to the conduct of monetary payment. Money's great phenomenological appeal, that it is explicit and unambiguous, is itself lost within a system, in which the winner is whichever actor can hide behind the greatest degree of complexity and the most advanced strategy.

Secondly, this economized version of liberal authority depends on a somewhat implausible assumption about the neutrality and independence of neo-classical methods, as practical procedures in public life. The entire authority of the competition agency (and subsequently, other regulators) comes to depend on the notion that economics cannot be manipulated, is impervious to political or contingent influence, and is conducted from some sort of external or transcendental standpoint. This is its ideal typical perspective, as this chapter has detailed, reinforced by engagement in the academic public sphere and various institutional mechanisms, such as chief economists on fixed term contracts. The fact that there is also a *market* for economics consultancy, through which dominant businesses can access technical arguments with which to defend themselves from regulation, renders the authority of the judicial neo-classical regulator hugely compromised. Moreover, as the 2007–09 financial crisis demonstrated, regulators are not as impervious to competitor or political interests, and nor do academic economists exist outside of the economic forces and influences that they seek to describe (Häring & Douglas, 2012). Although this hasn't been addressed here, there were clearly geopolitical and economic drivers creating pressure on the European Commission to import Chicago School analysis into its competition regulation. The Coasian paradox, that there is simultaneously no neutral model of competition, but that neo-classical economics can offer an objective view of it nevertheless, eventually collapses. As became revealed in the aftermath of the crisis, economists were as compromised by interests, competitive forces and pressures as anyone else. In a sense, they were consistent with their own worldview, in which incentives came to trump whatever vocation they might have had to the academic, Kantian public sphere (Mirowski, 2013). They too are internal to the game, even while they continue to credit their methods with a quasi-liberal fairness.

NOTES

1 'I remember having a case once where we were pretty much deciding that the merger wasn't problematic … and it looked like there were efficiencies that would certainly justify, even if it was more troublesome than it looked like on the face of the evidence. We had a conversation, sort of a wrap up with the parties and so we started to get into the efficiencies. And they denied any efficiencies, you know, because they were thinking about, boy, if we say this is efficient, you know, deep pocket theory, you know, the commission's gonna come down on us, this is a bad merger 'cause it's gonna create, you know, it's gonna give us an advantage over our rivals and that's a bad thing' (FTC economist A).

2 'Younger economists are urged to try and publish in refereed journals, to attend economic conferences, certainly in the area of industrial organization economics because this is an area where existing developments in theory inform ideas that may underlie future cases' (FTC economist B).

3 'It's an outside test, you know. The danger, you know, when I look at some people who work in the government and economists who work in the government – I look at some of the other agencies where people aren't as active, and you get a little, you know, you only talk to your colleagues, and you only talk to, you know, very narrow, small group of people, getting out there and publishing and presenting work at seminars, presenting work in commerce, that puts you out there in the larger body of the profession, and provides some outside validation, okay, you know, the way we're thinking about this makes sense, or are we just, you know, are we just talking to ourselves – and talking ourselves into something that doesn't make any sense' (FTC economist C).

4 'You can influence very early on in a case, and you can influence at the end … A lot of it was by me or by members of the CET working on cases and trying to make sure that the economic analysis was done right. There are always two rules in organizations – you can either be helping along to ensure that no mistakes are likely to take place or you can enter at the end and oppose it, and say I'm not going to accept this. And then the analysis will need to be redone or different actions will need to be taken from what they want us to take in the beginning. I think that 90% of the time I think it's trying to make sure that nothing goes wrong' (DG Competition economist A).

5 'You know, some agreement not to compete might look anti-competitive but when you think about what its function is it may be pro-competitive' (FTC economist D).

6 'In litigation, lawyers are still running the show in the sense that you're in a legal setting, a judge is making a determination of things and sometimes knowing all the facts, although may not matter to the economic conclusion, looks like it matters to the court and therefore you have to know many more details than an academic who is doing a paper' (DOJ economist A).

7 'Economics has had a tremendously disciplining influence from antitrust. And, you know, it says, you know, here's what you have to show – to show an antitrust violation, you've got to show that quantity's going to fall, prices are going to go up, consumers are going be harmed. And if you can't show that, move on, you know. If you get into this business of saying, well, this is really good for consumers on the whole, but it's bad for this kind of producer, or something, you know, you've lost that disciplining effect, and all of sudden now you're trying to weigh fairness versus efficiency' (FTC economist E).

4

THE VIOLENT THREAT OF MANAGEMENT

Competitiveness, strategy and the audit of political decision

In 1974, European political leaders attended a meeting of business leaders in Davos, Switzerland, that had been convened annually for the previous three years by the Swiss management scholar, Klaus Schwab. The meeting was then known as the European Management Forum, but changed its name to the World Economic Forum in 1987, in recognition of its expanding economic and political scope. Schwab had initially convened a group of business executives to address concerns surrounding the on-going productivity gap separating European from American corporations. But seeing this as a problem with broader public significance, politicians were soon invited to the Davos meetings, in the hope of articulating a shared agenda for raising business performance. In later years, 'Davos' would come to symbolize highly exclusive cross-sectoral networks, linking public, private and 'third' sectors, convening celebrities with CEOs and politicians (Lapham, 1998). What unites them is that they are all high profile *decision* makers.

In addition to the annual Davos meeting, the World Economic Forum (WEF) is best known for producing its Global Competitiveness Report, which it began to publish annually in 1979, overseen by Schwab and the Harvard Business School (HBS) strategy 'guru', Michael Porter. These reports measure, compare and rank nations around the world, according to a variety of economic, social, cultural and political traits that underpin business productivity growth, some of which (such as a society's entrepreneurial values) would seem to defy quantification. The authors, together with a network of associated think tanks and consultancies, then sell and push advice to policy makers in individual nations, on how they can carve a distinctive national path towards greater competitiveness. The term 'competitiveness' is often understood as synonymous with the economic term 'productivity', or more loosely with a nation's capacity to generate wealth (Thurow, 1985; Porter, 1990; Aiginger, 2006a). Existing prosperity, as measured by GDP for example, is viewed as the legacy of past decisions and investments, and no guarantee of future success. The concept of competitiveness is designed to capture the ingredients for *future* prosperity.

The notion of measurable national 'competitiveness' became a key rhetorical and political trope for US and European governments over the course of the 1980s and 1990s, offering decision makers a way of critically analysing public institutions and resources, that began from the premise that businesses now operated in a much fiercer and global competitive landscape, and had new possibilities for mobility. It would later become equally dominant in the framing of policy at other spatial tiers of policy making, including the urban, regional and continental (Brenner & Wachsmuth, 2012). The central question posed by competitiveness analysts was how public policy could be reoriented, to ensure that local enterprises were best able to compete productively with those located in other locales. The urgency of this challenge was asserted as more than merely 'economic', but of the highest political priority. The competitiveness paradigm simultaneously narrows the scope of political action (by stressing the lack of alternatives to competitiveness) while heightening the urgency to act in specific areas such as science policy, research and development (R&D), infrastructure, security, intellectual property rights and cultural policy. Investing in knowledge, and facilitating its transfer from universities into businesses, becomes one of the highest priorities for states wishing to win the 'race' of global competitiveness (Cerny, 1990; Jessop, 2002, 2012).

Of course the notion of politicians being actively lobbied by local big business or acting on its behalf dates back far earlier than the 1970s. Regulation and public policy always advantage one set of firms and interests over another (Jessop, 1990; Fligstein, 2001), and 'industrial policy' has long involved governments supporting 'national champions' and defending symbolically important industries, such as automobile manufacturing. The significance of the new competitiveness paradigm lay rather in its self-conscious construction of a common global language through which business and political leaders could discuss how public policy influenced corporate and entrepreneurial performance, and a measurement framework through which all public policy, public investment and executive political decision making could be subjected to a blanket economic audit. A new social science was invented to produce empirical representations of capitalism, that served the needs and anxieties of decision-making elites. The fate of nations (both as territories and cultures) became characterized as intimately entangled with the fate of enterprises, and vice versa. A new vision of political authority was invented, in which the nation (or city, region etc.) was comparable to a corporation, of which the political leader was the CEO and the citizens were employees. This 'corporation' contained various social, economic and cultural resources, which had to be analysed strategically, in terms of how they could be harnessed for future prosperity. Seeing as many of these resources (such as talented elites, world-leading firms, scientists and artists) were internationally mobile and limited in number, a competitive strategy would necessarily involve efforts to attract and keep these resources in a certain locale. An ontological parity was proposed between the authority of the CEO to manage and the authority of the political leader to govern, inflating the first with charismatic authority (as the management obsession with 'leadership' indicated), and deflating the latter through an expansion of managerial rationality into the political sphere. Both forms of leadership come to be defined by common problems of an uncertain future, heightened global competition and a requirement to take strategic decisions for collective long-term prosperity. And yet they are also underscored by a darker form of political authority, which became manifest in the strategic abandoning of unproductive resources and veiled hostility towards challengers.

The recurrent neoliberal problematic is that of how to represent or stabilize uncertainty, without determining it through political dictat: competitive processes offer to solve this. In his taxonomy of approaches to uncertainty, Knight recognized that businesses don't only depend on expert knowledge to rationalize uncertainty (i.e. representing it as risk), but can also actively reduce it through exerting control over their environment (Knight, 1957: 240). As Schumpeter argued, the greatest rewards go not to those who play within established rules, but to those who set new rules that others then have to play by. While the notion of government planning is taboo to the neoliberal mind, the notion of entrepreneurial or business planning is not, because where the former is alleged to repress difference, the latter seeks to enact change of some sort. *Planning for the new* represents an alternative – and paradoxical – means of approaching uncertainty, that is a further example of a market-based ethos that can be extended into non-market domains. If the state can also plan to unleash change like an entrepreneur (as opposed to plan to determine the future) then even public planners retain some authority within this convention of neoliberalism. Public spending on R&D is compatible with a Hayekian epistemology, inasmuch as the outcome of such investment is by definition unknown and unknowable (Davies, 2011c). Yet the legitimacy of such plans still requires a specific mode of critique and evaluation, so as to assess whether they are in the service of productive dynamism, or some less competitive political agenda. Providing this critique and evalution is the purpose of competitiveness theories and methodologies.

Given the one-off nature of innovation, and the qualitative differentiation involved in successful competitive strategy, there is something paradoxical about efforts to quantify and compare how well nations are performing in these respects. International competitiveness rankings render all national differences commensurable, but thereby eradicate the *incommensurable* qualities that make particular strategies valuable in the first place. They therefore wrestle with the problem of how to value and compare unique economic qualities, offering what Karpik terms 'judgement devices', which combine qualitative judgement with calculation (Karpik, 2010).

Returning to the themes of previous chapters, national competitiveness displays familiar characteristics of neoliberalism more broadly, in its effort to reinvent sovereign state authority in economically rational terms.[1] However, where Law and Economics sought to rationalize the judicial branch of government and regulators using neo-classical economics, national competitiveness sought to rationalize the executive branch of government using techniques and ideas derived from business strategy. Where the former seeks to economize *rules*, producing a form of neoliberal authority with a 'liberal spirit', the latter seeks to economize *decisions*, producing a form of neoliberal authority with a 'violent threat'. We can see this in four dimensions, as also explored in respect to Law and Economics.

Firstly, national competitiveness seeks to reduce political metaphysics to political physics, disenchanting executive political leadership through an expansion of economic logic. A number of theorists have analysed 'the political' as a singularly disruptive and unpredictable form of action, rooted in the capacity of individuals to take decisions or to act publicly (Arendt, 1958; Schmitt, 1996). Weber described charismatic political authority as a 'typically anti-economic force', possessing an excessive, non-rational character, which stemmed from the willpower of the leader himself (Weber, 1978: 245). In common with Schmitt, Weber saw the bare decision to employ violence as the definitive element of the political condition, at least in the modern era (Weber, 1991b). Liberal economics had long been suspicious of the executive branch of government, which it viewed as economically illogical and prone to mercantilist acts of protectionism and intervention. The task of liberal economics was to assert the primacy of positive-sum market competition over zero-sum political competition (Foucault, 2008). The executive would be persuaded to retreat, to stay out of the economic realm, as the liberal alternative to actively intervening in it.

The alternative offered by neoliberalism is to reinvent executive authority, in ways that are compatible with market logic. This is not achieved through the expansion of economics in any orthodox sense, but through theories of business strategy, focused more upon decision making in uncertain, dynamic situations than upon static quantitative analyses. Politics is not quite disenchanted by economics, but more specifically by *management*. The theory of competitiveness fuses together the entrepreneurial, strategic decision of the business leader with the political decision of the executive branch of government, evaluating them according to the single measure of strategic success, vis-à-vis competitors. In re-imagining the political leader as a CEO or entrepreneur, political and national-ist energies are *harnessed and diverted*, rather than thwarted, as liberal economics had sought to do. As with Law and Economics, this is a radically utilitarian move, in that the authority of the state comes to depend on its capac-ity to produce measurable economic benefits, in the same way that financial strategy requires a CEO to demonstrate value to shareholders. Competitiveness evaluations are audits of the value of public institutions and action. And in a typically neoliberal fashion, this subjection of the state to quantitative audit does not only occur in a narrowly 'economic' market realm, but also beyond, to encompass areas such as education policy or the arts.

Secondly, and consequently, this leads to an inflation in the authority and power of competitive strategy experts, techniques and discourses. As will be explored, the field of business strategy developed over the postwar period, to provide advice to business decision makers seeking to understand and influence the competitive environment in which their firms sat. The jump which occurred in the late 1970s, thanks to bodies such as the WEF and Porter especially, was that strategy experts expanded their remit, to provide advice to public policy makers. This wasn't simply a discursive or methodological shift, it was also dependent on the expansion of think tanks, business schools and policy commissions – part of what Thrift has termed 'the cultural circuit of capital' – which brought politicians, strategists and business leaders together to learn from one another as equals (Thrift, 2005). The authority of the strategist, in amongst all this, was to provide a clear-sighted view of the global competitive landscape, that regu-lated the uncertainty and anxiety of leaders in all sectors. Moreover, expert advice was tailored to the particular needs and qualities of the client nation, seeing as the promise that accompanied it was to define the nation's unique path towards competitiveness. As Jessop argues, the 'competition state' is required to develop its own distinctive 'self-image' in the world (Jessop, 2002: 124). The guru or expert therefore serves to help define national identity within a global economy: a service that in some instances becomes quite explicit, as the case of 'nation branding' experts indicates (Aronczyk, 2012).

Thirdly, national competitiveness made a particular Schumpeterian definition of 'competition' the test of valid action, on the part of firms and states. This definition was accompanied by various measures and methodologies, which purported to quantify and rank a nation's capacity to innovate. The achievement of the Schumpeterian entrepreneur is to offer a product or service that others don't or cannot, at least in the short term. As Chapter 2 argued, Schumpeter's theory rests on a philosophical anthropology of differentiation: a small minority of individuals have an uncommon psychological capacity to operate outside of existing conventions. On this basis, they are entitled to the monopolies that they create. One of the central messages that the competitiveness gurus sought to disseminate amongst policy elites over the 1980s and 1990s was that western economies could no longer compete internationally on price, but now needed to compete on quality, innovation and differentiation. Doing so involved identifying those elements of a population or locality that couldn't be easily mimicked by competitors, and then converting those into a source of competitive advantage. Ultimately, the global 'game' becomes one of whose society – and not only whose economy – can become most adaptable, networked and future-oriented. The Schumpeterian idea of the disruptive, self-governing entrepreneur provides the philosophical anthropology underpinning this vision, and the race is to see which nation can best release this economic heroism.

It is only this emphasis on Schumpeterian or entrepreneurial competitiveness that distinguishes this agenda from anti-market mercantilism or protectionism. It is precisely *because* the global free movement of goods, capital and elites is deemed unstoppable that policy makers are encouraged to consider which particular productive niche their cultural-political domain might be able to occupy. An assumption of a new global horizon for business is inbuilt into the newly designed methodologies of the competitiveness experts (Jessop, 2002: 116). The lesson is not to protect or subsidize local industry or devalue currency as a defence of competitiveness, although orthodox economists have spotted hints of such mercantilism in the rhetoric of competitiveness, and this rhetoric has proved convenient for those businesses seeking some form of direct state support (Krugman, 1994).

Finally, we can see that this tradition of management theory acquires a 'violent threat' of authority, as described in Chapter 2, once it is fused with executive political decision making. The competitive strategist's advice is never merely empirical, but carries the presumption of existential danger or opportunity: entire nations (or firms) will triumph or dwindle, depending on how well they and their leaders learn the lessons of competitive strategy. Schmitt's 'friend-enemy distinction' is reinvented, in terms of a strategic differentiation between 'us' and 'them', in the global competitive game. Charismatic authority, which Weber termed 'anti-economic', reappears in the policy seminar or think tank conference, as national economic strategy veers on the edge of national military strategy. As Harvey observes, 'the neoliberal state needs nationalism *of a certain sort* to survive' (Harvey, 2005: 85, emphasis added). In the form of the policy guru, network or think tank, advisors themselves come to embody the types of cultural and personality traits that are needed to succeed in the new era of global competitiveness. Gurus such as Porter are brands and entrepreneurs in their own right. While the politician's authority becomes rationalized in strategic, managerial terms, the strategist's authority becomes imbued with the distant threat of radical political action.

This chapter charts the development of the national competitiveness paradigm, via the business schools, think tanks, gurus and documents that have propagated it. Unlike the influence of Chicago Law and Economics over anti-trust, there is no clear example of a particular government agency being targeted, infiltrated or transformed by this convention of managerial logic. The ambition of the competitiveness experts is both higher than that and yet, from another perspective, more meagre. The ambition is higher, in that competitiveness is propagated as an ideal that matters urgently to everyone everywhere, no matter which sector, discipline or policy field they work in. There is an evangelical element to this tradition, that seeks to convert decision makers everywhere to a style of thinking and set of beliefs, using evidence in a pragmatic way to do so. But for the same reason, competitiveness analyses have very little potential to actually determine or underpin policy making, seeing as their principle role is to energize, enthuse, or if necessary frighten. Constructing a common reality, recognized by business executives and politicians equally, is the principle goal of any competitiveness agenda, part of which necessarily consists in simply getting them all in the same room to converse with one another.

The chapter is in three parts. The next section examines the theoretical underpinnings of national competitiveness analysis. In particular, I look at three ingredients that facilitated the expansion of business strategy into the domain of public policy, namely business strategy, the benchmarking of nations carried out by Richard Farmer and Barry Richman in the 1960s, and Porter's engagement with public policy during the 1980s. The second section examines how an economized vision of nation and political leadership was disseminated via cross-sectoral bodies such as think tanks and commissions. The third section explores the particular institutional, vocational and methodological dynamics by which this knowledge is produced and distributed, and the type of political and epistemological authority that is claimed for it. This is not knowledge that is offered with a spirit of disinterested 'objectivity' or 'neutrality', rather it is knowledge aimed at affirming and encouraging a national differentiation within a commonly acknowledged global contest. The chapter concludes by identifying the seeds of authority crisis that lie within this tradition of neoliberal reason.

THE FUSION OF POLITICAL AND MANAGERIAL DECISION

A common trait of politicians and managers is the capacity to take decisions on behalf of collective bodies, be they firms or societies. These decisions need to be recognized as legitimate, to a greater or lesser extent, and backed up with power, to a greater or lesser extent. But historically, management is a very recent form of power, dating back to the second half of the nineteenth century, when private business corporations began to emerge in the United States and Germany, with increasingly separate ownership and control (Chandler, 1977). The new class of professional managers was soon supported by the creation of business schools in the USA, beginning with Wharton in 1881, which initially sought to anchor managerial authority in broader notions of the public good, training future business leaders in ethics as well as the rudiments of business efficiency (Khurana, 2007). During the twentieth century, management and business schools drew on examples of effective political and military hierarchy and cooperation, importing psychological findings from wartime experiments in teamwork and leadership (Baritz, 1960; Rose, 1990). As a science and theory of authority, the field of management has spent the majority of its history importing examples and lessons from politics and the military, and not vice versa.

During the neoliberal era, however, the direction of travel was reversed. This was seen in a number of efforts to reinvent public sector agencies along private sector managerial lines, such as 'New Public Management' (Hood, 1991, 1995a, 1995b). The invention of privatization and public-private partnerships was a very visible example of the state being refashioned as a private actor. As Chapter 1 stressed, the crucial advances made by neoliberalism did not necessarily involve extending the market into every reach of state and society, but of reconstructing state and society in ways that are amenable to market-based techniques of evaluation. National competitiveness evaluation is one further example of this, in which a political community is treated as a quasi-firm to be managed and measured in a strategic fashion, in the hope of out-competing rival communities. National characteristics and political will become resources, to be evaluated and strategically employed, using techniques drawn from management and business schools.

So how did this reversal come about? How did a style of reasoning, aimed at the managers of enterprises, come to infiltrate the political and policy realm? Weber argued that a comparison of public and private sector bureaucracy was always more plausible in the American context, which can therefore be seen as one of the seeds of the neoliberal colonization (Weber, 1991b: 197). But given the copious ways in which governing an economy or society is *unlike* running a firm (many of which have been explained vociferously by orthodox economists), there is something deeply curious about this colonization of political reason by managerial reason, whose effects we shall explore later in this chapter. Genealogically, three theoretical and methodological preconditions can be identified.

The science of strategy

The rise of market research based on a science of consumer attitudes and behaviour during the 1920s demonstrated that firms needn't only depend on the laws of supply and demand for their success. It was possible for firms to understand and influence the nature of their external environment, and alter their activities accordingly. Yet prewar management in the United States was rarely concerned with the behaviour of competitor firms. And in the immediate postwar period, surging international demand, and comparatively homogeneous consumer groups, meant that US corporations remained profitable without giving much consideration to their competitive environment. The liberal economic assumption – that no individual market competitor is able to influence the overall shape of the marketplace – was held intact and, if necessary, enforced by highly interventionist anti-trust regimes. Accordingly, management theory was primarily 'intra-organizational' (Knights & Morgan, 2011).

Yet World War Two did spawn growing theoretical interest in a generic science of strategy, understood as the rationality of shaping and dominating competitive environments, including those of war. Game theory, beginning with the

1944 publication of *Theory of Games and Economic Behaviour*, can be seen as the first effort to bring all forms of competition within a single blanket theory of competitive strategy (Von Neumann & Morgenstern, 1953). While history had provided a number of influential theories of military victory which were later studied in business schools for strategic insight (most prominently Clausewitz's *On War* and Sun Tzu's *Art of War*), the attempt to codify and rationalize the principles of competitive strategy scientifically arose within the national-existential agenda of the Cold War. Military historian Liddell Hart's 1929 work, *Strategy: The Indirect Approach*, was re-published in 1941, and later provided an influential template for understanding the dynamics of competitive situations. Hart's founding principle was that a successful military strategy is one that minimizes the need for conflict altogether. The victorious competitor is one who positions themselves so as to *avoid* direct competition, except where necessary, an idea that would resurface in efforts to divert corporate or national strategies towards areas of specialized production where they are least likely to be challenged. The association of the term 'strategy' with military decision making held right up until the mid-1960s, when new business strategy consultancy firms (such as Boston Consulting) began to be established.

HBS would become the leading academic centre of business strategy thinking in the world. But strategy was initially approached as an issue that was not amenable to theoretical reasoning or models, due to the inherently contingent one-off nature of strategic challenges. The 'case method' of teaching – in which students study a large volume of material on specific and complex historical examples, on which they are then expected to form and defend judgements – was used to introduce business students to the problem of decision making, in inherently uncertain and unprecedented situations (Garvin, 2003). Part of the purpose of case teaching is to introduce students to situations in which empirical data are *never* fully sufficient to validate a given judgement. For those within the contest, uncertainty invites a *decision*, and not simply more evidence. As Schumpeter argued:

> As military action must be taken in a given strategic position even if all the data potentially procurable are not available, so also in economic life action must be taken without working out all the details of what is to be done. Here the success of everything depends upon intuition. (Schumpeter, 1934: 77)

As Hayek also argued, the partiality of economic knowledge means that the condition economic actors find themselves in is a practical one of what to *do*, and it is by no means clear that cold, 'objective', empirical knowledge necessarily serves the actor best. As John Gray argues, Hayek seems to have been appealing to a form of tacit or embodied knowledge, unmediated by methodology, which enables more instinctive action upon uncertain situations (Gray, 1998). Case teaching nurtures this pragmatic capacity.

The case method was imported from the Law School (where it had been used since the 1890s) to the Business School in 1920, and provided a template for the work on business strategy that was developed by George Albert Smith and Roland Christensen in the 1950s. Students were encouraged to question how well individual firms were matched to specific markets, on the basis of specific qualitative issues, such as technologies and supply chains (Ghemawat, 2000). This remained a teaching method, aimed at developing the judgement and confidence of future leaders, as opposed to a set of transferable theories. The purpose of a case is for students to arrive at their *own* theoretical principles via a process of empirical induction (albeit, facilitated by a teacher), and not to inform them of the rules of how competitiveness does or ought to work.

A number of things changed in the US business environment in the early 1960s, which created a market demand for strategic expertise and more generic methods of evaluation. As US firms grew, they became spread over larger distances, requiring more sophisticated forms of management coordination, which could not be simply dealt with through hierarchy. They also became increasingly multidivisional, and the separation of ownership and control developed with the dispersal of share ownership. In contrast to the emphasis on 'human relations' that had characterized management theory during the 1930s and 1940s, management theory experienced a rationalist turn in the late 1950s, importing insights from the behaviourist sciences that had expanded on the back of Pentagon funding (Barley & Kunda, 1992; Mirowski, 2005). By the mid-1960s corporations were conducting 'SWOT' analyses of their suitability for specific markets, while new consultancies emerged to produce quantitative analyses of the interactions between firms and their markets. Benchmarking (in which firms are compared to each other, across a range of numerical indicators) developed, to provide a statistical basis on which to assess a firm's advantages and disadvantages. Management became *inter*-organizational, in addition to being intra-organizational: competitors could not be controlled, but they could be strategically analysed and their decisions anticipated. The internal functions of the firm would now be critically assessed, in terms of whether they strengthened or weakened the firm's position in relation to those of other similar firms. Regardless of academic doubts about the plausibility of any theory of business strategy, the demand for such theories from business rose.

What is methodologically significant about business strategy for the transition to neoliberalism is that it offers an entirely new expert perspective on the marketplace that was inimical to liberal economics. In a naïve liberal view, the function of management is to run a firm as efficiently as possible, to reduce prices or raise output, for the benefit of consumers. Competition arises 'naturally' as a result of multiple enterprises all seeking to serve the same customers. The addition of antitrust acts to ensure that firms do *not* gain any control over the price mechanism of the market, and focus on delivering value to consumers, as the ordo-liberals for example had envisaged. But business strategists propose that firms also focus on *other firms*, in order both to reorganize themselves and influence the market, such that their advantage is *not* purely dependent on supply and demand, and they shape the structure of the market to their own advantage. The market is no longer acted within, but *acted upon*, and the horizon of competitive activity is that much broader than any individual market. As Schumpeter had envisaged, the arena of capitalist competition extends to include non-market institutions, networks, ideas and culture. Schumpeter had initially believed that it was individual entrepreneurs who would transform markets in this strategic way, but in his later work he recognized that innovation 'within the shell of existing corporations offers a much more convenient access to the entrepreneurial functions than existed in the world of owner-managed firms' (quoted in McCraw, 2007: 496). Corporate managers could seek new paths to dominate markets and reduce competition, without simply trying to fix prices.

The notion of corporate strategy greatly increases the requisite authority and celebrity of senior management, and nurtures the analogy between business leadership and political leadership. Traditionally, the task of the professional manager had been to ensure that a firm was fulfilling its various functions as efficiently and competently as possible. Authority was primarily bureaucratic and – in keeping with the nature of bureaucratic authority – relatively anonymous in nature. But strategy poses more fundamental questions, of what the firm's core product should be, which markets it should be in, what its long-term objective is, and how it intends to survive. The condition of rivalry between competitors means that the manager – or 'leader' as they increasingly understood themselves – is responsible for the survival and core identity of the firm, and not simply its competent operation. They decide where and what the firm is to be, which competitors it intends to fight, and which it intends to avoid. Defining the firm's identity in *intangible* terms (via its brand, its values), as opposed to technological or product terms, offers managers a source of stability, which does nothing to deny or reduce the disruptions and uncertainty that are afflicting the firm's tangible economic, social and technological identity. Every material aspect of the firm is potentially expendable, once its immaterial aspect is sufficiently secure. With the 'shareholder value' revolution of the 1980s, these managers also became responsible for offering a narrative about their firm to investors, which, if convincing, could allow them to inflate their own pay dramatically (Froud et al., 2006). The question of the 'fairness' of this rising pay does not arise, so long as they succeed in demonstrating unique personal qualities that others lack: psychological differentiation acts as an immanent justification of inequality. Drawing on an extensive infrastructure of consultancy, business schools, management theory and market analysis, managerial authority is imbued with a 'violent threat', whereby the existential fate of the enterprise is dependent on the decision of the heroic individuals at its top. As with the Schmittian political leader, the command issued by the strategic manager must be obeyed, on the purely immanent grounds that 'we' are in combat with 'them', and existence is at stake. The injunction is to obey, or else possibly perish.

The benchmarking of nations

If statistical measures of macro-economies and societies emerged gradually from the late nineteenth century onwards, national performance *indicators* only became publicly recognized in the aftermath of World War Two (Alonso & Starr, 1987; Innes, 1989; Desrosieres, 1998). GDP and unemployment figures became published at regular intervals, as ways of testing the value of economic policy. Qualitative differences between nations could be represented as quantitative comparisons, thanks to the commensuration provided by these indicators (Espeland & Stevens, 1998). But the question then quickly arose of how *else* available statistics might be compiled and represented, to test societies and policies differently, with different normative assumptions. The idea of 'social' indicators, to capture and compare non-economic value, was initially pioneered by the Eisenhower administration, before becoming adopted by civil society groups in the 1970s. The notion that a nation's competitiveness might be measured or 'scored' represents a similar example of such statistical innovation. The pioneering work in this regard was done by two management scholars, Richard Farmer and Barry Richman, in 1965–66 (Farmer & Richman, 1970, 1971). Farmer and Richman's work provided the example that the WEF (and subsequent competitiveness think tanks) would build on, in constructing entirely new methodologies, for the comparison and ranking of nations.

Anticipating the concerns of Schwab and the WEF, Farmer and Richman approached comparative political economy, by arguing that differences in the economic performance of nations must ultimately be explained by discrepancies in management, but that these must in turn be explained in terms of the conditions that nations offer to management. Management is 'the single most critical social activity in connection with economic progress', impacting on all types of organization (whether public or private sector) and all types of national political economy (including capitalist and communist) (Farmer & Richman, 1970: 1). The requirement to manage therefore becomes a form of global *a priori*, yet there is no theory available to address this, especially as orthodox economics largely overlooks this all-important entity. The lack of any 'general theory' of management, for use by all managers in all sectors and societies, meant that the most important discrepancies in economic performance went unexplained.

In pursuit of a 'general theory' of management, Farmer and Richman constructed a new methodology for the measurement and comparison of nations, with two key characteristics. Firstly, they deliberately ignored 'the personality, motivation and capabilities of individual managers', in favour of the 'external constraints' that shape and limit managers' decision making, where 'external constraints' refers to the national context in which managers operate (1970: 32). In one simple move, the world is stood on its head, such that everything that goes on outside of the limits of the organization is treated as simply a conditioning factor, to be understood in terms of how successfully it supports management. This is a bold methodological jump, which instantly colonizes every non-business sphere – including the political realm – with a managerial mode of evaluation. Nothing remains external to managerial logic, once the nation itself is evaluated in terms of the 'external constraints' it offers to decision makers in enterprises. The 'social' becomes represented as the servant of the 'economic', or as a potential resource for production (Jessop, 2002).

On this premise, there is no longer any 'separate' economic realm, but various spheres of social, economic, political and cultural activity, which combine to create a particular national (or local) ecology of innovation and business dynamism. As the WEF's first global competitiveness report argued:

> Traditionally, competitiveness is defined mainly in terms of the cost of production and productivity. However, we know today that many other elements come into play: the internal dynamism of a country, its socio-political consensus, the quality of its human resources, its commercial spirit, the manner in which it prepares for the future, etc. (European Management Forum, 1979)

The question is how to evaluate so many different fields of society, in ways that will prove useful. Farmer and Richman worked with four categories of evaluation:

'education'; 'sociological-cultural'; 'political-legal'; and 'economic'. Each of these is made up of sub-categories. As competitiveness institutes and think tanks multiplied over the course of the 1980s, more and more competing methodologies and weighting systems would be developed along these lines, identifying the 'pillars' or 'factors' that make up competitiveness. The competitiveness 'scoreboards' produced by WEF and IMD, and similar indexes such as the World Bank's 'Ease of Doing Business' rankings, distinguish themselves by the particular data sources they select, and how these are condensed down to the point of producing a single numerical evaluation of a nation. Competition between rival 'judgement devices' emerges (Karpik, 2010: 53). The goal in any case is to synthesize multiple statistical data, on heterogeneous socio-economic-political fields, and ultimately produce a single 'score' of a nation's overall performance.

Secondly, their methodology privileged quantification and comparability, regardless of how qualitative or apparently incomparable the objects being studied. Farmer and Richman purported to start with no presupposition about what constituted 'good' management, but simply wanted to produce a framework through which divergences in national managerial potential would come to light statistically. If an evaluation framework could be produced, that could engulf all cultures and political systems, it could seemingly offer a perspective from outside of any individual political or disciplinary tradition. Quantitative comparison becomes an end in itself, the assumption being that any individual nation must aspire to learn from or out-perform other nations. Producing tabular rankings of nations, with a 'winner' at the top, became the most publicly compelling technique of national competitiveness reports. The act of synthesizing data sources serves as an international comparison and objective test, whose own normative principles or authority retreat from view. The intrinsic valuation of national difference is replaced by an extrinsic evaluation.

A question which competitiveness experts subsequently had to confront was how to extend quantification into the *cultural* dimensions of particular nations and places. How to quantify a nation's business 'values' for example? Farmer and Richman used a method called the Delphi Survey, which became pivotal for competitiveness evaluations. The technique is used to poll a select group of elites – business leaders, policy makers and academics – on the 'constraints which do directly influence internal firm management in a given country' (Farmer & Richman, 1970: 329). The respondents are asked for their subjective evaluations of a particular nation, assuming that they (especially the business leaders) are sufficiently mobile as to have comparative experience of different nations. Where their opinions differ strongly, the difference itself is quantified, simplified and then sent back to the respondents for re-evaluation. The re-evaluations are received, compared, processed, and any remaining differences highlighted again. This process continues until the differences have been resolved, and subjective evaluations have been converted into an objective 'score' that can be attributed to a specific nation. The process is self-evidently a little clumsy – Farmer and Richman describe it as a way of attributing 'personal probabilities, which are then used as estimates of the objective probability statement' – but it succeeds in the all-important task of converting qualities into quantities, and thereby making nations entirely commensurable and rankable (1970: 333). What is being constructed here is a common empirical world, but one that is only inhabitable by a small group of elite decision makers. Once again, the Schumpeterian philosophical anthropology, which states that dynamic individuals operate outside of the normative framework of everybody else, is put to work in constructing a form of objective reality which is only recognizable by business and political leaders.

This is a manifestly constructivist and pragmatist project, in which methodologies are adopted and adapted in order to generate a quantitative, utilitarian audit of nations. Although Farmer and Richman's own work never gained great public policy influence, they had identified an important new means of putting public institutions and public goods to the test. A particular normative worldview, belonging to the managers of enterprises, is converted from a form of moral judgement, into a scientific tool, through which the worth of nations can be objectively gauged. The quality of a certain space or culture becomes first quantified and then compared, using benchmarking techniques that implicitly privilege the managerial gaze. This gaze is no longer just turned inwards upon the internal dynamics of a single firm, but also outwards upon the society in which it sits. The quantitative comparison, and hence ranking, of nations represents a symbolic step away from the liberal, Ricardian view of the global economy as a positive-sum game. Whether nations *are* actually in direct economic competition with each other is not confirmed, but benchmarking uses the power of comparison to identify priorities for action and communicate their urgency.

Michael Porter and national competitiveness

The fusion of managerial and political logic cannot only take place by subjecting public policy to economic evaluation, although that is a key part of it. The provision of statistical indicators and rankings of a nation's performance may provoke concern or excitement amongst political leaders, but they then require expert advice on what they should *do*. It is the immanent, self-validating problem of the decision that needs to be economically theorized, if executive political authority is to be reconfigured in market-oriented ways. The crucial contribution of Michael Porter was to provide a template through which policy makers and politicians could develop quasi-business strategies for entire nations, as well as cities, regions and neighbourhoods. By also founding and delivering a number of consultancy services to governments, Porter provided practical support for nations seeking to improve their competitiveness. His leap from the world of business strategy to that of policy consultancy and advocacy was possible because he distilled strategy to its simplest element: the problem of strategy is to *differentiate oneself qualitatively* in such a way that the threat of competition is reduced.[2]

Porter joined HBS in 1969 to do an MBA and then moved to the economics department, where industrial organization economics was still dominated by the Structure Conduct Performance theory of Bain. Bain's work, which remained influential in the US anti-trust agencies, showed how firms use their power to raise barriers to entry, and therefore require regulatory intervention. Porter adapted the same insights to show how individual firms could use their power to raise barriers to entry, and therefore return higher profits to shareholders and prosper in a more hostile environment (Stewart, 2010).[3] He thereby married the formalistic approach of orthodox economics to the pragmatic requirements of business strategy, producing a generic theory of business competitive advantage that appeared in his seminal 1979 'five forces' article (Porter, 1979).[4] As this article states, 'the same general principles apply to all types of business', a claim that directly contradicted the inductive assumptions of HBS strategy teachers of the 1950s and 1960s (1979: 3). At the same time, he inverted the assumption of Bainian economics, that high profits indicate illegitimate activity, and instead treated profitability as the raison d'être of management. In this respect Porter corroborated what the Chicago School were arguing in their critique of anti-trust, and anticipated the rise of 'shareholder value' thinking in the 1980s, which elevated share price to the status of ultimate corporate performance indicator.

Porter's most important innovation was to challenge the sceptical and inductivist epistemology that had previously dominated the academic study of strategy, as manifest in the case teaching method. Unlike neo-classical economics, with its shared presupposition of individual rational choice, strategy lacks any generally agreed methodological principles or presuppositions about the nature of competitive advantage (Froud et al., 2006: 23). But Porter recognized that principles and presuppositions were nevertheless needed by decision makers, and there was an opportunity for academics willing to *invent* them for practical use. Method and theory can be constructed anew, for the pragmatic purposes of reducing uncertainty to some extent – at least, to a greater extent than qualitative case studies offer to do. The question is who might possess the authority to construct such methods and theories, to which the answer is whichever scholar has the charisma and the political reach necessary to make them widely plausible. Porter applied this same inventive approach to the strategic analysis of nations, in developing the WEF's first Global Competitiveness report in 1979.

Porter's journey from business strategist to policy guru was initially conducted via elite networks, consultancy, policy commissions and think tanks over the course of the 1980s. A number of historical and political factors need to be taken into account in understanding this transition. His early career coincided precisely with the economic crisis of the 1970s, during which time large US corporations were mobilizing politically against regulation and behind the burgeoning conservative wing of the Republican Party (Phillips-Fein, 2009). The decline of corporate profitability, stagflation and the rise of Japanese exports to the USA, all raised nationalist anxieties regarding America's status in the world economy, that could quickly tip into protectionist rhetoric. Oil price rises showed that corporations could not simply rely on economies of scale to keep costs down, but needed to anticipate unusual threats from beyond their immediate market horizon. Porter's inversion of Bainian economics, from treating market power as a bad thing (for the public), to treating it as a good thing (for management), had a welcoming audience amongst corporate executives in the early 1980s, but a not unrelated question was how policy makers could act to defend the power of US firms in the global economy, other than simply imposing tariffs on Japanese imports. If strategy is reduced to the bare essentials, of finding areas of production which others can't mimic, Porter was quick to realize that this is something that can apply to entire nations, and not only individual firms. Both share the problem of how to define themselves as *different* in an increasingly globalized economy, so as to avoid competing directly through cost-cutting. This is a Schumpeterian affirmation of qualitative difference, applied to entire political territories as well as individual firms. Porter's 1990 work, *The Competitive Advantage of Nations*, completed his expansion of business strategy to the question of national decision making (Porter, 1990).

There is a necessary sociological presupposition in this analysis, which competitiveness consultants have expended great energy in stressing. This is that the arena of competition is constantly expanding, that levels of competitiveness are increasing all the time, that the pace of change is getting higher and higher, and that, while the risks of failure are growing, the rewards to the winner are greater and greater (e.g. Garelli, 2006). Innovation therefore becomes the only path to competitive advantage, because any static corporate strategy will quickly be mimicked by a lower cost rival. During the 1990s, Porter shifted his attention to how competitiveness can be upgraded, that is, constantly renewed as the only alternative to decline (Porter, 1998). Crucially, for his entry into policy advice and consultancy, Porter's implicit sociology also assumed that the significance of nations and localized production systems was growing in the global economy, and not declining (Porter, 1990). In a similarly formal style to how the five competitive forces influencing firm competitiveness were identified, Porter identified four factors which influenced a nation's 'competitive advantage'.[5] While the pace of change and scale of global competition were always rising, Porter argued that – contrary to a purely liberal vision of laissez-faire – national leaders *did* have a role to play in aiding their domestic industries, but not a protectionist one. Nations could be governed in ways that not only attracted productive enterprises, but also helped them to build and defend their own distinct competitive advantages. The idea that regional 'clusters' of businesses were key to national competitiveness became Porter's most recognized policy prescription (Martin & Sunley, 2003). What exactly any of this meant in terms of policies, however, was often vague, concealed behind rhetorical appeals to 'leadership', 'vision', entrepreneurial 'values', cultural re-definition and national boosterism.[6] Even proponents of Porter's 'cluster' theory were doubtful that policy could necessarily influence how such clusters develop.[7] Porter's message, that *both* corporate executives *and* state executives could act to influence the way in which global competition proceeded, was more important to winning influence than the empirical validity of the theories that he proposed to back this up. The theories were developed for a lucrative consultancy market of senior decision makers, for whom the liberal economic mantra of laissez-faire was of no practical use.

The political-economic contest

The effect of these various methodological developments was to represent firms and sovereign states as ontologically equivalent and symbiotically related. As the crisis of the 1970s appeared to demonstrate, national economic prosperity was dependent on the success of key industries and firms. But the success of key industries and firms was partly determined by the conditions and regulations created by public policy makers. A new type of political-economic contest is constructed and represented, which lies between market liberalism (positive sum market competition between firms) and political mercantilism (zero sum geopolitical competition between states).[8] In this contest, firms are quasi-political actors, seeking to position themselves in strategically advantageous positions in the global economy: states are quasi-corporate actors, seeking to do the same thing. Managers take decisions on how resources are allocated inside firms, while politicians take decisions on how they are allocated outside firms, and they each benefit from doing so with a shared goal in mind. This vision is neither as peaceful as the liberal ideal of unregulated 'free trade' nor as hostile as the Schmittian depiction of politics as existential combat. Instead, the economic and the political are fused together, into a Schumpeterian game in which the 'winner' is the firm or state that imposes its will on how and where wealth is produced.

Chapter 2 argued that competitions necessarily require some sense of *a priori* equality, as well as of empirical inequality, if they are to serve as coherent forms of socio-economic organization. There must be a normative, as well as an anti-normative, dimension. The Bretton Woods institutions, trade agreements and the World Trade Organization serve global capitalism with many of its formal international norms. Statistics on national performance (such as productivity and growth) make rival nations comparable before common standards of measurement. However, national competitiveness evaluations and rankings are invented to provide an entirely separate and neoliberal national measurement framework, that engulfs the social, the political and the economic, within a single audit of strategic dynamism. Moral values themselves are evaluated, for how strongly they promote the ethos of competitiveness. A nation's legal system is evaluated, for how strongly it defends property rights and business freedom, including market freedoms (the quality of anti-trust is given a score). The liberal rule of law is valued, but on the extrinsic and contingent grounds that it is beneficial for enterprise. The methodologies to do this are constructed in an institutional space that sits outside of conventional categories of state, business and academy, in cross-cutting think tanks and consultancies. These methodologies, and the global networks from which they emanate, then serve as the *a priori* for judgement that can then be cast upon any nation, city or region.

The necessary accompaniment to this new type of global audit is a global network of institutions, selling and pushing tailored knowledge and advice on how to act in response. Where a competitiveness evaluation must be imbued with some spirit of objectivity (albeit, an objectivity that is recognisable to global elites), the subsequent consultancy and advice are designed in a heavily partial fashion, that is sensitive to national political sentiments. *How* to make a nation competitively different from its 'rivals', through cultural policy, nation branding, a culture of enterprise and 'clusters' of innovation, is a practical challenge that competitiveness experts provide help with. The art of the competitiveness expert, whether in constructing measurement frameworks or in offering a definition of a nation's (or firm's) intangible cultural identity, is to provide a modicum of stability and existential security to a decision maker, while also stressing the irresistible hurricane of change that could yet engulf them. Uncertainty can be reduced through acts of formalistic simplification (such as Porter's resolutely simple theories of competitive advantage), but only for the pragmatic purpose of preparing leaders to re-enter the fray and face further uncertainty. In this way, the neoliberal problem of how to represent or stabilize uncertainty, without seeking to determine or reduce it, is addressed.

SPREADING COMPETITIVENESS

The empirical reality constructed and depicted by competitiveness experts is one that can only be inhabited by a global elite of decision makers, from businesses and governments. These decision makers are deemed to share a common existential fate, which is to define the communities they lead against a presupposed backdrop of ever increasing global competition. But how does this message access the elites it is intended for? How does this colonization of the political by business strategy actually proceed? The routes via which the discourse of national competitiveness has travelled are partly constitutive of the vision of the political that it propagates. The idea of strategic leadership, as self-legislating cultural differentiation in a global economy, demands and necessitates a break from other visions of politics, based in notions of representation, democracy or non-economic community. The 'violent threat' of management offers a vision of authority as reducible to the sheer contingency of the decision, that one individual takes on behalf of many others. It involves no justifications or appeals to the common good, as it originates in an existential affirmation of radical differentiation, that Schmitt identifies as the primary fact of politics.

The dissemination of competitiveness evaluations and rhetoric has occurred via channels and language specifically aimed at senior leaders, who may ostensibly be rivals, but share a common fate by virtue of their executive power. The evaluations themselves will be differentiating (splitting nations, firms and cities into 'winners' and 'losers', the 'competitive' and the 'uncompetitive'), but there is a limited, quasi-private community of those whose decision making needs to be reformatted against this backdrop. The function of competitiveness consultants is to constantly alternate between representations of equivalence and differentiation, on the one hand representing the shared global reality that all decision makers need to recognize, and on the other representing the qualitative and quantitative differences which define rival national communities in the global 'race'. This community of leaders – often associated with the WEF Davos annual forum – needs to be strategically separated off from the rest of the *demos*, whose political demands and representations are likely to interfere with the task of increasing the overall efficiency of a nation state.

Elite congregations

Think tanks were a crucial resource for the development of neoliberal thinking from the 1930s onwards, especially in Britain and the United States (Phillips-Fein, 2009; Plehwe, 2009; Stedman-Jones, 2012). The pragmatism and heterodoxy of neoliberal ideas meant that spaces were needed that sat outside of existing centres of intellectual and political authority, where debate could take place and ideas could be shared amongst intellectuals and interested parties. Think tanks are spaces for 'outsiders' who refuse to sit tidily in academia, business, media or government, but seek to influence all simultaneously (Medvetz, 2012). Hayek's Mont Pelerin Society, modelled on the socialist Fabian Society, aimed to provide a home for neoliberal intellectuals and critics from around the world, to aid them in developing a policy programme while they waited for an opportunity for influence to arise (Bergin, 2013).

The WEF might be described as a think tank, inasmuch as it employs academics (such as Porter) to provide policy narratives, reports and advice directly to governments, via the media. But it remains firstly a *forum*, in which a global elite can congregate to identify priorities for action. It is convened by management scholars, who have their own business interest in developing their consultancy brands, but those who attend are decision makers in the global game and not theoretical observers of the game. This is a different type of think tank from the famous incubators of New Right ideas, in which business (or conservative foundations, such as Ford and Rockefeller) provides funding to pay scholars to develop ideas. The model of the 'forum' is one in which scholars oversee an event, provide some simple empirical data to frame the event, and political and business leaders attend in order to develop a shared narrative about the future. The scholar is therefore in the position of facilitator or entrepreneur (much as they are when teaching cases in business schools) rather than supplier of objective knowledge or neutral theory. While such an event does not sanction

economic planning in any strict sense, it facilitates a degree of narrative homogeneity about the future across public and private sectors, tempering uncertainty
without seeking to deny or eradicate it.

Providing opportunities for leaders to assemble, outside of the orthodox routes
of lobbying and diplomacy which otherwise mediate the interactions of global
elites, is the primary institutional means by which competitiveness evaluations
have been disseminated. These assemblies occur with varying levels of formality
and regularity, and their exclusiveness is constitutive of their value and appeal.
In the history of competitiveness thinking, the key moments of policy influence
have been one-off national *commissions*, which follow the 'forum' model, with
select political, business and academic elites, who conclude the commission
with the publication of a document evaluating the nation's strategic strengths
and weaknesses in the global economic contest. Competitiveness forums and
commissions provide an example of what Thrift calls the 'cultural circuit of
capital': 'a continual critique of capitalism, a feedback loop which is intended to
keep capitalism surfing along the edge of its own contradictions' (Thrift, 2005: 6).
Knowledge is produced and dispersed within this circuit, but its practical function is also to support dialogue and linguistic homogeneity across multiple elite
institutions and cultures. The circuit is necessarily global, to provide a basis on
which to judge and act upon less mobile social and economic resources.

In the United States, where governments have historically not pursued active
industrial policies, the fear of declining relative productivity (relative to Japan
especially) was instrumentalized by business elites in order to engage the
Reagan White House in considering ways to improve national competitiveness.
In 1984 this led the White House to appoint John Young, the CEO of Hewlett
Packard, to chair a 'commission on industrial competitiveness' made up of business leaders and management thinkers, including Porter. The commission
reported 15 months later with *Global Competition: The New Reality*, laying out
a series of policy proposals to raise national competitiveness, focused on education, infrastructure and other public factors of productivity (President's
Commission on Industrial Competitiveness, 1985). In 1986, Young established
the Council on Competitiveness, the leading US think tank dedicated to evaluating and promoting American competitiveness, to provide constant data and
advocacy on competitiveness in Washington DC. From the early 1980s onwards,
a circuit of competitiveness advice and consultancy developed, within which
Porter was the most frequent broker. His Monitor consulting group was established in 1983 (providing consultancy on business strategy and national
competitiveness), from which OTF consulting was spun-off in 1991 (providing

consultancy to developing nations on competitiveness), and the Initiative for the Competitive Inner City was founded in 1997, building directly on an article published by Porter on this topic (Porter, 1995). The Porter 'brand' spanned business, academia and policy, demonstrating the types of personal qualities that are needed to succeed in this new era of competitiveness.

If competitiveness meant acting in pursuit of a more active industrial policy in the United States, for European policy makers it meant re-conceiving industrial policy for a global economy. And if it was pushed by business leaders 'upwards' towards the state in the United States, in Europe it was pushed by the European Commission 'downwards' towards national member states. A number of policy commissions were established by the European Commission during the 1990s, to assess what would be needed to develop Europe's 'competitiveness'. In 1990, the European Commission set out the new parameters of industrial policy, on the basis that 'competition is becoming ever more global and this trend is irreversible' and 'the role of corporate strategies is now determinant' (EC, 1990). Future industrial policy would have to involve 'maintaining a favourable business environment', much as Farmer and Richman's work had implicitly advocated in the mid-1960s. European nations were urged to shift from 'vertical' industrial policies (favouring certain firms or industries) to 'horizontal' industrial policies (favouring competitive markets and supportive infrastructure) (Aiginger, 2005). Tackling unemployment and low macro-economic growth, primarily through loosening labour market regulation and increasing market integration, remained the preoccupation for European competitiveness analysts during the 1990s. In this sense, the competitiveness agenda was initially more classically liberal in its European manifestation than in its American manifestation, and its expert advisors were drawn more from orthodox liberal economics than from business strategy. Only later, with the establishment of the distinctively Schumpeterian 'Lisbon Agenda' for competitiveness in 2000, did the European Commission begin to consider a more strategic role for policy makers seeking to spur innovation, differentiation and dynamic competition. From this point on, competitiveness would provide a justification for new types of state interventions, via universities, research and development, and support for new types of public-private collaboration.

Competitiveness institutes are constructed around the concerns and worldviews of elite decision makers from multiple sectors. Commissions such as the US Young Commission offered a voice to a select group, whose shared characteristic was seniority and celebrity. European competitiveness commissions represented subtly different institutions, with the inclusion of trade unions and more orthodox policy specialists. The WEF's Davos meeting is notorious for attracting pop stars and leading lights from all sectors, beyond the realms of business or public policy. The political implication in all cases is the same: professional identity or sector of responsibility is less significant than *power and weight of decision making*. The Schmittian burden to *decide on behalf of others* is what brings people together in competitiveness networks, seminars and institutions. The liberal boundaries separating the 'economic', 'political' and 'social' are dissolved by the distinctly neoliberal creation of networks and tools which extend a managerial-political calculus into all domains.

The cultural and spatial reach of these institutions must be somehow commensurate with their horizon of political action. Competitiveness discourse is a pragmatic reflection on the possibilities for economically efficient political action. Anything which lies beyond such perceived possibilities is beyond the scope of debate, but equally anything which lies within those possibilities is potentially relevant. Given that corporations and elite individuals are presumed to operate in a global space, so must policy makers be oriented towards it in their decisions and interventions. Think tanks with global reputations and evaluative reach (such as the WEF) serve to mediate a global debate about political-economic priorities, opportunities and threats, while also conducting the comparative audit of territories and states. Their perspective is offered from 'outside' of the competitive contest, frequently using the symbolically neutral territory of Switzerland as a base from which to do so. Individual gurus offer a perspective on the global economy and its future, that transcends institutional or disciplinary divisions.

In addition to globally-oriented think tanks and gurus, competitiveness institutions are created which map onto pre-existing political communities. Achieving concerted action in pursuit of competitiveness requires building on forms of collectivity that already exist. Competitiveness commissions and think tanks have therefore focused on *nations*, drawing *national* policy makers together, in addition to other tiers of governance such as cities and regions. There are cases of entirely new tiers of political action being imagined, constructed and governed, such as Britain's ill-fated 'Northern Way' or various attempts to nurture 'clusters' of business development, in line with Porter's advice. As Brenner argues, 'It is no longer capital that is to be molded into the (territorially integrated) geography of State space, but state space that is to be molded into the (territorially differentiated) geography of capital' (Brenner, 2004: 16). But politically, at least, competitiveness strategies have taken a stronger hold where they map onto spaces and cultures that have more obvious heritage.

Regulating leadership anxiety

The discourse of national competitiveness only makes any sense, if the central problem of politics is viewed as a Schmittian one of how to *decide* on behalf of others, and not (for instance) a Rousseauian one of how to represent the collective. Only if politics is conceived in Schmittian terms can it be reconceived in terms of competitive strategy, or can the analogy between a firm and a nation hold. We can see within competitiveness documents a nationalist rhetoric, compelling leaders to do whatever is necessary to defend their political communities against the 'threat' of rival nations. And commensurately, there is a suspicion of democratic and legal procedures that might threaten to undermine or divert this compulsion. A central objective for competitiveness rhetoric is therefore to produce an optimal sense of *anxiety* amongst political leaders with regard to competitiveness, that it is more than simply a matter of economic policy, but a fateful issue for their people and territory. It is through inculcating a sense of existential anxiety (which the consultant or guru then promises to temper) that business strategy succeeds in colonizing politics. Leaders are warned against ever feeling comfortable with the competitiveness that they have attained, as it can swiftly vanish or be overtaken by a rival. As Garelli argues, 'although being head of the class is certainly praise-worthy, nations and firms should also tackle a more fundamental question: *are we winning the right race and, if so, by how much?*' (Garelli, 2006: 25). Presenting empirical data as 'objective' or scientifically authoritative is less performatively effective than presenting it as uncertain and threatening, that makes some form of radical *decision* impossible to avoid.

Hayek, Schumpeter and leading members of the Chicago School all believed that modern democracy had a tendency to deliver economically irrational policies, ultimately tending towards socialism. The great weakness of democracy, by this account, was that voters prioritize immediate satisfaction over long-term political values and goods. As it seemed to the neoliberals and also to Schumpeter, socialism had the great electoral advantage of promising to deliver on the public's demands immediately, whereas the benefits of capitalism were only apparent to observers who could take a longer-term view. Stigler, for example, was resigned to the fact that a free market programme would never be popular: Hayek and Friedman both assumed that the success of neoliberalism would only be achieved via a programme of elite transformation, and not through any democratic movement. Friedman's infamous engagement with the proto-neoliberal Pinochet regime in Chile during the 1970s confirmed that political liberalism was not a precondition of his proposed policy programme (Mirowski, 2009). Competitiveness analysts have also viewed democracy as, at best, of secondary importance and, at worst, obstructive for successful economic policy making. Farmer and Richman's 'general theory of management' had benchmarked all industrial nations, capitalist and communist, in terms of how well they supported effective management. Democratic freedoms are external to the calculation of a nation's competitiveness.

Both business and political realms are represented by competitiveness experts as afflicted by problems of 'short termism'. Corporate managers run the risk of focusing only on existing market demand and their next quarterly report, and taking their eye off their longer-term strategy. Politicians face an analogous problem of focusing too much on their popularity and next election (Ketels, 2006: 132). This also distracts from the longer-term challenge of improving national competitiveness. Part of the justification for competitiveness institutes and think tanks is that they promise to insulate the competitiveness agenda from 'short-term' changes in the political weather (Ketels, 2006). Where the electoral cycle is measured in a temporality of four or five years, competitiveness is represented as a problem that needs acting on over significantly longer time periods.[9] Good competitive strategies are oriented around long-term horizons and necessarily uncertain outcomes. Democracy, including the electoral cycle, threatens these strategies.

Meanwhile, the political choices which *do* get made via democratic processes are shown to be inevitably dependent on competitiveness, regardless of the values that underlie them. If competitiveness is defined as a nation's capacity to produce wealth, then virtually any policy programme, whether of the Left or the Right, will be parasitical on competitiveness in some way.[10] In the USA the policy may be a tax cut, while in Europe it may be a social policy, but both are represented as dependent on a degree of competitiveness in the first place. National political communities therefore owe a constant debt to the enterprises which sit within their borders, and there is no coherent political position which does not place a high value on competitiveness. As the very condition of all democratic possibility, it must therefore be treated as beyond democratic debate.[11]

But it is not simply that democratic choices are dependent on competitiveness. The leadership anxiety that the competitiveness discourse targets is the possibility that the fate of the political community itself may depend on the leader's strategic decision making. In a number of ways, the urgency of addressing national competitiveness blends with more existential forms of politics. Urgency and the authority of leadership decision then become mutually reinforcing. The heightening of a sense of urgency (or even *emergency*) around national economic performance enables a form of Schmittian-managerial action to be ignited, where there is no public justification required, but simply a sense that 'we' are in combat with 'them'. The greater this immanent sense of rivalrousness, the more immediate is the injunction for elite action. And so at a rhetorical level, cherished forms of national identity are represented as under threat, as a result of diminishing competitiveness. Competitiveness reports which are addressed to American policy audiences make repeated analogies to the Cold War, and the 'Sputnik moment' when the technological challenge of the Soviet Union became most visible (e.g. President's Commission on Industrial Competitiveness, 1985; Kao, 2007). Meanwhile, European leaders are urged to pursue competitiveness, or else confront the end of their social model. The threat of lost competitiveness exceeds any narrowly economic or measurable concerns. What begins as an analogy between states and corporations takes on an existential hue, where competitive strategy is (re)imbued with the rationality and rhetoric of military strategy. The veiled threat is that the loser in the international 'race' for competitiveness might be weakened in the more existential sense, that they may become technologically incapable of defending themselves.

Is this allusion to warfare merely rhetorical and analogical, or is there a genuinely biopolitical or mortal dimension to these national performance evaluations? History shows that the statistical project of measuring and comparing national economic aggregates has often been motivated by strategic military requirements (Desrosières, 1998). The integration of economics and statistics in the 1930s and 1940s was partly a requirement of wartime government (Backhouse, 2006). Statistics put nations to the test, as non-violent audits or trials, which indicate the likely outcomes of more fateful and less measurable contests, hence we might say that a 'violent threat' has always hovered behind the project of aggregating national capacities. We have seen that falling competitiveness is represented as more than a narrowly 'economic' issue. And arguably, it has existential implications and causes, which lay bare the Schmittian underpinnings of competitive strategies. US competitiveness is tied up with the vitality of its military-industrial complex: rising competitiveness is achievable through Pentagon investment in research and technology, while declining competitiveness could ultimately affect American military pre-eminence.[12] To ignore US competitiveness is deemed to put national security at risk (Cole, 2012). Meanwhile, European competitiveness is tied up with its response to its ageing population: a low birth rate and a ticking pensions 'time bomb' are the primary conditions forcing political leaders to act, to increase competitiveness. The political threat in each case is existential and Schmittian in character. American competitiveness is distantly indicative of its capacity to annihilate its enemies, while European competitiveness is hampered by its inability to replace its friends.

MEASUREMENT AND CONVERSATION

Empirical data perform differently, depending on their pragmatic situation or the mode of unspoken authority that accompanies them. Neoliberalism seeks to substitute economic facts for political rhetoric or judgement, but how these facts are generated, mobilized and represented depends on what their practical and political purpose is. The previous chapter argued that neo-classical economics provided a liberal principle of equivalence, which could resolve conflict in a quasi-juridical sense. The facts produced by competitiveness consultants are entirely different in their pragmatic orientation. National competitiveness evaluations and comparisons are produced in order to *frighten, enthuse and differentiate* their chosen audience, while at the same time defining the broad global arena within which differentiation must take place. The quantitative evaluations are not offered with a spirit of neutral objectivity, but with a threat of imminent danger. Yet they must at the same time be intuitively convincing.

The epistemology and methodologies of national competitiveness evaluation are riven by a fundamental tension between qualitative affirmations of national-cultural differentiation, and quantitative judgements, rankings and comparisons. From a neoliberal perspective, qualitative differentiations are to be welcomed and celebrated, as long as they are manifest in entrepreneurial forms of distinction, which are oriented towards the global contest. The purpose of quantitative audit and rankings is not to arrive at some stable objective facts, which can be a matter of broad public consensus: competitiveness consultants are often surprisingly dismissive of the validity of their empirical methodologies. The task is to provide an empirical representation of the global economy, that is designed to catalyse entrepreneurial competitive energies on the part of policy makers and political leaders. The pragmatic purpose of competitiveness 'scoreboards' is not to achieve a form of peaceful consensus, via the provision of an agreed-upon principle of equivalence, but to nurture existential anxieties on the part of leaders, which might drive a greater concern and enthusiasm for competitiveness.

Institutional conditions of differentiation

In the previous chapter, we saw how anti-trust economists are encouraged to participate in academic public spheres and how quasi-academic activities (such as seminars and theoretical research) are reproduced within government agencies. The legal authority of the government agency is strengthened, if its economic experts can gain credibility amongst their disciplinary peers, and then bring their skills to the service of agency lawyers. Competitiveness experts have their own distinctive way of gathering, legitimating and distributing knowledge, which is animated by a desire to energize decision makers, rather than provide a neutral or objective view of the world that withstands scientific scrutiny.

In the first instance, these experts must construct a method through which diverse sources of data can be weighted and combined. Each think tank or guru develops their own methodology, which instrumentalizes a non-empirical belief about the sources of advantage and disadvantage in contemporary capitalism. These are then circulated via the circuit of think tank seminars, policy consultancy markets and lobbying networks. Rival theories of competitive advantage necessarily end up in competition with each other. Hence, Porter became known as someone who would recommend business clusters as the path to national productivity improvements, and Richard Florida became known as someone who would explore urban strategy in terms of attracting a 'creative class' of residents. These are not testable hypotheses, but narratives that presume to account for unstable and rapid fluctuations in the geography of capital.

Accompanying each narrative must be a technical apparatus of measurement and comparison, which is sufficiently flexible to be applied across time and space, but sufficiently stable to represent socio-economic inequalities. The unique brand of the guru or think tank is mirrored in unique means of combining and weighting statistics, so as to provide an evaluation rooted in a particular substantive view about capitalism and its future. In general terms, gurus provide this substantive view, legitimating it through their own charismatic authority and sense of clarity, while an associated team of technical experts provides supportive quantitative analysis. A division of labour develops, between the prominent individual providing a qualitative narrative, which must be sufficiently compelling as to convince its audience, and the technical analyst providing an accompanying evidence base. The combination of the two means that data are provided not only as empirically credible, but also as substantively meaningful.

Achieving this balance between empirical and ontological plausibility is the art of the competitiveness expert. Empirical data are used to the extent that they support a policy narrative, or open up valuable questions about future decisions, but are never analysed for the sake of it. Data must be processed in ways that reduce the complexity of uncertain situations, rather than increase it.[13] Narratives are developed to the extent that they provide a shared reality, within which data can be discussed, and shared problems identified and described. Orthodox economic data (for instance on trade deficits) might be accompanied with a narrative or question about what they *really mean* or whether they are *really worth* considering at all.[14] The 'scores' and national rankings that are the most publicly visible output of competitiveness think tanks are recognized by their proponents to be of limited value, beyond raising the political profile of competitiveness as a concern.[15] The hope is that they will lead decision makers to engage in a more detailed discussion about how they can respond to the challenge of competitiveness. Seeing as competitiveness experts are also commercial consultants, this is partly a business strategy in its own right, which can lead a guru and his associates to win lucrative consulting work.[16] How methods and narratives are constructed is also, therefore, partly a response to a competitive consultancy market: methods and narratives have to be differentiated from one another, if each consultant is to maintain a clear 'brand'. The fact that rival competitiveness evaluations are based on different techniques of data analysis, with different assumptions about sources of competitive advantage, is a function of the fact that onto-empirical worldviews are competing against each other in a marketplace for policy advice. In certain instances, experts might even protect their methods with intellectual property rights.[17]

Clients and audiences for competitiveness research also serve as a source of empirical data and substantive meaning, for the experts that advise them. They provide case studies and examples, which can be used by consultants when advising other clients or audiences. Crucially, they serve as the consultant's sensors for *new* challenges or threats that might be emerging. Their anxieties and perspectives on the future can inform how a competitiveness narrative is developed and changes over time. The dialogical nature of seminars and consultancy relationships means that competitiveness experts gather disparate subjective impressions of the world as they travel.[18] By synthesizing these into a coherent 'story' about capitalism, they then reflect back a representation of the world that is immediately plausible, though subtly altered. The 'delphi survey' technique (which constructs quantitative evaluations through elite surveys) codifies a methodological approach, which uses audience perspectives as a basis for representation.

The discourse of competitiveness is thus characterized by flux and fluidity. Methods are necessarily plural rather than standardized. Narratives and empirical data blend together. Knowledge moves through commercial and non-commercial routes simultaneously. Academics, business leaders and political leaders are brought together via seminars, gurus and think tanks, to address shared concerns and priorities. An opinion or subjective perspective might be shared in one elite forum, and then repeated as a form of evidence in another forum. This 'cultural circuit of capital' is often referred to with the term 'conversation' by its participants, such that their aim is to 'start a conversation about competitiveness' in x territory, or to 'reflect on the on-going conversation'. In line with the dynamic perspective on global capitalism that underpins competitiveness theory, a constantly evolving world is met with a constantly evolving 'conversation' to represent it.

Economizing political decision

A critical distinction between the competitiveness expert and the academic economist is that the former is sympathetic to the political vocation to act purposefully upon economy and society.[19] Knowledge is tailored pragmatically to serve decision making, rather than as an end in itself. And yet the aspiration is that decisions will become economically rational, oriented around maximizing the productive potential of local spaces in a global economy. The authority of the competitive state derives from its capacity to decide on a strategic path, which will lead to rising wealth, or at least offset the 'threat' of faster-moving or lower cost overseas rivals. But what, then, does the authority of the competitiveness advisor consist in? On what basis does the competitiveness advisor claim to know or see what this strategic path might be? Given the unknowable uncertainties of global capitalism, which the competitiveness expert is keen to stress, what counts as a valid representation or credible advice? Something must remain stable amidst so much flux, if epistemological – and hence political – authority is to remain feasible.

The key trait of competitiveness expertise that is employed to respond to this anxiety is its own entrepreneurship. The uniqueness of the expert is constitutive of the authority of his advice. The advisor possesses authority by virtue of being unconstrained by all forms of disciplinary, institutional, sectoral, cultural and spatial boundaries. By constantly transcending every division or binary opposition, the expert gains a perspective from a position external to the cultural locale of the elites they are advising. Firstly, this means abstaining from any disciplinary commitment to scholarly method.[20] Instead, as we have already seen, a distinctive method is constructed on the back of a substantive ontological narrative about the mechanics of global capitalism. Secondly, it means being able to communicate across sectors, so as to facilitate a 'conversation' between business, academia and government. The competitiveness expert refuses to be placed in any of these categories. And finally, the entrepreneurial expert must be at least as geographically and culturally mobile as those who are drawing on their expertise.

Competitiveness experts thus presume to operate in a meta-institutional, meta-cultural space, from where they can survey comparative inequalities. From this space, they get a view of 'winners' and 'losers' and a sense of the challenges that are coming over the horizon. However, they must be capable of descending to engage with clients and decision makers, so as to help reorient their goals in ways that are compatible with global competition. Their authority is ultimately of a charismatic form, inasmuch as it is their personality, self-belief and powers of convincing representation that offer a reason to believe and follow. Precisely because they do *not* rely on any *a priori* language or rules, but draw only on the existential resources of themselves and the fact of global capitalism, they provide a form of expertise that offers ontological security and meaning, rather than mere empirical calculation. Methods, such as those of neo-classical economics, are internal to the flux of capitalist evolution. The only stable methodological premise in a capitalist world, as for Schumpeter, is the force of the entrepreneurial will to reinvent and transcend divisions. In scholarly terms, competitiveness gurus engage in what Weber bemoaned as 'academic prophecy, [which] will create only fanatical sects but never a genuine community' (Weber, 1991a: 151). However, it is because of the need to align knowledge production with the perspective and existential anxieties of elite decision makers, whose ultimate capacity is to order violence against enemies, that this affective and prophetic stance is adopted.

CONCLUSION: THE VIOLENCE OF DECISION

Convention theory stresses that coordinated social and economic activity depends on reaching agreements, which requires the offer of acceptable justifications and often evidence for a given course of action. Individuals need to share certain principles of equivalence, which become tangibly manifest in measures and tests, such that they can agree that certain things, people and actions carry value. A degree of publicness is needed, for justifications to be aired, listened to and – if necessary – challenged. Where justifications are withheld, and the public spaces of possible dispute are closed down, then people enter what Boltanski terms a 'regime of violence' (Boltanski, 2011), in which they can behave as they please 'without being burdened by the requirement to explain' (Boltanski & Thévenot, 2006: 38). Within the regime of violence, there is an absence of any external, transcendent philosophical principle regarding common humanity, but an affirmation of the sheer contingency of the situation at hand, which needs acting upon as a matter of immediate necessity. The Schmittian political agent exists within the regime of violence, even when physical force is not being used, because purely decision-based politics admits no normative justification. It is mandated purely with respect to the 'friend-enemy distinction', which arises as a matter of contingent differentiation. What is culturally *uncommon* to the parties involved is what dictates action, rather than what is morally common to all parties. Boltanski argues that, in the regime of violence, the philosophical difference between people and things is abandoned, and individuals act upon one another in a non-discursive, purely material fashion.

In this precise sense, the Schumpeterian entrepreneur and the business strategist also operate in a regime of violence, in the sense that their authority to act derives purely from contingent differences between competitors, and their own contingent qualities of charismatic personality. People become mere factors of production or 'human capital'. While the majority of individuals continue to act in accordance to norms (within a 'regime of justice'), leaders, strategists and entrepreneurs draw on their exceptional personal qualities to act *upon the rules, from outside of the rules.* As for the Schmittian sovereign, their decision is generative of a new set of norms; that decision cannot be mandated by any norm. By distilling the problem of management to that of decision making under conditions of uncertainty, business strategy invites business executives to conceive of their authority in a regime of violence. There are no justifications or proofs offered for the strategic decision that is made: there is no time or capacity to compile sufficient evidence, for why *this* course of action is superior to *that* one. The action is self-legislating. The analogy between the existential condition of the military leader and that of the corporate leader or entrepreneur which is repeated by Schumpeter, and recurs in strategy thinking, means that an ontological gulf opens up, not only between the identities of competing firms, but also between those elites compelled to *decide,* and the vast mass of employees who obey rules as they are created. This is an anti-normative vision of managerial authority.

This is already deeply problematic in the context of business. It affirms a radical existential separation between senior 'leaders' and those that simply 'follow' (which is then mirrored in how income is distributed within the firm). It affirms actions which are not limited by a regime of justification, in the sense that they are not open to themselves being judged or measured, at least not by those within the firm (judgement is ostensibly performed by shareholders). Modes of institution that do not seek legitimacy leave themselves open to crises of legitimation, unless sufficient power is available to prevent or delay critique. One advantage that business leaders have in operating without justification, and purely on the basis of decision, is the capacity to transform the enterprise, alter its market productive functions, downsize its employees, such that it evades critique. Managers retain the option to simply eradicate certain employees, as an alternative to morally engaging with them. The resilience of highly innovative firms can be explained partly in terms of their ability to evade the constraints of justification, through a constant redefinition of their modes of valuation (Boltanski & Chiapello, 2007: 534).

If this is problematic as a mode of managerial authority, it encounters its own specific and graver contradictions when imported into the executive branch of government, as national competitiveness consultants sought to do. The analogy between the firm and the nation, the CEO and the political leader, has been widely criticized by orthodox economists, on the basis that it encourages forms of anti-trade protectionism and subsidy in defence of global market share (Krugman, 1994). But reconceiving of executive political authority in the language of business strategy also means abandoning notions of representative democracy or other theories of legitimate power. Even the Weberian notion of modern bureaucratic authority is too uniform and inflexible to guarantee survival in the competitive landscape asserted and represented by competitiveness gurus. The struggle posed by the narrative of competitiveness is a struggle for economic survival, with the hint that this is ultimately a struggle for a nation's *existential* survival. Political elites gain exceptional quasi-wartime powers, against such a backdrop, and lose any constitutional relationship to the political community they lead. Their allies in the 'battle' or 'race' for competitiveness are the business leaders, with whom they share a common form of charismatic-managerial authority. Through economic critique, the competitiveness agenda seeks to channel executive political powers towards dynamically productive paths.

The analogy between a firm and a nation (or other political territory) encounters the most serious tensions with respect to those resources which hamper competitiveness. Business strategy encourages managers to evaluate how well suited their firm's existing resources and activities are to their competitive emerging competitive environment. Certain resources can be abandoned (out-sourcing, down-sizing), and others acquired (M&As), in response to such an audit. The same is not true with respect to nations. The geography of the competitive state concentrates political capital behind the *most competitive* cities, clusters and regions, in contrast to a Keynesian spatial strategy which spreads wealth via industrial policy (Brenner, 2004). What then becomes of the uncompetitive spaces or populations? The Schumpeterian logic of competition gives an unlimited political mandate for those individuals or communities with the psychological strength to enact 'new combinations', who operate outside of existing routines and regulations. By some rhetorical sleight of hand, this may involve the executives of large firms, and not only those creating new ones. These routine-less individuals possess the ultimate worth in the global economy, because they are not governed by any stable standard, but capable of constant reinvention. Others, in the Schumpeterian economy, must simply try to keep up, adopting the new conventions as and when they are invented. But what of the individuals who are without value, in this contest, either because they are inflexible or because their inventiveness is more politically disruptive, and not simply in an entrepreneurial sense (Skeggs & Loveday, 2012)? In an economy oriented towards the exploitation of uncommon human traits ('talent', 'leadership', 'innovation'), what value remains placed upon *common* human traits? The danger faced by an antinormative capitalism is that it 'finds itself stripped of the justifications that make it desirable for a large number of actors' (Boltanski & Chiapello, 2007: 35).

The strategic, competitive political authority depends on affirmations of difference, rather than appeals to justice. The capacity of such authority to stave off or delay crises of legitimation depends on its reserves of sovereign power, and its capacity to mobilize these within the economic game, in support of certain territorially specific strategic goals. As the next chapter will explore, the neoliberal response to the financial crisis which began in 2007 has been to refuse critical judgement, in favour of *even more decisive* acts of competitive differentiation. This Schmittian politics, in which executive decision overrides public justification and critique, is now more naked, as Western political leaders simply declare that the market-based order will survive as a matter of necessity. However, this invites and affirms equally nihilistic forms of friend–enemy combat by populations, such as the 2011 rioters, who are not included in the shrinking group whose worth is being defended by executive dictat. When the state renounces general principles of justification and critique in favour of immanent executive freedoms, then it will encounter equally non-critical forms of response, which may be potent, destructive and differentiating without contributing to measured 'competitiveness'.

NOTES

1 It needs stressing that the language and measurement of 'competitiveness' have been equally, if not more, influential at sub-national scales of governance, such as cities and regions. However, for sake of brevity, I henceforth refer to 'national competitiveness' or the 'state', to explore how this particular scale is reconfigured, save for where some other scale (such as the European Union) is being discussed.

2 'Competitive strategy is about being different. It means deliberately choosing a different set of activities to deliver a unique mix of value' (Porter, 1998: 45).

3 'From the start, my goal was to integrate what we knew about the economics of markets and industrial organization and what we knew about companies and business strategy' (quotes in Gavel, 2000).

4 The 'five forces' which govern the level of competitiveness of a given industry are: 'threat of new entrants'; 'bargaining power of customers'; 'threat of substitute products'; 'bargaining power of suppliers'; 'jockeying for position among current competitors'. Firms need to act upon these different forces, to relieve the pressures that competition places on them.

5 The four factors are: 'factor conditions' (e.g. skills, infrastructure); 'demand conditions' (the home market); 'related industries' (presence of other successful industries nearby); 'firm strategy, structure and rivalry' (governance and culture of a nation's firms).

6 'Government's proper role is as catalyst and challenger; it is to encourage – or even push – companies to raise their aspirations and move to higher levels of competitive performance ... Government plays a role that is inherently partial' (Porter, 1998: 185).

7 'There is increasing evidence and agreement among researchers that clusters exist and that they feature a number of positive economic effects. There is less systematic evidence and agreement that policy interventions are possible and that they can generate value by speeding up the process of cluster development or increasing the effectiveness of existing clusters' (Ketels, 2003: 14).

8 'To be competitive America will have to sail between the Scylla of protection and the Charybdis that "left alone, the market will take care of it"' (Thurow, 1985: 2).

9 Porter argues that 'building strong regional economies takes decades' (Porter, 2001a: xiii).

10 IMD competitiveness rankings include a measure of how well a nation's political parties understand economic challenges (Garelli, 2006: 198).

11 '... competitiveness is not an end in itself; it is a means to an end ... Being competitive is what pays for whatever public or private goals we choose to pursue' (President's Commission on Industrial Competitiveness, 1985: 7).

12 'To do nothing is to lose not only economic leadership but political and military leadership too' (Thurow, 1985: 60).

13 '[It's about] trying as much as we can to come up with ways of saying "what are the one or two really interesting things that it's worth going forward with?". It's trying to understand and look at how we can learn something new. But doing it so that we don't have a list of 75 indicators. That doesn't help. It's nice, it's comprehensive, but it's not really useful' (US competitiveness consultant A).

14 'So I think there are some issues that seem to always stick around and there's always a challenge and people on [Capitol] Hill are wanting to know more to try to understand better ... And then others sort of wane and come and go. I mean, the whole offshoring thing two or three years ago was very hot; less so today. Trade deficits, what does that mean? Some years it's like it's a, you know, it's a disaster, other years, oh, they're sustainable and trade deficits don't mean anything in the 21st century economy' (US competitiveness consultant B).

15 'If I'm known at all in the media it's from the indicators, but I really use the indicators as a hook. I understand the limitations of them. They're really a hook for people to start taking the whole agenda seriously' (UK competitiveness consultant A).

16 '[What's] been incredibly effective is when we've been able to say "don't just hire [guru x] for the speech, but hire the consulting company". Hire the consulting company to come in and help you understand what your region is, help you develop a plan, have [guru x] come in and be the – I like to call it the igniting event – it energizes the hell out of everybody and as soon as he's done, everybody's really excited and saying "wow we really need to make something happen", and we can say "in the lobby there are little booths with all the things we've identified that we need to do in this region, go and sign up for the one you want to work on". So that you're not doing what happens so often which is he goes and gives a speech, and everybody gets excited, then he leaves, then nothing happens. And so when people like to see things changing in their region and in their community, that you need to do some work ahead of time and to follow up' (US competitiveness consultant A).

17 'As opposed to a lot of other consulting firms, [our institute] has really rigorous techniques which we branded. We have business process patents. Not only do other firms have nothing like them, most consulting firms don't even have patents' (US competitiveness consultant C).

18 'We convened a group down in Silicon Valley a few days ago ... of futurists, economic development analysts, large companies like Google, small high-end entrepreneurs in the biotech and nanotech space, and people who have worked with other global agencies, to say "how is innovation happening here in 2007 in Silicon Valley and the Bay Area, and how does that relate to what's going on globally?" So we're going to publish that and there'll be on-going discussions around that, and one of the things that the participants tell us is that actually the interaction with each other is what they value. They wouldn't have the ability to get together across all those different sectors and have that conversation' (US competitiveness consultant D).

19 'Too many economists say, okay, you know, if we don't exactly know we don't do anything. And I think if you work with politicians long enough you can see that that's really not an option. They will do something, and, you know, they're under pressure, even good people, with bad people it's even worse, but even good people that have the right intention and are smart, they will be forced to do something. So the question is what can we do for them – give them in terms of tools and thinking so that at least there is a likelihood that when they do will move in the right direction' (EC competitiveness advisor A).

20 'So as you can probably tell from me right now, I can talk about anthropology, I can talk about economics, and I sure as hell can talk about business strategy. As it turns out there are actually eight domains that will opine about prosperity, none of which will listen to any of the others' (US competitiveness consultant D).

5

CONTINGENT NEOLIBERALISM

Financial crisis and beyond

The classically modern schema of judgement – or crisis – operates according to a certain rhythm, that is found in both the normal governance and the reform of capitalism. Stable empirical and normative situations are periodically punctuated by new events or phenomena, which introduce uncertainty. There is a moment of doubt regarding the empirical nature or value of this interruption, a brief period in which shared reality is suspended. This moment of uncertainty is resolved through the use of some broader principle or measure, through which its quality or quantity can be ascertained, thereby stabilizing the situation once more. The situation is *judged*, a statement is made, and a consensual reality can take hold again, until a new interruption occurs. In order for judgement to succeed in achieving this, it is necessary that there is some agreed-upon external or 'higher' basis on which the judgement can take place, and that the judge is considered to be sufficiently distant (neutral, objective) from the issue at hand as to be able to act in the common interest. This sequence reproduces the form of Cartesian skepticism and Kantian critique, in which doubt is resolved into certainty through the abstract premise of the autonomous reasoning mind itself.

As convention theorists explore, this sequence is constantly at work in how institutions perpetuate themselves. People and things are constantly subjected to critical evaluations, so that their quality and quantity can be confirmed. These are what Boltanski terms 'reality tests' (Boltanski, 2011: 105). Neoliberalism is a project of taking measures and principles from the marketplace, and using these to perform judgements across social and political spheres, including of the state itself. Uncertainty is only to be empirically resolved using economics (and associated methodologies), so that competitive dynamics can be preserved. Ostensibly, neoliberals claim to value uncertainty positively, inasmuch as it is injected by complex and constantly changing consumer preferences and entrepreneurial strategies, which markets and economics are uniquely able to represent without determining. Yet the same sequence of judgement is also manifest in more radical, historic moments of uncertainty, which throw doubt upon the existing tools and principles of judgement, and open up political questions about *how else* judgement might be performed, by whom, and with what tools and principles. This is a form of historical punctuation of normality, associated with the notion of a capitalist crisis, which opens up space for radical critique or 'existential tests' (Boltanski, 2011). Crises of this form are really moments of *meta-evaluation*, in which there is no available judge – other than history or political action – to resolve doubt and restore certainty. Multiple moral and technical modes of judgement arise, side by side, and offer rhetorical and aesthetic reasons to be adopted, until a degree of consensus re-remerges. Capitalist crises are resolved when new economic theories, principles and tests have been agreed upon, as a basis on which normal evaluation can then progress (Boyer, 1989; Aglietta, 2001; Boyer & Saillard, 2001). Alternatively, capitalism itself is succeeded.

Two forms of uncertainty therefore need to be distinguished with respect to neoliberalism. Firstly, there is 'competitive uncertainty', or uncertainty that arises within the arranged economic 'game' as a result of multiple actors, all pursuing conflicting and distributed agendas. This is the form of uncertainty that neoliberals have always celebrated, not least because they claim to have the tools through which this uncertainty can be rendered periodically empirical, intelligible and manageable. Competitive uncertainty is a consequence of perspectival pluralism, and requires certain artifices and interventions to guarantee it. Secondly, there is 'political uncertainty', or uncertainty that challenges the very terms on which doubt and judgement are to be performed. This is what opens up space for 'meta-evaluation', *radical* critique, in which standard methodologies, moral principles and anthropological presuppositions can be thrown into doubt. Applied neoliberalism seized the political uncertainty occasioned by the crisis of Keynesianism during the 1970s to offer new ideas, principles and techniques through which states could proceed with a common agenda (Hall, 1986, 1989). Many assumed that neoliberalism had itself reached a similar point of crisis with the banking crisis of 2007–09. Had the banking crisis followed the classically modern sequence followed by the crisis of Keynesianism, there would have been a rupture, succeeded by a period of political uncertainty and theoretical pluralism, succeeded by the emergence of a new regime of evaluation, leading to a new stable reality.

Yet as many theorists and commentators have since recognized, neoliberalism has appeared to avoid its moment of historical reckoning (Crouch, 2011; Engelen et al., 2011; Mirowski, 2013). Rather than a period of 'political uncertainty', in which principles and techniques of evaluation are themselves subjected to critique and debate, new forms of state intervention have developed in order to defend the status quo and prevent the moment of radicalized judgement. So how has this occurred? And what form of neoliberalism arises as a consequence?

The argument made in this chapter is that a new form of *contingent neoliberalism* has emerged, which renounces the classically modern schema of judgement, offering only cultural-political affirmations of certain forms of conduct and certain representations of reality. A politics of *anti-crisis* arises, through which the very authority of doubt (and hence of critical judgement) is challenged, and the time and space of political uncertainty are closed down. This rests on what Boltanski terms 'systems of confirmation', which are tautologous statements – or 'truth tests' – seeking to demonstrate that 'this' is all there 'is', to offset the disruption represented by radical uncertainty (Boltanski, 2012: 72–73). Mirowski has explored the strategies through which the 'neoliberal thought collective' set about seizing control of how the crisis was interpreted and acted upon, albeit after a short period of confusion (Mirowski, 2013). In particular, he shows how a pincer movement between a classically neoliberal Hayekian argument (which would suggest doing nothing to rescue the financial system) and a monetarist and neo-classical argument for emergency rescue measures (as actually occurred) ended up allowing the latter to pose as the more public-spirited and reasonable position. But in any case, the sense of a political exception was crucial to the state's ability to act, in accordance with key neoliberal prescriptions.

Yet this necessarily alters the type of authority that can be claimed for the forms of economic evaluation previously endorsed by neoliberalism. They become contingently propped up, so as to avoid crisis, rather than used as principles through which crisis might be confronted and resolved. This anti-critical strand of neoliberalism inevitably infects how 'competitive uncertainty' is represented and experienced as well. The competitive 'game' loses its aspiration to be a general basis on which to distribute goods and recognition, and becomes performed without any appeal to the broader public good. 'Competitive uncertainty' is suddenly treated with greater suspicion for fear that it may create the conditions of 'political uncertainty', hence the resolutely anti-Hayekian political decisions to save banks, industries and currencies from the uncertainty of markets. Conversely, the empirical representations of the 'game' (prices, economic evaluations, scores) are also treated with greater suspicion, as an effect of political strategies, rather than as objective or 'neutral' judgements. Economic methodologies lose their aspiration to transcendental finality, and serve as instruments of more naked power struggles. For example, the empirical judgements produced by credit rating agencies are no longer credited with any *a priori* authority or 'ultimate' validity, but become means of briefly stabilizing an untrustworthy reality. The judges in this instance have lost 'objectivity', and are dragged into the 'game' by letting their own strategic agendas shape the evaluations they produce (Häring & Douglas, 2012). Rather than doubt resolved by judgement, there is simply a feeling of general unease.

To put this another way, the 'liberal spirit' of neoliberal authority which was already rendered very frail by the Chicago School economic critique of law and regulation is abandoned altogether. There is no longer an *a priori*, transcendental principle through which the critique of political metaphysics by economics is enacted. Rather, economic reason itself is the target of political rescue acts. The disenchantment of politics by economics is transformed into contingent strategies for enchanting economics with political substance and reinforcing it with power. In its anti-crisis formation, neoliberalism exists without *any* principle of equivalence, with *no* appeal to common humanity, but purely via contingent acts of preservation of the status quo. In doing so, a philosophical anthropology of difference structures the types of expert knowledge and policy intervention that sustain neoliberalism, without any accompanying philosophical principle of sameness.

This can be witnessed in contingent and exceptional appeals to the very forms of 'political metaphysics' that neoliberalism had once hoped to eradicate or hide. The project of replacing politics with economics, judgement with measurement, can now only persist if some open acknowledgement of the latter's political, performative and normative dimensions is made. And yet rather than reopen spaces and moments of political and normative argument, which might risk the abandonment of much economic rationalization, contingent political and normative capacities are now mobilized in order to defend and sustain the governing orthodoxy, on purely contingent grounds. Where Hayek had hoped to invent technical apparatuses in order to defend the liberal philosophical 'idea' of unplanned coordination, the contemporary neoliberal problem is how to harness political and ethical resources in order to defend extant technical apparatuses. Two manifestations of this are explored in this chapter.

Firstly, the tacit dependence of economic calculation on common normative pre-suppositions has now become entirely explicit. However, this is not being addressed from the perspective of moral or pragmatist philosophy, but rather from that of empirical psychology. With the rise of behavioural and happiness economics, visions of a rational economic actor have mutated from the status of methodological presuppositions (as they were for Coase) to the status of *norms for behaviour*. Homo economicus is no longer assumed, but *taught, nudged, mimicked and nurtured into existence*. It becomes apparent that individuals need to be helped to act in their own interests, indeed they need help in identifying what that interest even is, or else they can lapse into forms of self-destructive nihilistic behaviour. Psychological expertise can help reconstruct the necessary ethos on which calculative market individualism depends, though through no less techno-cratic means. This represents what I term 'neocommunitarianism' (Davies, 2012).

Secondly, the tacit dependence of neoliberalism on sovereign power has now become entirely explicit. However, it is important to recognize which variety of sovereign power. It is not the sovereignty of law, which the ordo-liberals had hoped might formalize the market system as an open competitive game, but the sovereignty of executive decision. Following the collapse of Lehman Brothers in September 2008, rapid executive action was presented as necessary in order for the market system – including its regulatory principles – to survive at all. In this sense, a *state of market exception* was declared, and arguably remained in place (Davies, 2013). The 'violent threat' of neoliberal authority is now relied upon to uphold the market order. From a Schmittian perspective, this is always tacitly assumed, in that legal normativity is existentially dependent on executive and military defence, but not vice versa. In a sense, the logic of national competitive-ness, explored in the previous chapter, potentially then offers the basis of a post-liberal, more mercantilist neoliberalism, in which rules are only recog-nized and enforced to the extent that they offer a local strategic advantage. The next section addresses the nature of the financial crisis in more detail, and then explores how 'neocommunitarianism' and the 'state of market exception' are manifest in governmental rationalities and actions.

CRISIS AND ANTI-CRISIS

In the months that followed the bankruptcy of Lehman Brothers on 15 September 2008, the news headlines were dominated by two contrasting ontolo-gies of political agency. The first was a form of Nietzschean, hedonistic individualism, whereby individual bankers were represented as having allowed their exuberance to overwhelm them, making reasonable calculation of risk impossible. Many of these bankers were named and nick-named: Dick Fuld of Lehmans, 'Fabulous Fab' Toure of Goldmans, 'Fred the Shred' Goodwin of RBS. Email records and taped telephone conversations revealed that the inner workings of the banking world were not organized around cold, rationalist calculations of utility optimization, but were instead often driven by surges of egoistic desire, demonstrations of power and hostility towards rivals. It wasn't simply that the markets for financial products suffered from 'information asymmetries', which left customers less able to calculate the value of products: it transpired that Goldman Sachs referred to their customers as 'muppets', offering opportunities for exploitation. The *dramatis personae* of this crisis were individuals, caught on tapes and emails, conspiring to enrich themselves personally, through manipulating rules and methods. At a certain point, the competitive ethos reaches a limiting point, where it attacks its formal conditions of possibility.

The second was the Hobbesian Leviathan of the modern, sovereign state, which came to the rescue of the financial system, on the understanding that the banking crisis would quickly bring down the entire monetary system if it were not acted upon. For years, neoliberal states had prided themselves on critically evaluating and auditing the efficiency of public spending, and had adopted self-imposed rules of fiscal constraint. Many of the hallmarks of neoliberal 'governance', such as out-sourcing, privatization, public-private partnerships and private finance initiatives, were initially invented for the purposes of trimming accounted-for public spending, sometimes by just a few hundred million dollars worth. During the 1990s, this economized and economizing state led many political theorists to divert attention away from sovereignty and towards measured forms of governance and governmentality (Rhodes, 1996, 1997; Rose, 1999; Rose & Miller, 2008). In its effort to behave 'as if' it were a market actor, the state treated the pursuit of administrative efficiency as critical to its authority. The shock, therefore, of discovering that states could, in extremis, find *hundreds of billions* of dollars worth of money through the force of executive decision was a stark reminder of the fact that states possess an ontological substrate that is entirely unlike that of private market actors.

In Britain, for example, the National Audit Office (NAO) calculated that, by the end of 2009 alone, the financial crisis had already cost the UK Treasury £850bn or 60% of GDP (NAO, 2010). The NAO reported that this expense was in fact 'justified' – but its order of magnitude placed it beyond the limits of conventional public management evaluation. Britain's public debt roughly doubled as a proportion of GDP, as a result of the financial crisis, the sort of fiscal shock that has previously only occurred as a result of a world war (BBC, 2012). As with the existential national politics of world wars, the state dealt with the financial crisis only by appealing to its immeasurable sovereign potentiality. But unlike in war, this sovereign mobilization remained immaterial or metaphysical: the collective recognition that sovereign states *do* still exist as immeasurable potentialities, in spite of the neoliberal emphasis on the visible and the measurable, enabled states to make credible promises on a scale that no other actor could. With the effective promise to underwrite the entire financial system, states explicitly made sovereignty a condition of economic possibility. Since then, this trick has been pulled in other ways too, as with the practice of 'quantitative easing', in which central banks take on debt in order to inject more money into the economy. Sovereignty is a shared illusion with possible material effects, which can plausibly retreat into the background for long periods of time, but is magically and swiftly rediscovered when other shared illusions – such as money – start to disintegrate.

With banks established as limited liability businesses, and balance sheets greater than the GDP of their host nations in many cases, it was clear that their managers and shareholders would never carry the costs of very large risk-taking, making high-risk strategies quite rational (Haldane, 2012a). This facilitated the vast 'privatization of gain and socialization of loss', as it became commonly referred to. One of the striking features of this crisis was the appearance of sublime numerical *ratios* between the numbers of individuals 'winning' ('the 1%') and the numbers 'losing', of how particular strategies of personal enrichment became a matter of fiscal concern. One calculation showed that if British bankers had paid themselves just 10% less between 2000–07, the banks would have had £50bn of additional capital available to them – precisely the figure the UK Treasury supplied as equity finance to Lloyds-TSB and RBS during October 2008. The crisis was characterized by such examples of *extreme rationality*, in the literal sense of the logic of *ratio*, with private individual actors generating costs that only the most powerful public institutions could then carry.

This flipping between the agency of individuals and the agency of sovereign states was not simply a consequence of the scalar ratios involved. The costs of the banking crisis have turned out to be extremely large, arguably of a scale that only sovereign bodies could carry. But in the moment of crisis itself, this was not why sovereign powers had to be mobilized. The problem at the time was that the full scale of those costs could not be reasonably known or estimated at all: their magnitude had become sublime, in the Kantian sense of a phenomenon from which cognition flees in terror. The complexity of the financial instruments that banks had invented, made up of lengthy chains of derivation, meant that the value of their assets and liabilities was not calculable. Yet this wasn't the 'competitive uncertainty', generated by the plurality of perspectives and agendas present in and around markets, and on which the financial system feeds through esoteric forms of quantification and derivation. It was 'political uncertainty', in the sense that the 'game' no longer appeared viable at all, because it had undermined its own conditions of possibility. The reason for this flipping from 'competitive uncertainty' into 'political uncertainty' was that uncertainty was now being generated *by the very calculative tools that had been constructed in order to manage it*. As theorists of performativity have explored, in financial institutions economics had become a constitutive part of the reality it once sought to describe or model, and was ultimately then unable to continue to act as an 'objective' means of description (MacKenzie, 2006; MacKenzie et al., 2007). Quantitative economic evaluations were still manifold, everywhere across the financial services industry, in banks, credit-raters and regulators. But the *value of those evaluations* had become impossible to specify. As MacKenzie has argued, economics went from being 'performative' to 'counter-performative' (MacKenzie, 2011). It was rendered a form of groundless mathematical babble, according prices and values to various entities and possibilities, but no longer able to do so with any credibility or authority. The financial sector still had techniques of validation, but it no longer believed that these techniques were themselves valid. In such a situation, where the 'value of values' is the object of critique, a problem of acute relativism – or perspectivism – ensues.

A sovereign response to the financial crisis was therefore necessary not simply because of its scale, but because of the acute evaluative chaos that had arisen. If banks had merely come to confront an 'uncertain' future (in the sense of 'competitive uncertainty'), then they could have done what they always did, which was to build statistical risk models in order to quantify possibilities and then securitize them via markets. But where those very practices of quantification and securitization had generated the uncertainty, then evidently that response would not be adequate. The shared objective reality produced by economic calculation had been fractured, creating an intrinsically unquantifiable cost. The only certain means of alleviating an unquantifiable cost is via a promise made by an unquantifiable power, that is, the sovereign state. The effective promise made by sovereign powers during autumn 2008 and subsequently was that no matter how big the scale of the crisis might turn out to be, the scale of the state response would be even bigger. One form of irrational power – the exuberant, hedonistic Nietzschean individual – is met with another form, that promises to always be quantitatively greater – the sovereign. The very aspect of sovereignty that had long bothered neoliberals, namely its incalculable and 'metaphysical' quality, is what rescued neoliberalism from collapse in 2008.

As Chapter 1 argued, the project of neoliberalism, as a deliberate disenchantment of politics by economics, was always dependent on convenient forms of amnesia about its conditions of possibility. These conditions are at least twofold. Firstly, the expansion of economic rationalization into socio-political territories requires some shared normative sense regarding the authority of economic methodology and evaluation. Technical rationality and method do not simply advance by force of power, or at least, they cannot rely on doing so. Before a technique can be implemented, there must be a shared sense that it is the right technique to use, that it is being implemented correctly, and that its results will be a legitimate basis for consensus. This is a central insight of convention theory. Economics can only produce a shared reality that 'holds together' coherently if individuals already possess a shared normative commitment to certain ways of doing things. This shared normative commitment cannot be derived from technical devices or methodologies themselves, as it is fundamentally pragmatic. Nor can it be entirely articulated in language. But without it, devices of measurement and evaluation become tools of violence, to be used by one agent against another, rather than as a basis for consensus-formation. In its intellectual foundations, neoliberal technique (economics, price, governance) was justified with reference to liberal ethos (freedom, individualism, rights), but gradually, as the latter was lost to Chicago School positivism, amnesia took hold and economics was asserted as sufficient unto itself. The consequence is an economics without any pragmatic connection to consensus-formation. Groundless babble is the inevitable endpoint of this.

Secondly, the expansion of economic rationalization into the state itself is implicitly dependent on the complicity of the authoritative sovereign powers that are set to be economized. As Chapter 3 examined, law cannot be subjected to economic critique without judges becoming sympathetic to the logic and justifications of economics. And as Chapter 4 examined, executive decision cannot be subjected to a strategic managerial analysis, without political leaders becoming sympathetic to the dynamism and charisma of business leadership. Sovereignty has always hovered behind and alongside the neoliberal project, invisibly, despite what Foucault describes as the instinctive ridicule that neoliberals have levelled at the very idea (Foucault, 2008). While the expansion of economic rationalities has drawn on state power, this needs to be forgotten if the vision of a wholly economized world is to remain plausible, at least for periods of time or in specific locations.

The disturbing of neoliberalism, if not quite its crisis, consists of these convenient amnesias becoming untenable, and preconditions coming to light. We
are reminded of the normative preconditions of effective economic calculation, by the spectacle of large numbers of individuals exercising their choices
in wildly self-destructive and de-stabilizing ways. The financial crisis was one
very destructive example of this, but so are the various other crises of individual choice that afflict Western societies, such as the rising obesity epidemic
or the depressive elements of consumerism. Rendered merely empirical, techniques for calculation and evaluation become arbitrary: the value of evaluations
is thrown into radical Nietzschean doubt, and it becomes impossible to say
that healthy choices are more valuable than unhealthy ones, or a stable financial system is more valuable than an unstable one. This explains the rising
policy interest in the conditions of choice and calculation in recent years, as
manifest in the rise of 'nudge' theory (explored next). Meanwhile, we are
reminded of the sovereign preconditions of extensive economization, by the
fact that states are now constantly called upon to maintain the credibility of
currencies, markets and individual banks. Financial credit and credibility
survive because nation states have declared that they must. Those with the
ultimate power express a simple and tautologous *affirmation* of a given economic reality, rather than offer an objective judgement of it, that might
withstand critique.

The neoliberalism that survives such a crisis is one that lacks any broader
sources of justification, which necessarily involve claims about the common
good for all. In this sense, it is post-liberal, in that it lacks an immanent liberal
philosophy of the *a priori* equality of competitors. In place of justification is a
politics of contingency, which treats economic rationalization as a particular
cultural-political procedure, that history just happens to have delivered to us and
requires safe-guarding. The presuppositions of this rationalization – individual
and sovereign – become acted upon, so as to prop it up. Evaluative economic
language, like all languages, has an arbitrary quality, which may not reveal the
'true' worth of things, but is at least something we potentially hold in common.
Market-based techniques and principles of evaluation lack any outward justification, or sense of their superiority over rivals, but because they are already
dominant, so they must be propped up further. Where pre-2008 neoliberalism
exercised amnesia about its normative or sovereign preconditions, now those
preconditions are absolutely crucial to how neoliberalism survives. Indeed, we
might now speak of economic calculation being *fused* with its own preconditions, as the next two sections explore. Economic evaluation and calculation
become a form of normativity, that individuals are taught to practice and repeat;

economic risk management *becomes* the constitution of executive sovereignty. Let's address each of these in turn.

NEOCOMMUNITARIANISM

As a number of institutionalist and regulationist scholars have explored, the expert framing and interpretation of capitalist crises are constitutive factors in how they proceed and are eventually resolved. Such hermeneutics of crisis can produce the foundations of new regimes of economic regulation, hence the emergence of national competitiveness theories, for example, originated in a narrative regarding the failures of corporate and national strategy during the 1970s. On the other hand, regimes of governance and evaluation can be strengthened and sustained if they can discover their own forms of self-criticism (Boltanski & Chiapello, 2007). The survival of neoliberalism through various failures occurs thanks partly to the development of a specific interpretation of these failures, which recognizes the contingent limits of market-based economic rationalities, but so as to bolster and not challenge them. This interpretation is offered by economic psychology, and in particular by behavioural and happiness economics, with growing support from neuro-economics.

If a historic crisis throws the value of valuation mechanisms into doubt, then those mechanisms can be rescued if their own critique or 'meta-evaluation' can be anticipated and predetermined. Offering a *psychological* explanation of why consumerism and financialization encounter crises has proved to be a crucial strategy in avoiding a more radical critique of the status quo. Theories rooted in biology and biological metaphors concerning the brain, behavioural 'epidemics', financial 'ecology' and genetics have complemented these psychological narratives. At the same time, this allows for a critique of neo-classical economics that effectively keeps the discipline intact (Mirowski, 2013). Common to these various perspectives is an assumption that the methodological presuppositions of neoliberalism *ought* to have been true, but are empirically compromised by various anomalies that show up in laboratory experiments, surveys, brain scans (Rose, 2010) or critical situations. These anomalies can be corrected or accommodated, if experts and policy makers can understand the various contingent preconditions of economically rational behaviour. Psychological presuppositions regarding competitive behaviour are lifted from the realm of methodology, where they are implicitly assumed to apply to all people in all times and places (as for Coase), and subjected to empirical tests of their own, enabling their scope of validity to be specified. These tests involve new types of surveillance and audit, such as Randomized Controlled Trials and 'in vivo' economic experiments, in order that particular behavioural responses can be empirically gauged (Muniesa & Callon, 2007). It transpires that different people pursue different strategies or rationalities, depending on different cultures, circumstances, brain types (or brain injuries) or social influences (e.g. Levinson & Peng, 2006). Efficiency-maximization and competitive strategy can remain the substantive goals of public policy, but the conditions that support them are revealed as culturally and biologically contingent. What Weber would identify as the 'vocational' precondition of economics – the implicit 'metaphysical' orientation that accompanies tangible acts of rationalization – is addressed instead as an empirical psychological or neurological problem.

Viewed from the perspective of economic psychology or neuro-economics, calculated, competitive and strategic individual behaviour can no longer be presumed on principle. It no longer serves as a principle of equivalence, through which judgement and comparison can be performed. Instead, its conditions need interrogating, in order that they might be defended and extended by various means. In certain respects, this represents a major departure from core tenets of neoliberal thought. Hayek's commitment to individual choice and competitive process was sufficiently deep that it offered no basis from which to criticize the actual decisions or outcomes that emerged as a result. He (in common with Chicago economists) recognized no authoritative basis from which to differentiate a 'good' from a 'bad' decision or preference. Outcomes of competitive, choice-based systems were *de jure* legitimate, as long as those systems were genuinely competitive. By contrast, the tools of economic psychology offer a basis on which to evaluate the quality of choices, and understand how decisions are influenced. The 'paternalist' implications of economic psychology, as a basis on which to 'improve' decision making, have been criticized by neo-classical economists on normative liberal grounds (Saint-Paul, 2011). But in another sense, the privileging of the choosing, consuming, strategizing *mind* as the central organizing principle of the economy is entirely in keeping with the neoliberal tradition. Offering sustenance and support to the psyche and/or the brain is viewed as a means of preserving a system that depends on psyches and brains functioning with a degree of predictability. At some point, the neural drivers of choice-making behaviour may be identified with sufficient precision, that rational choice theory can be built on biological foundations, without the need for formal hypotheses (Shizgal, 1997; Montague & Berns, 2002; Berridge, 2003); Coase himself expressed some hope that this might happen.[1] This is a critique of neoliberalism that potentially preserves it in its practical form, though not its normative form. Moreover, in its attempt to secure a competitive market ethos through technical governance, it maintains the empiricist epistemology identified with neoliberalism in Chapter 1.

The effect of this partial critique is that the market-based principles and techniques of evaluation are represented as spatially and temporally specific in their validity, losing the transcendental capacity (and methodological imperialism) that the neoliberals had initially bestowed upon them. This can be understood as a form of neocommunitarianism, inasmuch as it highlights the unavoidably local, social and learnt nature of economic rationality. The communitarian critique of liberalism is that liberal philosophers in the Kantian tradition have ignored or misunderstood the historical and cultural origins and preconditions of their own conceptual apparatus. Hence, they have also under-estimated the extent to which norms of justice and rights are rooted in traditions and practices, whose authority is contingent not universal. My argument is that the psychological critique of neoliberalism is similar *in spirit*, challenging its presuppositions, so as to reaffirm its principles in contingent, rather than universal, terms. As with the market exception, this results in a radically contingent defence of market-based forms of valuation, as being little more than an arbitrary but nevertheless viable tradition to be upheld and repeated. The liberal spirit of neoliberalism, based on the presumption of common calculative capacity, disappears, to be replaced by a cultural anthropology of different habits and rationalities. To explore this proposition further, we need to review key tenets of communitarianism, which provide an implicit moral coherence to neocommunitarianism.

Communitarianism

'Communitarianism' here refers to a genre of responses to Rawls's 1971 statement of liberal political philosophy, *A Theory of Justice*. Philosophers, including Alasdair MacIntyre, Charles Taylor and Michael Sandel, drew on Aristotle, Hegel and Heidegger to denounce the ahistorical abstractions that underpinned and organized Rawls's work, arguing instead that political philosophy needed to be rooted in the specificities of time and space (Taylor, 1992; Sandel, 1998; MacIntyre, 2013). Unless political philosophy were attuned to its own historical tradition and the ethical resources of specific political communities and traditions, it ran the risk of empty nihilism and/or violent imperialism. The communitarian critique was not necessarily of liberal practices, institutions or policies themselves, but that liberals in the 'deontological' Kantian tradition inhabited by Rawls approached moral and political questions in entirely the wrong way, from entirely the wrong starting point.

The challenge that Kant set for liberalism, and which Rawls attempted to meet, was to establish an entirely *a priori* basis for moral and political rules, as opposed to an empirical one. If the foundations and principles of justice were derived from contingent circumstances, then they could make no claim to apply to all people, in all situations, and were therefore not compatible with the very idea of law or right. Rawls famously constructed a theory of justice on the basis of an imaginary 'original position', in which individuals agree to a legal and economic framework without any knowledge of their contingent empirical circumstances. Such a framework would be one that no reasonable person could refuse to be judged under. However, it is presupposed by those in the Kantian tradition that political authority derives from applying general rules to particular cases, that is, through a 'descent' from an abstract idea of the common good to an evaluation of a single action or situation. As Boltanski and Thévenot argue, all arguments about justice share this grammatical quality, in which a general proposition about *all humanity* is put forward, as a basis from which to judge specific issues. The general rule is assumed to precede any individual situation, and the task of philosophy is to focus on the design of *a priori* rules. Chapters 2 and 3 argued that neoliberalism takes this philosophical tradition and reproduces it in a technical, economized form, where efficiency tests, imbued with a liberal spirit, become the transcendental basis of legal authority.

If, on the other hand, rules are recognized as *emerging from* contingent, empirical situations, then the task of philosophy looks very different, and generalizable judgement is no longer privileged as the primary problem of political philosophy or politics. There is no 'external' or 'neutral' basis on which to conduct a critique, and the possibility of 'objective' or 'critical' distance is lost. The authority of a procedure – be it legal or methodological – no longer consists in its capacity to accommodate *all* events or phenomena, but in the fact that it is a meaningful ritual for those who practise it. The value of a rule or technique comes to consist of its performance and repetition, rather than in its capacity to classify all contingent possibilities. Repetition is crucial in keeping doubt (and hence, ultimately, nihilism) at bay, but viewed differently this also means keeping critique at bay. As Boltanski argues with regard to 'systems of confirmation', repetition's only role is '*to make visible the fact that there is a norm*, by deploying it in a sense for its own sake, without it being given any external function' (Boltanski, 2011: 104). Where contingent difference is simply being affirmed, rules are *only* performative.

From this latter communitarian perspective, laws are emergent, evolving properties of historical sociology. There is nothing 'ultimate' or *a priori* about them, and their constitutional authority is no higher than informal norms or *mores* of social interaction. Thus the grammar of critique – that is, of judgement – is no longer what organizes communitarian political rhetoric. Rather than appealing to 'higher' laws, so as to evaluate the action of the other, the communitarian citizen performs a ritual so as to win cultural recognition from the other. Should two different sets of rules come into contact with one another, recognition is withheld, and difference may be acknowledged. Rather than Schmitt's 'friend–enemy' distinction, which is consummated in violence, this is an Aristotelian 'friend–stranger' distinction, which will hopefully be consummated in forms of diplomacy. Equally, a communitarian rule cannot fail as dramatically as a liberal rule can fail. If the rule cannot be applied (due to some event or action that seems to defy classification) this simply reveals something about the empirical and performative character of that particular rule. If a procedure or method encounters a phenomenon or behaviour that threatens its applicability, then this discovery reorients or delimits how the procedure or method is practised. Individuals and communities are constantly learning. The notion of a *crisis* or historic judgement therefore does not register in the same way, as normative frameworks are constantly evolving in an organic way, as lived rituals rather than abstract premises. The value of valuations is not thrown into the grave doubt of crisis, so long as those valuations still facilitate some mutual recognition on the part of those who practise them.

Strictly speaking, communitarianism does not represent a *critique* of liberalism, but really a genealogy or deconstruction of it, inasmuch as it does not offer some alternative principle for judgement. Instead it challenges the very possibility of there being stable, *a priori* principles for judgement, and the very possibility of an 'objective' perspective upon or 'critical' distance from one's situation. Communitarianism is not so much uncritical, in a purely agnostic sense, as *anti-critical* in an affirmative sense. This challenge has two important recurrent features, which we will see reappearing in the 'neocommunitarian' response to neoliberalism, which simultaneously localize neoliberal evaluation tools and seek to rescue them.

Firstly, communitarians claim that liberalism (in the Kantian and Rawlsian tradition) is founded on an unrealistically empty theory of the self, as a disembodied, ahistorical choice maker. Where Rawls defined individuals by their shared capacity to reason, and not the values or goals that they hold, communitarians responded that values and goals were constitutive of individual identity. Religious, moral or political beliefs are not selected as a matter of free will, but are important conditions of human fulfilment and identity. An individual, as imagined by liberals, would suffer from existential crises of having no sources of intrinsic purpose or value. In the hands of some communitarian philosophers such as Taylor and MacIntyre, this is a critique that is extended to secular modernity more broadly. The Cartesian attempt to found objective certainty on the premise of subjective doubt is historicized, and the primacy of doubt is itself thrown into question.

Secondly, communitarians argue that human beings only ever exist in relationships with others. They do not enter these relationships as if via choice or contract, as Rawls's philosophy proposed, but find themselves already in them. It is through others that we learn who we are and what we value. Reason, including secular critical reason, is learnt and acquired through mutual recognition, rather than bestowed as a condition of being human, as Kantian liberals had deduced. By the same token, there are no political or moral values that precede or transcend human community, community is instead a condition of political and moral principles. The error of liberalism is in seeking the principles of justice from outside of the practices of ethical and political action.

In the face of crisis, in which the value of values is thrown into doubt, communitarianism offers stability through denying the foundational authority of critique. With contingent and shared ethical practices as the only *a priori* available to human beings, as they happen to exist, critical philosophy and judgement lose their privileged position in the constitution of moral and political life. The value of values is suddenly very obvious: they are generative of particular identities and relations, and cannot simply be thrown off. The risk is that values and procedures come to appear as arbitrary cultural inheritances, whose authority lies simply in being communally recognized. Belief can flip quickly into radicalized doubt – a choice that MacIntyre represents as one between Aristotle and Nietzsche (MacIntyre, 2013). Liberal institutions equally are valued and valuable only to the extent that they make us who we are. And to the extent that the crises of neoliberalism throw the value of its valuations into doubt, one means of rescuing neoliberalism is via a neo-communitarian strategy that asserts the socially binding nature of certain rituals of calculation. Market-based rationalities are affirmed as a collective inheritance, rather than offered as a transcendental basis from which to carry out generally valid, 'objective' judgements.

Non-critical audit and homo psycho-economicus

In his famous testimony to the US Congress in October 2008, Alan Greenspan, former Chairman of the Federal Reserve, offered his own immediate interpretation of the banking crisis. He confessed that he had made a 'mistake' in trusting that the 'self-interest of lending institutions' was sufficient for them to preserve the overall viability of the financial system (Committee on Oversight and Government Reform, 2008). This remark raises interesting questions about how an institution might exercise '*self*-interest'. But it also demonstrates the capacity of psychological rhetoric and categories to provide a hermeneutics of the crisis on behalf of policy-making elites. If the limits and failures of market-based techniques and rationalities can be attributed to minds, selves or brains, then neoliberalism itself can be modified in view of contingent calculative anomalies, but also preserved as a particular tradition of practice.

Elsewhere, various crises of neoliberalism are interpreted and acted on in psychological terms. If Hayek and the Chicago School had hoped to make the private choosing or knowing mind the central barometer of value across society (indicated in observed behaviour and price), problems such as obesity, depression, hedonistic rioting and financial short termism suggest that the psyche or brain is not sufficiently robust or calculative to perform this constitutional function. How individuals *actually* exercise choice, how much utility they *actually* experience as a result, how they *actually* adapt their behaviour to experience and the lessons of others, become crucial empirical questions, if regulations and policies are to continue to be premised upon a particular, market-based vision of individual action. These empirical psycho-economic questions had been addressed on behalf of private companies since the 1920s, in the guise of human resource management and market research, but never in any systematic way by the state (Baritz, 1960; Davies, 2011a). Some causal understanding of the unconscious is needed, if policies based upon rational choice assumptions are not to be overwhelmed by irrational psychic forces. With this knowledge, either those regulations and policies can be adjusted accordingly, or new interventions can be designed to try and counteract individual or collective 'irrationalities'. Thus a new model of subjectivity arises, that might be termed '*homo psycho-economicus*', which is provided by a combination of methodological assumptions of economics, wedded to contingent empirical findings of economic psychology and, where possible, neuroscience.

Under the influence of Jeremy Bentham and the German psycho-physicist Gustav Fechner, the early British neo-classical economists of the 1870s and 1880s hoped to build a theory of value and method of valuation directly on empirical psychology (Maas, 2005; Colander, 2007). The continental pioneers of neo-classical economics, Menger and Walras, were far less concerned with the mental substrates of choice or value. And with psychology emerging as a distinct social science in its own right, and laboratories providing a new mode of empirical enquiry to replace introspection, economists began to abandon their concern with the psyche from the 1890s onwards (Bruni & Sugden, 2007). In the 1930s, Lionel Robbins proposed the 'revealed preference theory of choice': that observable behaviour was sufficient data on which to base economic theories of what individuals want or value, representing the final divorce of economics from psychology (Maas, 2009). But emerging in the 1970s, happiness and behavioural economics represented the gradual rediscovery of psychology by economics. In 1974, Richard Easterlin published an article demonstrating that economic growth did not translate into increased psychological welfare (Easterlin, 1974). In 1979, Daniel Kahneman and Amos Tversky published an article showing that individual decision making is more influenced by relative losses and gains, than by absolute levels of reward, and is therefore context-dependent (Kahneman & Tversky, 1979). Both of these papers used empirical data to challenge the methodological premise of neo-classical economics, namely that the choices made by the individual mind are a perfect indicator of value. The 'revealed preference theory of choice' is discarded. Behavioural and happiness economics emerged as growing and distinctive fields over the course of the 1980s and 1990s (Heukelom, 2011).

The notion that a methodological premise is not empirically valid should not be surprising, given that its function is to facilitate cognition and not constitute it. The question is how can such knowledge be acquired and, subsequently, how might it be acquired and employed by the state. How, for example, does the authority of the state change, if it no longer assumes that individuals are equipped to make utility-optimizing choices? And what techniques of knowledge accumulation and processing does it depend on? For happiness economics, the key technique was initially the survey. Market research surveys and opinion polling had also arisen as early as the 1920s, as notions such as 'attitude' were invented by social psychologists (Rose, 1996a; Danziger, 1997). The first national surveys on happiness were first introduced in the mid-1960s, by Albert Cantril and the polling company Gallup, producing the data that Easterlin then based his analysis on. Statistical agencies and household panel surveys began to collect more regular data on happiness from the mid-1980s onwards, enabling the rapid growth of happiness economics, beginning with a 1994 article on happiness and unemployment (Clark & Oswald, 1994). The other technique that economics imported from psychology was the laboratory experiment. This began with the study of games and mathematical psychology at the University of Michigan during the 1950s, in which experiments were created in order to test how far individuals diverged from instrumentally rational choice (Heukelom,

2010). Experimental economics focuses upon the divergence between how abstract mathematical economics states individuals ought to act, and how they do in fact act, under various circumstances. In this way, rational choice is converted into a normative ideal, against which patterns of behaviour should be judged, rather than as an abstract premise through which economic states of affairs should be judged. Along with the mind, the context of individual activity, or what would later become known as 'choice architectures', is brought back into economics, as the explanation for differing forms of behaviour (Thaler & Sunstein, 2008).

The main object of empirical enquiry becomes the behavioural anomaly. Where individuals are found not to behave as neo-classical economics assumes they do, this represents a potential opportunity for a third party to work on assisting with the construction of their calculative capacity. The Coasian view of a freely competitive society, as set out in 'The Problem of Social Cost', depends on the notion that all individuals are equally endowed with a calculative capacity. Hence, the dominator and the dominated can strike some sort of agreement, which compensates the latter, removing the formal requirement for regulatory intervention. The implausibility of this presupposition is tacitly recognized in behavioural economics, given that the dominated receive additional support to behave in a rational, utility-maximizing fashion. Their calculative 'equipment' is reinforced via supportive 'choice architectures' and policies for improving 'financial literacy' and various other literacies. What this ignores, of course, is that the dominator is not simply better at calculating in a psychological sense, but that this is because of extensive legal, technological and political equipment, which isn't simply carried around in the mind as a heuristic, but actively shapes the material environment in which competition takes place (Caliskan & Callon, 2009).

The influence of economic psychology within much public policy rose sharply during and after the financial crisis of 2007–09. Various areas of governance and policy, which had long operated according to a logic of 'incentives' (in which individuals are assumed to respond rationally to changes in cost and benefit), were criticized and rethought, on the basis of empirical evidence on behaviour, happiness and brains (e.g. Dolan et al., 2010). Economic psychology was proposed as a basis on which to reform corporate governance (PwC, 2012), consumer protection (Mulholland, 2007; OFT, 2010), welfare-to-work (Black, 2008), financial regulation (Shiller, 2008) and so on. Importing recommendations from the previously left-field 'social indicators' movement, official statistical agencies in Britain, France, the United States, Canada and Australia began to collect data on happiness, and publish official indicators of national wellbeing (e.g. Fitoussi et al., 2009). The potential to achieve cost savings through importing lessons from behavioural economics became a *cause celebre* of the Obama administration in the USA and the Cameron government in the UK, both of which employed authors of the popular *Nudge* as advisors. The successes of 'nudges' were generally gauged in terms of how well they influenced 'more rational' behaviour, such as paying one's taxes on time or signing up to a defined contribution pension scheme (Langley & Leaver, 2012).

A significant consequence of this renewed empirical interest in the mind is a (re)discovery of the 'social' – or at least relational – dimensions of human behaviour and subjective experience (Mulgan, 2012). This is where the potential break between neocommunitarianism and neoliberalism becomes most apparent. Neoliberalism, as we have seen, sought to expand market-based economic rationalities into all corners of life, and was *particularly* hostile to the notion of distinctive 'social' rationalities, which provided the logic of socialism. Neoliberalism began from a critique of the possibility of efficient 'socialist calculation', and was propagated as a strategic stripping-out of distinctively 'social' policies or 'sociological' knowledge (Mises, 1990; Rose, 1996b; Fine, 2001). Hayek represented social science as a crypto-socialist project of converting the subjective perspective of an intellectual minority into bogus truth claims, with broad political reach (Hayek, 1942, 1949). But paying empirical attention to the mind, behaviour and the brain quickly reveals the importance of relationships, learning, mimicry and group norms in determining habits and tastes. Social relations are revealed as a crucial resource for individual wellbeing (Cacioppo & Patrick, 2009). A growing burden of mental ill health (especially anxiety and depression) afflicts many neoliberal societies, which can be reduced to a set of neuro-chemical imbalances as favoured by many pharmaceutical companies (Healy, 1997), but is more promisingly looked at in 'social' terms, as manifest in the growing movement towards 'social prescribing' whereby singing, gardening or dancing are prescribed by doctors to raise levels of physical and mental wellbeing. 'Behaviours' and moods, whether 'good' or 'bad', are shown to travel through social networks like contagions, with important lessons for health policy and financial regulation (e.g. Lo, 2004; Christakis & Fowler, 2011). Biological metaphors of 'contagion', 'toxicity', systemic 'resilience' come to organize how the 'social' is newly conceived. This is the 'social', not as understood in a Durkheimian sense, but in the sense of social network analysis, as mathematically traceable webs of linkage (Freeman, 2004). The role for public policy, under neocommunitarianism, becomes one of seeking to catalyse or 'nudge' positive contagions of rational, utility-increasing behaviour, in the hope that these travel through social networks and gradually oust negative ones.

But the question here is how does the government expert *know* when it is the suitable time or place to intervene in these organic processes? Under neoliberalism, socio-economic activity is subject to a quasi-juridical ritual of audit (Power, 1997). This follows the modern critical sequence described at the beginning of this chapter, of certainty, doubt, crisis/judgement, resolution, certainty. At regular intervals or at pre-designated moments, an evaluation is carried out, to test the worth of certain behaviours, so as to render these objective and public. A complex and uncertain situation is represented via a numerical 'score', briefly removing its uncertainty. But the rise of homo psycho-economicus necessitates a very different style of audit, which is oriented around questions of systemic sustainability or resilience. What is being gauged is the compatibility of multiple rationalities at multiple scales. Is the behaviour of individual banks consistent with the resilience of the financial system as a whole? Are individual nutritional decisions consistent with bodily health in the long term? At what point does individual utility-maximization come into conflict with collective wellbeing? These involve what I would call a form of 'non-critical audit', which is a constant monitoring of activity, but one that is unpunctuated by any recognized moments of judgement/crisis. There is a perceived need to stay constantly abreast of how individual and collective behaviours are evolving and aggregating, but without any sense of when or on what basis to form a judgement on this empirical data.

The technologies of non-critical audit are emerging rapidly, thanks heavily to the digitization of socio-economic relations. The mapping of social networks can now be done at a scale and speed that the social sciences had never imagined, prior to social media (Savage & Burrows, 2007). The auditing of psychological mood can be conducted on a constant basis, without the periodization that goes with surveys, using technologies such as iPhone Apps and 'sentiment analysis' algorithms designed to assess the mood of very large numbers of Twitter or Facebook users. The Hayekian problem, of how legitimately to represent uncertain situations, receives new technical solutions that owe nothing to markets or economics, but from the mathematical analysis of Big Data that accumulates from companies such as Google. The Bank of England has begun to draw on Google search data in constructing their economic forecasts, for instance tracking the number of searches for terms like 'estate agent' (McLaren, 2011). Meanwhile, as public policy makers become more interested in the vagaries of behaviour, so they import techniques from medical research, namely Randomized Controlled Trials (RCTs), whereby rival policies are introduced simultaneously, such that knowledge about their empirical efficacy can be accumulated. Where the behaviour in question is digitally-mediated (for instance, through an e-government service or an interaction with an electricity provider), RCTs are possible without any cost, seeing as surveillance of the behaviour occurs by default. The promise of the 'smart city', for example, is one in which *so much activity* is digitally mediated, resulting in *so much data* accumulating, that services, design and policy can be perfectly calibrated around constantly emerging patterns of behaviour.

But still the question of judgement or the critical test is not addressed directly. Under neoliberalism, normative and political judgement is replaced by some form of numerical test, either that of the market itself (i.e. price) or that of economics and associated techniques. The era of 'non-critical audit', exemplified by a belief in Big Data, does not use numbers *instead of* judgement, but really just so as to *delay* judgement. For an example of this, consider the case of 'macro-prudential regulation', which was quickly identified as the regulatory model that could prevent another financial crisis after 2007–09 (Saporta, 2009; Clement, 2010). Macro-prudential regulation would involve regulators and central banks intervening when the behaviour of *some* financial institutions appears to be destabilizing the financial system as a whole. It looks beyond orthodox, quasi-juridical forms of audit, in which every financial institution has to pass the same audit to prove their worth, towards a form of non-critical audit, in which large quantities of data are collected and studied for signs that the financial system may be becoming unstable. It recognizes that the similarity of risk models at work within the financial system can lead individual institutions to pursue strategies that are individually rational, but collectively irrational. But this also means recognizing that not every financial institution is as systemically important as another, and not every moment in the financial cycle is as critical as any other. The hope might be that data-mining of the financial system as a whole, combined with some form of representation of the system's current 'behaviour' or 'mood', might make it possible to determine *when to act* and *on which institution*. But, as one behavioural finance theorist argues, 'market efficiency is not an all-or-none condition but is a constant characteristic that varies continuously over time', which removes the neoliberal technical rationality that justifies government intervention (Lo, 2005). The greater the amount of data accumulated, the more this exacerbates rather than alleviates the expert question of what to do.

Homo psycho-economicus, supported by an infrastructure of non-critical audit, generates a mode of government that is 'neocommunitarian' in its implicit ethos, because it stands in relation to neoliberalism, just as communitarianism stands in relation to Kantian liberalism. Neoliberalism (and its apparent failures) provides economic psychologists with their empirical orientation: what are the socio-cultural conditions and limits of sustained, rational, welfare-enhancing decision making? This question only arises to the extent that neoliberalism takes such decision making as read, and suffers various negative consequences as a result. In response, economic psychology finds technical and empirical fault with neoliberalism in two key areas, which echo the communitarian critique of liberalism. Firstly, the technical methodologies of neoliberalism are criticized for resting on an implausibly empty theory of the self, as nothing but an atomized choosing calculator. Chapter 2 argued that the neoliberal valorization of competition shifted from a commitment to markets as institution to a commitment to competitiveness as a psychological attribute. However, few of the theorists involved had ever paid much attention to the empirical plausibility of the psychological precepts that they assumed.

Secondly, and consequently, the rise of economic psychology as a policy discipline undermines the transcendental *a priori* ideal of the neoliberal state. Elevating competition (however defined) as the central organizing principle of society was expected to produce a state that was neutral or 'ignorant' regarding what 'good' outcomes would consist of. For Hayek, competition itself was the moral and empirical discovery process, and the state was merely its *a priori* facilitator. But evidence from laboratories, surveys and big data analytics offers a very different perspective, which reveals the capacity of individuals to routinely and collectively act against their own best interests, assuming some standard for what their real interests actually are. While not quite ethical, in a communitarian sense, or substantively rational, in Weber's sense, this return of teleology into economic policy making is nevertheless a significant departure from neoliberal agnosticism regarding outcomes. To be sure, this teleological rationality remains technocratic, with the socio-economic telos captured in metrics of 'wellbeing', 'resilience' and 'sustainability', and the means of pursuing these goals remain organized in terms of incentives, choices, strategies and individual agents. But in acknowledging that economic reason has a normative and teleological dimension, and not merely an instrumental or formal one, the contemporary state has experienced a subtle but important new orientation away from purely market-based modes of evaluation.

This represents a new and more fearful orientation to uncertainty. Where neoliberalism had valorized uncertainty, so long as it was an effect of competition and organized within the rubric of markets, rankings and economic tests, neocommunitarianism rests on a recognition that this 'competitive uncertainty' can tip into a more radical, 'political uncertainty' that is *genuinely* disruptive, and not simply in an entrepreneurial sense. The capacity of human decision making to generate more profoundly disturbing or unsettling outcomes, which may be self-destructive (as with hedonistic consumption) or systemically destructive (as with financial exuberance) or both, means that policy makers become concerned with *how the competitive game is played*, and not simply with helping to distinguish the 'winners' from the 'losers'. In this sense, uncertainty itself becomes managed and ritualized, via new empirical representations of 'irrational' and 'social' forms of behaviour. A key element of the Hayekian neoliberal project is discarded.

STATE OF MARKET EXCEPTION

The banking crisis was swiftly framed by political leaders in starkly existential terms, with Ben Bernanke, Chairman of the US Federal Reserve, declaring after the Lehmans' collapse that unless action were taken instantly, 'there will be no economy on Monday' (quoted in Bryan et al., 2012). The viability of the entire financial system was in doubt, and emergency political action was required to prevent a catastrophic failure. One of the first normative and regulative principles that was suspended as a result of this apparent emergency was that of competition enforcement. In Britain, the fatal condition of HBOS bank in September 2008 meant that the government encouraged a takeover by Lloyds-TSB which would otherwise have been blocked by the competition authorities. The Prime Minister personally brokered the deal, exploiting 'national interest' clauses in competition law to do so. As we shall explore further on, the European Commission meanwhile deemed it necessary to suspend the State Aid rules that prevent member states from giving subsidies or favours to specific firms, so that states could rescue their financial sectors by whatever means they deemed necessary.

The vision of the state as a neutral enforcer of competition, without regard to the consequences, winners or losers, was at the heart of the founding neoliberal and ordo-liberal vision. It was especially powerful in the German and European Union contexts, at least until the infiltration of utilitarian Chicago School ideas and techniques during the 1990s. As Chapter 3 examined, this commitment to an *a priori* rule of market law was attacked and largely dismantled by Chicago economists and their acolytes in the legal profession. And yet some notion of a fair and competitive *a priori* is necessary if competition is to survive as an organizing principle of both socio-economic order and state authority. On the face of it, the fact that competition enforcement was amongst the first political casualties of the financial crisis (at least for a period of time) may indicate that the neoliberal paradigm (or at least its specifically *liberal* element) had been dramatically terminated, or at least suspended.

The crisis was accompanied by a number of other instances of highly unusual, emergency interventions by executive state authorities. Besides the bailouts of banks and insurance companies, in which a handful of political decision makers agreed to provide vast sums of equity finance, credit and guarantees to failing financial institutions, special executive powers have been claimed and exercised in other instances too. In October 2008, the British government drew on anti-terrorism laws, in order to freeze £4bn of assets in a failed Icelandic bank. In 2011, the elected Prime Ministers of Italy and Greece were both replaced by recognized economists, as part of the effort to sustain the Euro in the face of supposed Southern European fiscal profligacy. This threw a thoroughly more Hobbesian light upon the potential 'performativity' of economics. Executive decision making was no longer being economized and authorized by the strategic framework of national competitiveness evaluation: it had become stripped bare as a purely contingent force for the rescue of economic normativity. But by directly replacing elected executives with economists, and using exceptional powers to rescue risk-management institutions, sovereign decision was fused with economic rationality.

This phenomenon, of extraordinary emergency powers being claimed for the sake of saving the juridical status quo, is the definition of exception, as theorized by Schmitt and subsequently Giorgio Agamben (Schmitt, 1996; Agamben, 2005). The difference under neoliberalism is that the juridical status quo is permeated by economic rationality. Hence, when speaking of a 'state of market exception', I refer to the fact that the market-based norms, procedures and techniques of economic evaluation that characterize regular neoliberalism, are suspended for their own sake, in favour of a logic of necessity. As was explored with reference to 'national competitiveness', neoliberalism already acquires a form of self-legislating executive authority, borrowed from the Schumpeterian notion of the entrepreneur and business strategy. The case for 'competitiveness' is depicted as something of a national emergency, even during times of relative economic peace: in that sense, the 'market exception' simply ups the ante, raises the stakes, and compels even more decisive action on the part of leaders. To understand this state better, we must first address the state of exception in its original juridical sense, and the types of rhetorical strategies that accompany it.

The state of exception

The application of rules involves a Kantian problematic of how to subsume particular instances under universal principles. In Kant's critical philosophy, this practical problem mirrors an epistemological one, of how particular phenomena can be classified within general epistemic categories. Yet the claim put forward by convention theory is that the two problems are really identical, as they are both fundamentally practical in nature. Science (and social science) can only take place through the practical application of methodologies, leading to the public demonstration of proofs that can withstand further critique. What Boltanski and Thévenot refer to as 'tests' are those material tools and practices which subject individual situations to moral-empirical judgements. The term usefully bridges both 'juridical' situations (such as courtrooms) and 'scientific' situations (such as laboratories), and highlights the various commonalities in how such situations are framed, initiated and concluded.

Judgement therefore requires a 'descent' from a general principle to a particular occurrence, which strips the latter of its particularity by classifying it. But if something occurs which seems to threaten the very possibility of applying the law, the problem of judgement becomes very different. The situation must be judged purely in terms of its particularity, without recourse to any higher principle. In a laboratory situation, this might be the appearance of a new phenomenon which breaks some basic law of scientific theory, and thereby threatens to bring down an entire paradigm of research. In a juridical situation, it may be some type of act that is so threatening towards the rule of law, such as terrorism, that it must not be dealt with within standard legal process. Such situations demand that the particular case be judged purely in terms of its own particularity, and not with recourse to any available law or principle. A new law may need to be invented specifically to deal with this one case. This is closer to Kant's model of aesthetic judgement, in which particularity is not subsumed within a general category, but judged as a singularity from which a new general principle can be extrapolated (Kant, 2007). The juridical recognition of pure particularity is the basis of the state of exception, as understood by Schmitt and Agamben.

Politics, for Schmitt, is ontologically constituted by the 'friend-enemy' distinction, which finds its full consummation in mortal combat. The critical political distinction is therefore between those whom I am willing to fight for, and those who I am willing to fight against. This being the case, contingent existential political *decisions* are always prior to the implementation of laws. The very existence of law is dependent upon the possibility that violence can be used to defend the polity against an enemy. This is not to say that law itself is constituted by violence or contingency. During periods of peace and stability, the rule of law is perfectly plausible from a Schmittian perspective. The separation of powers between the executive and the judiciary can become a practical reality, such that the executive is constrained by normativity. However, it remains constantly implicit (or sometimes explicit) that the executive retains the capacity to suspend the law, in order to save it from some type of unprecedented disruption or threat. Law rules with a general form, but it only rules particular territories and populations: universality is secondary to 'pluriversality'. Moreover, Schmitt argues, law only rules for limited periods of *time*. It can be interrupted at any time by a sovereign decision to declare an exception, which is foundational: 'Sovereign is he who decides on exception', thereby deciding to suspend the constitutional separation of law and violence (Schmitt, 1996: 5).

The judgement that is made, in declaring a state of exception, is that it is *necessary* (Agamben, 2005: 24–25). This type of judgement cannot be made with recourse to some other norm or law, because it concerns an event that disrupts the very possibility of legal normativity. The logic of political necessity concerns unique occurrences, which demand to be acted on in ways that are specific to themselves. These events neither comply with laws nor break them, but introduce a set of possibilities that are entirely at odds with the law as constituted. As Agamben argues:

> In truth, the state of exception is neither external nor internal to the juridical order, and the problem of defining it concerns precisely a threshold, or a zone of indifference, where inside and outside do not exclude each other but rather blur with each other. (Agamben, 2005: 23)

In this 'zone of indifference', justifications are neither required nor possible, because there is no general grammar or classificatory system through which the exception can be proved or subsumed. The declaration of exception rests on a purely political judgement of necessity, which lacks any preconditions beyond itself. Agamben notes that some legal constitutions include a formal provision that the constitution may be suspended in exceptional circumstances, while others do not (Agamben, 2005: 13–21). But the fact that exception is recognized as a formal possibility does not mean that it is somehow 'within' the rule of law, any more than a lack of formal recognition renders it 'external' to the rule of law. Exception is consistent with the logic of law, without being strictly legal or illegal. It is impossible to conceive of a law that did not imply the possibility of exception, even though legal rationality itself cannot entirely articulate what the juridical status of exception actually is.

The state of exception is typically defined temporally, although it may have specific spatial characteristics as well. Agamben offers the example of the

Roman institution of *iustitium*, in which the law would take a 'holiday', during which acts were no longer judged in terms of legality/illegality. He also observes that states of exception have often arisen as a consequence of monetary collapse, as occurred at the end of the Weimar Republic. In the USA, meanwhile, the possibility of an exception was first acknowledged with the Civil War, and has always been associated with the peculiar political circumstance of wartime. Framing objectives in the language of 'war' has become the primary rhetorical strategy through which American political leaders have sought to free themselves from the constraints of the constitution. Whether as holiday, monetary restoration or war, it is expected that exception will come to an end, and legal judgement will be restored. But specifying when the period of exception ends is never straightforward, and it is possible to live in a state of exception where law survives only through constant non-legal sovereign interventions and decisions.

It is crucial that a state of exception can only arise with a *sovereign* decision, that is, it must be backed up with sufficient violence (or its threat) to be realized. A revolutionary who believes in the 'sovereignty' of the people can declare a state of exception, but only if the people have sufficient means of violence to realize it. Otherwise they are merely in the realm of civil disobedience or criminality. When the sovereign declares a state of exception, their declaration is valid to the extent that they can back it up with violence. By contrast, a historical 'crisis' occurs when a system of judgement ceases to work, opening up a space of political uncertainty in which new systems of judgement might arise. Such situations are not constituted by violence, although they open up space within which violence is one possibility. When an orthodox economist confronts events that their theory deems impossible, this creates a space in which alternative theories can be propagated and the dominant theory attacked. The orthodox economist can try different ways of defending their theory, such as adapting it or seeking to constrain the empirical data. The novel occurrence can be quickly classified as a particular variant of a more familiar occurrence. These strategies may well succeed in rebuffing attacks on their own, or else they may eventually lead to a Kuhnian 'paradigm shift'. But what the economist cannot ordinarily do is to declare that it is necessary to suspend norms of scientific validation, as he lacks the power to realize this suspension. An economist (or any other type of scientist, evaluator, critic or judge) who sought to do this would be viewed as having accepted defeat.

A declaration of exception is therefore a form of violent *anti-crisis*, in which judgement is debarred or delayed, for fear that it would otherwise be destroyed. The speed of events or proximity of a threat is deemed so severe, that achieving a critical or objective distance from them is deemed impossible (or too existentially dangerous). Kant argued that the sublime occasions a form of pleasure, as a result of cognitive judgement being first overwhelmed by something too vast or powerful to grasp, and then retreating in terror, before taking comfort in rediscovering its own transcendent ideas of reason (Kant, 2007). The state of exception follows a similar path, in which law looks to be destroyed by some unprecedented event or aggressor, but is then rescued by a sovereign decision to suspend juridical rule. For a historic crisis to occur, a regime of judgement must be allowed to fail, producing a situation of political uncertainty in which a new mode of judgement might emerge. Events or rivals must have time to overwhelm the legal, critical or scientific apparatus (as the case may be), such that its failure to classify people or things can become fully and publicly manifest. The crisis itself will be experienced as a moment of radical contingency and openness, in which there is no dominant 'higher' principle on which a shared evaluation can be based. It is this full and public failure of rule that the state of exception prevents. As with a crisis, exception also introduces a period of radical contingency, but without the openness to alternative principles of judgement. The contingency is rather of sovereign executive will, and not of some democratic pluralism. Thanks to their entangling with sovereign powers, it is into this ambivalent state of exception that neoliberal principles and techniques of evaluation were thrown by the bank failures of 2008.

Rescuing market rule

One of the central tasks that neoliberal critics of the state set themselves was to fuse together law and economics, as Chapter 3 explored. The ordo-liberals set about doing this by using rule of law to formalize market mechanisms, inflating the price mechanism with a form of juridical authority. By contrast, the Chicago School sought to demolish the very notion of law's substantive rationality, by reducing it to an instrumental logic of incentives and neo-classical calculation. This latter movement came to predominate in competition authorities from the late 1970s onwards, yet by doing so it effectively elevated neo-classical methodology to the status of a quasi-juridical procedure. Where law has been successfully economized, the calculated maximization of efficiency comes to replace the pursuit of 'justice' as the test of legitimate action. The normativity of economic evaluation serves as a quasi-constitutional template for the state.

In contrast to the strict rule of market law proposed by the ordo-liberals and early Hayek, this test represents a very weak form of normative constraint. In the state envisaged by Chicago economists, law is only authoritative to the

extent that it has demonstrably positive economic effects. All it takes is economic evidence to be constructed demonstrating the inefficiency of a law or
regulation (measured in Coasian terms of aggregate consumer welfare) and its
authority is lost. Corporations marshalling well-paid private consultants can
often succeed in doing this. The *liberal spirit* of neoliberal authority is rendered
very frail by the Chicago critique. The authority of anti-trust law therefore
comes to derive partly from the 'violent threat' of executive power, the claim
that *competition is good for competitiveness*. Michael Porter and a number of
other competitiveness experts have argued that the normativity of regulation
can have a positive effect on the productive and entrepreneurial capacity of state
territories (Porter, 2001b). Economically rational anti-trust enforcement is
viewed by national competitiveness evaluations as a positive strategic attribute
of a state. Market law receives a positive evaluation, to the extent that it raises
the overall productive capacity of a state-space. In this sense, the neoliberal
state's *liberal spirit* is tacitly sanctioned by its *political threat*. To put this another
way, the fairness of market competition is valued to the extent that it supports
greater local entrepreneurial dynamism, but not vice versa.

The logic of the political-strategic decision is therefore prior to that of legal-
economic rules, in a way that echoes Schmitt's theory of sovereignty. The
Schmittian sympathies of neoliberal scholars such as Hayek and Friedman have
been noted, resting in a deep pessimism regarding the capacity of societies to
remain 'open' and 'competitive' without constant enforcement and protection by
executive powers (Mirowski, 2009; Spieker, 2012). The possibility and eventual
necessity of exception are therefore already contained within the logic of neoliberalism. As an empirical manifestation of such an exception in practice, the
case of European Commission State Aid rules, and their effective suspension
during the banking crisis, provides an empirical case through which to examine
this (Davies, 2013). The reason why this is so instructive is that, in this case, we
get a clear view of the interface of executive decision and market law. And what
becomes apparent is a shift from ordo-liberal, to Chicagoan, to *exceptional*
modes of economic jurisdiction.

State Aid rules seek to maintain a competitive order across the European Union,
by preventing member states from offering 'aid' to individual firms or industries,
and originate in the 1957 Treaty of Rome that first founded the common
market.[2] The body responsible for enforcing the rules is the anti-trust directorate,
DG Competition. Initially, 'aid' was defined in normative terms, as something
which disrupted the equally normative principle of competition, as the form of
market organization. This definition was formal, rather than empirical, but

would include subsidies, tax breaks, trade protections or any type of state action that appeared to disrupt the authority of the price mechanism. As a classically ordo-liberal case of states seeking to construct a binding 'economic constitution', the vision behind State Aid rules was of a common European space in which the market offered the primary institutional mechanism for coordination. Executive political action would be constrained by market law. But in its original statement, this constitutional framework contained various provisions for states to exempt their policies from its constraints, that is, to employ evaluative criteria other than those associated with markets. Aid 'having a social character' would always be permitted, offering a justification for European welfare states, that is also in accordance with ordo-liberalism (Bonefeld, 2013). In addition, a further five categories of exemption are formally recognized in the treaty, one of which is aid 'to remedy a serious disturbance in the economy of a Member State' (EC, 1992: 87 (3)). This exemption was used from October 2008 onwards, in order to permit exceptional state acts of financial rescue which otherwise would have counted as anti-competitive. This is an instance of an economic constitution which formally acknowledges the possibility of its own suspension, but as Agamben argues, even without such an acknowledgement, sovereigns would retain such an option regardless.

As a purely formal commitment to the principle of competition, the State Aid rules did not initially represent a very powerful restraint on the executive powers of member states. The exemptions available, the lack of accompanying implementation guidelines or 'soft law' (until the 1990s) and the ambiguous sovereignty of the European Commission meant that DG Competition had little capacity to enforce the rules. There was no instance of unlawful aid ever being repaid by its recipient until 1984 (Luengo, 2007). The rules state that DG Competition must always be *notified* in advance of aid being given, such that an evaluation of its compatibility with the single market can be given (EC, 1992: 88 (3)). As a formality, notification enables a considered judgement to be passed, even if it is typically to recognize that the aid is legitimate. The strong emphasis on notification is therefore a requirement for *public explanation*, as a constitutive element of legitimate sovereign action within the European community. Lack of notification represents as much of a challenge to the Commission as the aid itself, given that it renders the possibility of judgement impossible (EC, 1980). The Commission's *a priori* commitment to a competitive European order underpins a ritual of notification and evaluation, but initially offered no technical or empirical test with which to assess whether a particular instance of state aid is anti-competitive or not. Nor did it offer any basis on which to offer a positive evaluation of state aid.

With the growing influence of neo-classical economic evaluation within DG Competition, the critique of aid became increasingly empirical (or 'effects-based') in nature, with the argument that aid is typically inefficient. The DG began to conduct an annual audit of aid from 1988, which initially discovered that state aid was worth the equivalent of 3% of European GDP. The critique of aid shifted from an ordo-liberal one, that it disrupts the market form, to a utilitarian one, that there is too much of it and its costs are not being accounted for. The influence of, firstly, competitiveness concerns across the European Commission and, subsequently, Chicago economics within DG Competition resulted in a more economics-led approach to the problem. Aid and competition were no longer judged normatively, but in terms of their benefits or harms to European consumers, which could be quantified through regular audit. At the same time, this widened the scope for legitimate state interventions, where states were raising competitiveness through public support for R&D and innovation (EC, 2005). Critically, this new economic approach led to the publication of a new 'compatibility test', which would be applied to evaluate individual aid proposals, to assess whether or not they were legal.[3] The test was a form of economic cost-benefit analysis, which would seek to evaluate the overall efficiency of the particular state proposal. Legal procedure, as laid down in the 1957 Treaty, was thereby complemented with an economic methodology, providing DG Competition with a normative-empirical procedure by which to conduct its evaluations. European member states become constrained by empirical economics, and not just by law.

Guidelines issued in 1999 stated that DG Competition may take up to two months to evaluate whether or not a proposed aid was legal (EC, 1999). The economics-led approach made the process substantially more complicated, as DG economists were required to gather and analyse data, which would then be fed into the legal procedure. Where states were claiming that aid had a positive effect on local competitiveness, this added further complexity, as economists sought to quantify 'dynamic' effects, such as innovation. One indicator of the exceptional nature of autumn 2008 was that DG Competition promised to grant permission for aid in a matter of hours or over a weekend, making it clear that any normal procedure for evaluation had been suspended.

State rescue packages for financial institutions were already underway during late September and early October 2008, before DG Competition had issued any guidance on whether or not these were legal or not. Executive decisions by member states had *de facto* over-ridden the economic constitution of the European Union, demonstrating that the exception is effected by those with the sovereign power to do so, not by those with the normative authority to. Hence, the most urgent task for the Commission at this time was not to delimit state aid or even to evaluate it, but to take urgent action to ensure that European Law could accommodate whatever was deemed *necessary*. Following pressure from member states, a Communication issued by the Commission on 13 October formally acknowledged the treaty clause referring to aid needed 'to remedy a serious disturbance in the economy of a Member State' (EC, 2008a). In this context, the activity of member states was no longer being evaluated, either in a normative or an economic sense, but sanctioned by the unique and *exceptional* nature of the situation.[4] States were no longer invited to justify their interventions, either in a legal or an economic sense, but merely to act however they deemed *necessary*.[5] The document makes no reference to 'efficiency', 'costs', 'benefits', 'competitiveness' or to the compatibility of state aid with market competition. Hence, economic evaluation was suspended as well as law.

The effective orientation of the state aid authorities at this time was away from the defence of competition (however defined) and towards the defence of the state aid rules themselves. When the *new* Communications referred to the 'compatibility' of a piece of aid, they were not referring to its compatibility with competition or the European single market, but its compatibility with the Treaty of Rome. Under the exceptional circumstances of the financial crisis, necessary actions are, as Agamben puts it, neither inside nor outside the law but in a 'zone of indifference'. The question for those responsible for applying the law was how to ensure that it could return once this period had ended. The stress upon notification remained as great as ever, even though an evaluation would clearly be impossible given the time constraints.[6] The priority was simply that the law's existence was recognized, even while its procedural implementation was effectively suspended. The judgement of what was 'necessary' now lay in the hands of member states: DG Competition merely asked to be kept informed, so that the barest form of procedure could be sustained. For example, the British government notified DG Competition that it intended to buy £35bn-worth of shares in two banks on Saturday 11 October, and the DG granted permission on Sunday 12. A shadow of constitutional norms is maintained during this exceptional time, but no test is being applied. Actions are simply declared and affirmed (albeit publicly) but not justified in any critical sense.

How long does this state of exception last and how far does it extend? One criterion by which aid to banks would be considered compatible with state aid rules was that it be reviewed at least every six months (EC, 2008b). In December 2008, the Commission announced a new Temporary Framework authorizing necessary rescue packages in the 'real economy' (i.e. non-financial firms), such as loans and guarantees that the financial sector was itself unable to offer (EC, 2008c). This framework expired on 31 December 2010, and subsequent communications were issued to provide guidance on the phasing out of aid to financial institutions (EC, 2010). Statements made by the Commission therefore indicate a desire to terminate the formally recognized exception to market-based principles and techniques of valuation. But this doesn't mean that these principles and techniques are now restored to the status of state-endorsed norms. On the contrary, the exception does not need to be legally validated or recognized to persist, that is its definition. From a Schmittian perspective, the legality of sovereign rule always tacitly allows for non-legal acts. But moments of rupture and publicly declared states of exception create the possibility of permanently exceptional states, in which executive political power acquires the legal right to act purely out of necessity, and without justification. Whether or not the Commission would recognize this as an accurate depiction of European neoliberalism post-2008, it may be what has emerged.

European State Aid rules are an unusual case, inasmuch as their sovereignty is at best ambiguous. The implementation of these rules has always been somewhat dependent on a degree of compliance from those they seek to constrain, as the emphasis on advance 'notification' indicates. In their ambiguity, they capture something about the contradictory nature of neoliberal authority, in which positive economic reason is offered in place of sovereignty, but then requires sovereign backing in order for its enforcement. As an attempt to elevate market principles above nation states, but with no 'higher' power to enforce them, the European project is riddled with this problem, and the financial crisis has rendered it naked. When the threat to market principles appears existential in nature, that is, when the entire possibility of market-based evaluation is thrown into doubt, those principles need to be suspended, and executive powers mobilized in whatever way is deemed 'necessary'.

Historic crises or paradigm shifts threaten to evaluate the evaluators, through periods of political uncertainty and radical critique. The financial crisis could have represented such a moment of judgement, when a dominant economic rationality was thrown open to critique. That this did not occur (at least to the extent that many first predicted) was thanks to the contradictory entangling of economics and state sovereignty that constitutes neoliberalism. Both law *and* economics were suspended, so as to prevent their failure becoming publicly manifest, and the logic of executive necessity took over in their place. A market-based economic rationality was not simply one evaluative logic amongst many, to be dispensed with once it had failed: it was elevated to the status of quasi-constitutional state norm. As such, in a situation of emergency, it became more important to secure that norm by any means necessary than to apply it.

In the state of market exception, the 'violent threat' of the neoliberal state's authority becomes more nakedly political. The logic of business strategy, whereby the nation is managed like a corporation, morphs back into something approaching military strategy, in which all reserves of sovereign force must be drawn on to defend the existing market and economic infrastructure. Economic logic becomes fused with executive decision, such that anything political leaders decide to do is *de jure* economically rational during such a state of emergency. Fear of what political uncertainty might produce given time – for instance, a new political-economic paradigm – means that it must be shut down as swiftly as possible, even if that means (paradoxically enough) a return to quasi-socialist acts of public expenditure and economic planning in key areas of the economy such as finance. Political decision prevents a period of political critique, with the result being that there is no meaningful 'crisis' to speak of. This also means that there is no higher principle available through which economic rule can be justified any longer.

CONCLUSION: POST-LIBERAL NEOLIBERALISM

Since 2008, Marxist scholars have debated whether neoliberalism is alive or dead or in some type of 'zombie' state, in which a deceased economic paradigm continues to regulate and govern us (Peck et al., 2010; Harvey, 2011). Clearly the existential state of neoliberalism, however defined, is somewhat ambivalent. This chapter confirms something like a 'zombie' diagnosis, to the extent that the organizing categories and valuation devices of neoliberalism are no longer trusted to function of their own accord, without being propped up with various forms of contingent political intervention. In order to operate with normative authority, the neoliberal system relied on the fact that two of its preconditions were conveniently forgotten about and concealed. These were, firstly, the sovereign state, which hovers as an immeasurable force in the background of all governmental strategies of economization, and secondly, the choosing competitive individual mind, which is implicitly relied on to act in a vaguely predictable and self-interested fashion. The pretense that society and politics could be reorganized along the principles of the market was viable, so long as these two forces remained both vigilant and also seemingly absent. The rescue of neoliberalism has involved a new focus upon both, as explicit conditions of the status quo's survival. 'Neocommunitarianism' and 'market exceptionalism' are the concepts that I have developed to try and capture how this contingent rescue act has proceeded.

This contingent neoliberalism survives through a radical rejection of the modern sequence of crisis, as a periodic interruption and recreation of stable objectivity and normativity. The assumption that neoliberalism would meet its fate, just as the Keynesian-Fordist paradigm had during the 1970s, was implicitly derived from this modernist or dialectical notion of history and epistemology. But the sheer affirmation of a given reality, and an appeal to the bald necessity to carry on as before – repeating certain forms of calculation, reciting certain narratives – offer a political alternative to crisis and critique, which closes down the time and space of uncertainty, through exceptional and culturalist acts of state intervention. The infrastructure of economic evaluation can survive only if it can avoid the 'meta-evaluation' represented by a historical crisis. This calls for philosophies and strategies which abandon the primacy of evaluation altogether. As Mises remarked in his 1920 pamphlet that launched the 'socialist calculation debate', 'the static state can dispense with economic calculation'; absent change or progress, and credible techniques of valuation are no longer required (Mises, 1990: 16). To the extent that neoliberalism has now become a ritual to be repeated, not a judgement to be believed, the fact that its tools no longer function is by the by. One thing that is common both to Schmittian political theory and to behaviourism is an acute focus on the moment of *decision* (Schwarzkopf, 2011). At various political scales, from executive leader down to individual consumer, it is in the contingency of decision that neoliberalism's faith is now placed.

So what form of authority does this leave us with? Is it even a form of 'authority' at all, or is it merely a condition of political expediency or emergency? The first thing to note is that the 'liberal spirit' of neoliberalism, as described in Chapter 3, is now weaker than ever. The example of European State Aid rules demonstrates how the liberal ideal of a single, stateless competitive order can be very rapidly abandoned, once that order becomes subject to a sufficiently dangerous threat. In the state of market exception, there is a rapid reappearance of national sovereign boundaries and political identities. The psychological critique of economic rationality also contributes to this new 'cultural turn' within neoliberalism, whereby contingent differences in calculative capacity start to appear, and nothing can be presumed about humans *qua* humans any longer. The methodological basis to evaluate and judge all competitive activity equally is being dissolved. In its place are descriptions and 'rules of thumb' regarding how communities can best be supported, in different situations.

The political philosophies of communitarianism and exception have various things in common. They both take *difference* as their starting point for political theory and political action, rather than an assumption of common humanity. They both challenge the Cartesian and Kantian project of modernity, which treats rational human subjectivity as a stable epistemological and moral basis from which to reorganize society. This fiction of a stable, exterior subject, whose judgement can be relied on as a constitutional principle for politics and political philosophy, is replaced with various ontological portraits of individuals in various types of political communities, with various uneven distributions of physical power. These are forms of authority which do not operate using a grammar of justification or evaluation. Instead, they are performative, repetitive and potentially violent. To question the validity or authority source of those performances, repetitions and violence would be partly to miss the point. Nevertheless, such questions must be raised if critique is not to be silenced all together, in favour of tradition and stability, as the next chapter will explore.

The contingent neoliberalism that we currently live with is in a literal sense *unjustified*. It is propagated without the forms of justification (be they moral or empirical) that either the early neoliberals or the technical practitioners of neo-liberal policy had employed, in order to produce a reality that 'holds together', as pragmatist sociologists like to say. The economized social and political reality now only just about 'holds together', because it is constantly propped up, bailed out, nudged, monitored, adjusted, data-mined, and altered by those responsible for rescuing it. It does not survive as a consensual reality: economic judgements regarding 'what is going on' are no longer 'objective' or 'neutral', to the extent that they once were. The justice of inequality can no longer be explained with reference to a competition or to competitiveness, let alone to a market. Thus, power may be exercised along the very same tramlines that it was during the golden neoliberal years of the 1990s and early millennium, and the same experts, policies and agencies may continue to speak to the same public audiences. But the sudden reappearance of those two unruly uneconomic actors, the Hobbesian sovereign state and the psychological unconscious, suggests that that the project of disenchanting politics by economics has reached its limit. And yet crisis and critique have been strategically deferred or accommodated. What resources are there available for this to change, and to what extent are these distinguishable from neoliberalism's own critical capacities?

NOTES

1 'It may be, therefore, that ultimately the work of socio-biologists (and their critics) will enable us to construct a picture of human nature in such detail that we can derive the set of preferences with which economists start. And if this result is achieved, it will enable us to refine our analysis of consumer demand and of other kinds of behaviour in the economic sphere. In the meantime, however, whatever makes men choose as they do, we must be content with the knowledge that for groups of human beings, in almost all circumstances, a higher (relative) price for anything will lead to a reduction in the amount demanded' (Coase, 2005: 201).

2 'Any aid granted by a Member State or through State resources in any form whatsoever which distorts or threatens to distort competition by favouring certain undertakings or the production of certain goods shall, in so far as it affects trade between Member States, be incompatible with the common market' (EC, 1992: Article 87).

3 The test is as follows:

1 Is the aid measure aimed at a well-defined objective of common interest?

2 Is the aid well designed to deliver the objective of common interest, i.e. does the proposed aid address the market failure or other objectives?

(i) Is the aid an appropriate policy instrument to address the policy concerned?

(ii) Is there an incentive effect, i.e. does the aid change the behaviour of the aid recipient?

(iii) Is the aid measure proportionate to the problem tackled, i.e. could the same change in behaviour not be obtained with less aid?

3 Are the distortions of competition and effect on trade limited, so that the overall balance is positive? (EC, 2008a).

4 'As regards the financial sector, invoking this provision is possible only in genuinely exceptional circumstances where the entire functioning of financial markets is jeopardised' (EC, 2008a: 3).

5 'Given the scale of the crisis … the Commission recognises that Member States may consider it necessary to adopt appropriate measures to safeguard the stability of the financial system' (EC, 2008a: 2).

6 'It is of paramount importance that Member States inform the Commission of their intentions … The Commission has taken appropriate steps to ensure the swift adoption of decisions upon complete notification, if necessary within 24 hours and over a weekend' (EC, 2008a: 12).

AFTERWORD: CRITIQUE IN AND OF NEOLIBERALISM

Neoliberalism, as this book has sought to demonstrate, is replete with its own internal modes of criticism, judgement, measurement and evaluation, which enable actors to reach agreements about what is going on. These are especially provided by certain traditions of economics and business strategy, which privilege competitive processes, on the basis that those processes are uniquely able to preserve an element of uncertainty in social and economic life. The role of the expert – be it in the state, the think tank or university – within this programme is to produce quantitative facts about the current state of competitive reality, such that actors, firms or whole nations can be judged, compared and ranked. For Hayek and many of the early neoliberals, markets would do this job instead of expert authorities, with prices the only facts that were entirely necessary. But increasingly, under the influence of the later Chicago School and business strategists, the 'winners' and the 'losers' were to be judged through the evaluations of economics (and associated techniques and measures), rather than of markets as such. Certain forms of authority are therefore necessary for this 'game' to be playable. Economized law is used to test the validity of certain forms of competitive conduct; audits derived from business strategy are used to test and enthuse the entrepreneurial energies of rival communities. But the neoliberal programme initially operated such that these forms of authority could be exercised in a primarily technical sense, without metaphysical appeals to the common good, individual autonomy or the sovereignty of the state that employed them.

As the previous chapter argued, various crises (primarily, but not exclusively, the 2007–09 financial crisis) have exposed neoliberalism's tacit dependence on both executive sovereignty and on certain moral-psychological equipment on the part of individuals. A close reading of neoliberal texts and policies would have exposed this anyway. In which case, the recent 'discovery' that neoliberalism depends on and justifies power inequalities, and not markets as such, may be superficial in nature. Witnessing the exceptional measures that states have taken to rescue the status quo simply confirms the state-centric nature of neoliberalism, as an anti-political mode of politics. As Zizek argued in relation to the Wikileaks' exposures of 2011, 'the real disturbance was at the level of appearances: we can no longer pretend we don't know what everyone knows we know' (Zizek, 2011b). Most dramatically, neoliberalism now appears naked and shorn of any pretence to liberalism, that is, it no longer operates with manifest *a priori* principles of equivalence, against which all contestants should be judged. Chapter 2 identified the 'liberal spirit' of neo-liberalism with a Rawlsian assumption that contestants are formally equal before they enter the economic 'game'. Within the Kantian or 'deontological' tradition of liberalism, this is the critical issue, and it played a part in internal debates within the early neoliberal movement. For those such as the ordo-liberals, who feared the rationalizing potential of capitalist monopoly, the task was to build an economy around such an *a priori* liberal logic. Ensuring some equality of access to the economic 'game', via the active regulation of large firms and 'equality of opportunity' for individuals, is how neoliberalism's liberalism has most commonly been presented politically. As Chapter 3 discussed, the American tradition of neoliberalism – as manifest in Chicago Law and Economics – abandoned this sort of normative liberalism, in favour of a Benthamite utilitarianism, in which efficiency claims trumped formal arguments. The philosophical and normative elements of neoliberalism have, in truth, been in decline since the 1950s.

The 'liberal spirit' of neoliberalism was kept faintly alive by the authority that was bestowed upon methodologies, audits and measures of efficiency analysis. The liberal *a priori* just about survived in the purported neutrality of economic method (of various forms), to judge all contestants equally, even while the empirical results of these judgements have increasingly benefitted already-dominant competitors. This notion relied on a fundamental epistemological inconsistency of neoliberalism, between the Hayekian argument that there can be no stable or objective scientific perspective on economic activity, and the more positivist argument that economics offers a final and definitive judge-ment. American neoliberalism broadens the 'arena' in which competition is understood to take place, beyond definable markets, and beyond the sphere of the 'economy', enabling cultural, social and political resources to be legitimately dragged into the economic 'game', and a clustering of various forms of advantage in the same hands. Monopoly, in Walzer's terms, becomes translated into dominance.

The loss of neoliberalism's pretence to liberalism transforms the type of authority that can be claimed by and on behalf of power, be it business, financial or state power. It means the abandonment of the globalizing, universalizing, transcendental branch of neoliberalism, in which certain economic techniques and measures (including, but not only, prices) would provide a common framework through which all human difference could be mediated and represented. Instead, cultural and national difference – potentially leading to conflict – now animates neoliberalism, but without a commonly recognized principle against which to convert this into competitive inequality. What I have characterized as the 'violent threat' of neoliberalism has come to the fore, whereby authority in economic decision making is increasingly predicated upon the claim that 'we' must beat 'them'. This fracturing of universalism, in favour of political and cultural particularism, may be a symptom of how capitalist crises often play out (Gamble, 2009). One reason why neoliberalism has survived as well as it has since 2007 is that it has always managed to operate within two rhetorical registers simultaneously, satisfying *both* the demand for liberal universalism *and* that for political particularism, so when the former falls apart, a neoliberal discourse of competitive nationalism and the authority of executive decision is already present and available.

One argument against the 'sociology of critique' is that it involves a capitulation to the forces of power that 'critical sociology' was traditionally pitched against. But unless we take seriously the capacity of regimes of economic power to assert themselves successfully in coherent normative, political and philosophical terms, then we will be unable to explain why they are quite as resilient as they are. The political success of neoliberalism lies partly in its capacity to harness arguments about *both* justice *and* political transformation, and to locate these within an economic contest, such that the demand for justice is reframed in terms of 'meritocracy' and the urge for political action is channelled into 'strategic leadership'. Recognizing the internal modes and conventions of critique, that are immanent to neoliberal authority, helps to cast some light on the great question of recent years – why has the pre-2007 paradigm survived to the extent that it has? But it may also help us to imagine how critique – be it liberal or otherwise – might be better disentangled from the institutions and regimes that have sought to possess it. While there is an obvious and necessary role for critique of neoliberalism today, there is also some benefit in a hermeneutic excavation of the forms of critical authority that neoliberalism has claimed ownership of, but is now gradually relinquishing, or which it has struggled to possess in the first place. So what do these look like, where might they be found, and how might they differ from their economized, neoliberal manifestations?

THE FATE OF LIBERAL CRITIQUE

Neoliberalism's relationship with liberalism was always somewhat ambivalent. The moral metaphysics of the latter was treated with suspicion, by the pragmatists, behaviourists and positivists of the neoliberal movement. Outside of ordo-liberalism, rules and laws were only rarely recognized as legitimate in and of themselves (for instance, in the case of anti-cartel rules). Following the banking crisis, it now seems that neoliberalism has been de-coupled from liberalism altogether. This has opened up space for nascent political movements to challenge capitalism, from within the 'liberal spirit' of critique. Arguing that the system, as currently organized, is not 'fair', that the rules 'ought' to apply equally to the rich as to the poor, that the game has been 'rigged' by elites, represents a manifestation of liberal judgement operating in a manner that is antagonistic to neoliberalism, and not constitutive of it. Critiques of tax avoidance by the wealthy are typically liberal, in the sense that they demand a restoration of the rules, imposed with a spirit of *a priori* equality. According to this critique, elites had been gradually and tacitly exempting themselves from the liberal spirit of neoliberalism for many years, prior to the financial crisis of 2007–09.

These same critiques also point precisely to how neoliberalism could in principle rebuild itself in an authoritative fashion. As Boltanski and Chiapello argue, 'the price paid by critique for being listened to, at least in part, is to see some of the values it had mobilized to oppose the form taken by the accumulation process being placed at the service of accumulation' (Boltanski & Chiapello, 2007: 29). The critique of 'unfairness' in the current political-economic system achieves so much public reach because neoliberalism has, at least for the time being, been denuded of its liberal qualities. Preserving it in its 'contingent' form has become the goal of neoliberal government, and not running it in its quasi-transcendental, universalizing form. But if the rules were applied fairly again, if economic judgement (by regulators, credit-raters, auditors etc.) came to be restored to the status of a 'neutral' and 'objective' perspective, and if elites were subjected to the same set of rules as everyone else, would that really bring the normative critique to a resolution?

The danger with this liberal critique of neoliberalism is that it can overlook Michael Walzer's distinction, noted in Chapter 2, between 'dominance' and 'monopoly'. Monopoly is a form of inequality that is limited in its institutional reach, and therefore confronts other forms of inequality, that are antagonistic to it. Hence money does not translate directly into political power, which does not translate directly into cultural capital, though in no case is the good distributed equally. Dominance, on the other hand, involves one form of monopoly dictating all others. In totalitarian regimes, political power strives to dictate all other distributions of worth and recognition, and under existing neoliberalism, economic and monetary evaluation, and hence economic inequality, infiltrates previously separate spheres. This was not necessarily how neoliberalism had to turn out. The tradition of neoliberalism manifests in ordo-liberalism, Simons and the early Hayek proposed strict limits to markets and market power, overseen by judicial rule. The price system could not practically be used to value *everything*. But increasingly it was economic evaluation, and not markets as such, that became the critical neoliberal test of worth, and with sufficient methodological innovation, there is nowhere that economics cannot be extended. Not everything can become commensurable within the market price system (for instance, 'public goods' such as pollution and national security cannot be bought and sold), but everything can become commensurable within economic analysis, even culture, as the study of national competitiveness demonstrated.

Dominance, in this sense, invariably undermines the conditions of liberal legitimacy, because it eventually seeks to dominate even its own adjudicators, and therefore its potential validators. Under neoliberalism, economic evaluation tools and money become the supreme mechanisms of comparison and commensuration – so powerful, in fact, that they infect the bodies responsible for representing and judging the market economy itself, such as accountants, auditors and credit raters. For example, the quest for fees on the part of service providers and evaluators is such that the 'objectivity' of evaluations and report can no longer 'hold together' as a viable convention. In 2013, the UK's Competition Commission expressed concern that the major accounting firms were too socially connected to the major banks to be able to audit them objectively (Competition Commission, 2013). Legitimate power, in a liberal sense, requires some 'other' through which its legitimacy is judged, tested and made publicly apparent. Some sort of constitution or normative framework must be external to the power that is to be judged. But this means that there must therefore be more than one form of power, more than one source of authority, or else the validity of political action cannot be gauged. Ultimately, there can be no single ultimate source of authority, a paradox that is also responsible for the Schmittian exception, an ontologically ambivalent situation that is neither internal nor external to the juridical order.

Critique of neoliberalism cannot simply focus on its general 'unfairness', as if legitimacy could be restored if everyone were 'playing by the same rules'. The problem is that the production and enforcement of rules is now *internal to the game*.

There is no longer a juridical outside, thanks to strategic acts of rationalization and positivist critiques of the very idea of any 'higher' or 'juridical' source of authority, external to economic processes. Chicago Law and Economics scholars explicitly attacked substantive liberal notions of justice, rights and procedural legitimacy. While not addressed in this book, the Virginia Public Choice school similarly dismantled notions of the 'public interest' or ethos of government officials, through expanding neo-classical economics into political science (Amadae, 2003). Meanwhile, the authority of the entrepreneur or business leader to *create* the rules that others then have to play by is a similarly immanentist and economistic account of normativity.

The vision of a 'meritocratic' society undermines its own conditions of possibility, if there is only a single sphere of competition to be dominated. Only if there are *multiple and incommensurable* spheres of inequality, with multiple measures, judges and notions of value, can liberalism be practically saved in any meaningful way. This means radically reducing the scope of economics again, and rediscovering rival measures and theories of value. A liberal separation of powers needs to be mirrored in a liberal separation of valuation techniques and principles, probably also of monies. The social indicators movement, which offers alternative and sometimes incommensurable audits of national 'performance' and policy, provides an example of how this can be done (De Neufville, 1975; Innes, 1989). The growth of social valuation techniques, such as social impact assessment and social return on investment, shows that the value of the 'non-economic' can be recognized and measured independently. But regardless of the critical imperatives underlying these techniques, they too are liable to be co-opted, in support of some broader notion of economic efficiency. The 'neocommunitarian' discovery of the 'social', described in Chapter 5, is a manifestation of this. Competitiveness evaluations also include plentiful 'non-economic' resources and data, in their assessment of a nation's overall competitiveness.

When intrinsic values are reduced to metrics of value, the danger of this type of commensuration with economics and prices is ever-present. But if values are not reduced to metrics of value then they forego certain rhetorical and performative opportunities, that a numbers-obsessed public sphere might otherwise offer. A statement such as 'art for art's sake' can be portrayed as elitist, while a legal-normative commitment to human rights or juridical procedure can appear to be a special minority interest or lobby group that is 'out of touch' with public sentiment. Intrinsic valuation has lost publicly plausible metaphysical substrates, but extrinsic, utilitarian valuation is pure babble, unless it has some tacitly assumed connection to a reality which exceeds it. The performative and rhetorical capacities of numbers are now becoming explicit, in ways that make the possibility of 'pre-interpretive' empirical 'facts' about society far less plausible. Civic movements, from across the political spectrum, now generate their own numbers for rhetorical purposes – such as the '99%' – and circulate them via social media, in ways that are aesthetically designed to gain attention and persuasion. The rhetorical and political elements of economic theories and methodologies have also moved to the foreground, corroborating studies of economic performativity (Callon, 1998), such that theories are now publicly discussed in terms of whether they can survive politically, rather than whether or not they are objectively valid. The discovery in April 2013 that a key paper, endorsing austerity policies and which the IMF and British Treasury had both attached great authority to, was based on a calculative error attributable to an Excel spreadsheet, is one dramatic example of how the performativity of economics and calculative devices is now a mainstream political issue (Reinhart & Rogoff, 2010). Mainstream policy thinking is beginning to address the role of models and measures in financial life (e.g. Haldane, 2012b).

Neoliberalism is therefore becoming a victim of its own success, in making quantitative economic evaluation the 'ultimate' test of validity across all realms of governance and decision making. The price paid for this economic imperialism is that, once the language of 'price', 'competitiveness' and 'efficiency' is the lingua franca of public political discourse, then it itself becomes imbued with all of the ambiguity and rhetorical cleverness for which political speech was feared by the neoliberals. It is no longer clear on what basis an academic economist – or any other academic – can claim sufficient distance from economic events and policies, in order to speak with 'objective' authority on a state of affairs. Chapter 3 described how anti-trust agencies went to great lengths to allow in-house economists to operate in a secluded, quasi-academic culture of esoteric theoretical debate. But the authority of academic theories is no longer taken for granted, and alternative, 'amateur' and civic methodologies are emerging to challenge those of the 'professional' social sciences. This was a matter of public debate following Barack Obama's 2012 Presidential election victory, which had been predicted with unnerving precision by Nate Silver, a blogger who analysed various large data sets. As methodologies and measures multiply, so the possibility of building a liberalism upon quantitative measure becomes more distant and not less, if there can be no *a priori* agreement that the measure is the right one, and is being applied in the right way. The 'audit society' promised to replace judgement with numbers: now we encounter so much enumeration, that we face a severe question as to how to judge *which numbers* genuinely matter, and *how much* they matter. The rise of 'Big Data' is exacerbating this. A purely immanentist and political view of numbers emerges instead, meaning that it is no longer clear where any new liberal 'equivalence principle' will emerge from. No doubt it may reappear in the language of neuroscience, with accompanying measures of value. But for the time being, we might ironically paraphrase Milton Friedman's 1953 methodological essay and say that 'over numbers and measures, men can only fight'.

THE FATE OF POLITICAL ACTION

I argued in Chapter 5 that a form of 'contingent neoliberalism' now existed, a combination of a 'state of market exception' and 'neocommunitarianism'. Both of these, in different ways, seek to base economic rationality on some tacitly political notion of *the decision*. It is only the decision of executive sovereign powers to rescue and preserve the neoliberal status quo at all costs that keeps it alive: this is the state of market exception. Meanwhile individuals have to be taught and nudged to decide (or 'choose') in a certain utility-maximizing way, as a matter of cultural preservation: this is neocommunitarianism. A longer-standing neoliberal tradition (examined in Chapter 4) had also granted a certain political authority to decision making, in the form of the strategic leader or entrepreneur, who could rearrange social and economic institutions according to their own will. The national competitiveness paradigm sought to persuade national leaders to view their own roles in similarly business-oriented Schumpeterian terms. One question, as we consider the possibility of alternatives to and within neoliberalism, is how might the notion of political decision making or action be harnessed in ways that broaden the horizon of political possibility. This is partly about de-coupling the notion of the 'political' from that of entrepreneurship, and de-coupling the notion of the 'social' from that of cognitive and behavioural psychology, where neocommunitarianism has placed it.

Achieving this will require a critical reexamination and rethink of the Hayekian understanding of uncertainty, in both its political and its economic forms. Hayek's core proposition, which weaves through subsequent neoliberal thought with various mutations, is that economic uncertainty will protect against the imposition of political plans. Therefore, the preconditions of economic uncertainty need to be constructed and secured by any means possible. But as Hayek himself was aware, this is itself a project of political planning, and its success lies in the fact that it has come to appear immutable and permanent. Arguably, it is now *so* politically successful (at least judged in terms of its elimination of political alternatives) that it suffers the same fate of the socialist planning that the neoliberals were initially inspired to combat, in that it is undermining the possibility of economic progress and innovation. In the United States and Europe, the neoliberal project has become both politically *and* economically stagnant, suggesting that its political substrate (which insists that there is only one way to govern the economy) has now overwhelmed its economic veneer (which initially suggested that the future was radically uncertain). As Graeber succinctly argues, 'whenever there is a choice between one option that makes capitalism seem the only possible economic system, and another that would actually make capitalism a more viable economic system, neoliberalism means always choosing the former' (Graeber, 2013).

Neoliberalism rests on an idiosyncratic political anthropology, in which individuals and groups confront the future by way of plans. The assumption is that human beings are predisposed to impose their will upon others, that is, they are not 'naturally' liberal, so must be placed in frameworks which force them to be. Challenging neoliberal politics must therefore also involve offering an alternative political anthropology, in which political actors are capable of injecting vitality and surprise into society, without necessarily dominating one another, either as managers or as tyrants. This needs to be fed into the design and governance of economic institutions. This more Arendtian vision of politics bestows a capacity for decisive, inventive, autonomous political action upon all humans, and not only on those who are 'leaders' or 'sovereign' in the Schmittian sense. The notion of the 'plan' as the enemy of economic liberty now appears somewhat outdated, following the demise of state socialism. The more urgent object of critique is the political insistence that the same dominant economic powers must be protected and secured at all costs, for the forseeable future. This is neoliberalism's own equivalent of the 'plan', which now resembles Brezhnev-era state socialism, in its empty insistence that the future must be *the same as* the present. Businesses themselves impose bland and deadening plans upon society, via credit relations, consumer contracts and work contracts, which are all designed to restrict the individual's freedom of choice and not expand it. It is not the dynamism of the price system that is likely to upset this repetition of the present, but the dynamism of political action and the invention of alternative economic institutions, which do not concentrate the capacity for 'decisions' and 'action' only in their 'leaders' or their 'entrepreneurs'.

Entrepreneurship, as an ethos, contains a Schmittian 'violent threat', inasmuch as the entrepreneur acts without justification, in ways that are animated entirely by a desire for victory, rather than for peace or fairness. The entrepreneur simply desires that the economic status quo get re-made, including its rules and conditions. For this reason, there is undoubtedly political potential in entrepreneurship to introduce something radically new, and not simply 'more innovation' in the sense favoured by business and neoliberal policy makers. Entrepreneurship *potentially* moves beyond a zone of 'competitive uncertainty' (of the form valorized by Hayek) and into one of 'political uncertainty', which challenges the very terms on which choice, freedom and evaluation are organized. In this respect, entrepreneurship has always posed a tacit threat to neoliberalism, while also being celebrated. This threat is managed by offering celebrity, extreme wealth and political status to successful entrepreneurs (for instance, inviting them to Davos), as ways of channelling the entrepreneurial and militaristic ethos into the existing 'game', as opposed to creating new political conditions altogether. The phenomenon of 'social entrepreneurship' (in which non-monetary goals are pursued by new enterprises) represents a small shift away from this. However, were the disruptive entrepreneurial ethos channelled into the creation of radically new institutional forms, currencies, forms of property and rules of exchange, then it potentially would abandon the limits of 'competitive uncertainty' altogether. The creation of 'real utopias', such as democratically governed firms and public budgets, offers glimpses of this (Wright, 2010).

The political shortcoming of entrepreneurship is that it remains, for the most part, hampered by its assumption that the new can only be brought into existence by a small minority of individuals, whose authority stems purely from their 'talent', 'decision' or 'strategy'. To date, this has largely remained a feature of the social entrepreneurship and social innovation movement. A Schumpeterian anthropology, which affirms the facticity of human difference – in which most are inclined to obey routines, but a small few are inclined to invent new ones – underpins most visions of entrepreneurship, splitting political-economic agents into a small minority of narcissistic innovators, and a large majority of depressive followers. For this reason the term 'entrepreneur' may be too compromised to be politically transformative. The same may be true of the 'innovation' and 'creativity' that are so beloved of corporate elites. But if an alternative political anthropology were harnessed and channelled into the design and construction of new economic institutions, one which started from the (liberal-spirited) assumption that *all* individuals have ideas, decision-making capacity and value to contribute (albeit of incommensurable varieties), this might disrupt in ways that are genuinely uncertain, both in an economic and a political sense.

At present, the actions and decision making of the 'non-entrepreneurial' majority are viewed via the lens of economic psychology, whether that be Human Resource Management and marketing on the part of business managers, or 'nudging' and cognitive behavioural therapy on the part of public policy makers. This is a critique 'within' neoliberalism which poses its own particular challenge for the critique 'of' neoliberalism. The assumption of the applied economic psychologists is that most people do not really know what they want, do not really know what they are doing, and are unhappy due to cognitive or neurochemical malfunctions. The recognition on the part of policy makers that consumers and citizens can be psychologically manipulated, through the provision of cognitive cues or drugs, represents a peculiar neoliberal acquisition of a theory of critical realism (or false consciousness), which is entirely opposed to the early neoliberal assumption that there was no higher basis on which to base knowledge, beyond ordinary consumer perspectives. Just as political action needs to be decoupled from a specific notion of entrepreneurship, that presumes some heroic vision of an unaccountable leader, so also does it need to be de-coupled from this notion of a choice maker, who suffers from certain neurological or cultural defects of cognition. This would mean highlighting the ways in which individuals *do* know what they want, and *do* know what they're doing, but are severely limited by circumstances, and not by their brains or their cognitive equipment. It requires illuminating the latent relationship between unhappiness and critique, such that a phenomenon such as depression can be reactivated as resistance, rather than as re-engagement. A new variety of liberal agency therefore needs to be rediscovered or invented, in which rational action is taken seriously as a sociological, political phenomenon, and is not reduced to the normative prescription of a mathematical equation, to be used to test choice-making in laboratories against. Convention theory is an important resource here, as it takes the statements and judgements of all actors seriously, without ever presuming that they are invalid by virtue of their context. The attempt to understand what people are doing, on their own terms, takes on a newly political dimension, in societies which have made 'behaviour change' a crucial goal of public policy.

AFTER COMPETITION AND COMPETITIVENESS

Chapter 2 argued that competition is privileged under neoliberalism, because of certain paradoxical qualities that distinguish it. Firstly, enforcing competition appeared to offer the state a unique economic role, that was both active and passive at the same time. Secondly, it seemed to secure a paradoxical combination of equality and inequality amongst persons, whereby they are formally equal, but contingently unequal. And thirdly, it appeared to offer a logical route between an 'over-socialized' vision of capitalism (in which it is the outcome only of rules and hierarchies) and an 'under-socialized' vision (in which it is determined only via individual rationality). Contrary to the depiction of neoliberalism as a form of Darwinistic or naturalistic faith in competition, which arises as soon as the state 'gets out of the way', it is important to remember the constructivist elements of this approach to competition, and its reliance on the state to secure and enhance competitive processes (Mirowski, 2009). As I argued through Chapters 2, 3 and 4, the politics of competition and competitiveness consists of creating a necessary tension and balance between the 'liberal spirit' (formal equality) and the 'violent threat' (contingent inequality) of political authority, which serve to harness (and hence also constrain) both.

One lesson to be taken from neoliberalism, for political movements which seek to challenge it, is that both individual agency and collective institutions need to be criticized and invented simultaneously. Political reform does not have to build on any 'natural' account of human beings, but can also invent new visions of individual agency. The design and transformation of institutions, such as markets, regulators and firms, do not need to take place separately from this project, but in tandem and in dialogue with it. A productive focus of critical economic enquiry would be those institutions which neoliberal thought has tended to be entirely silent on. These are the institutions and mechanisms of capitalism which coerce and coordinate individuals, thereby removing choices from economic situations. The era of applied neoliberal policy making has recently started to appear as one of rampant 'financialisation' (Krippner, 2012). So it is therefore peculiar how little attention is paid within neoliberal discourse to institutions of credit and equity, other than that they should be priced and distributed via markets. Likewise, the rising power of corporations has been sanctioned by theories that actually say very little about firms, management, work or organization, but focus all their attention on the incentives and choices confronting a few 'agents' and 'leaders' at the very top. Despite having permeated our cultural lives with visions of competition, and also permeated political institutions with certain economic rationalities, the dominant discourse of neoliberalism actually contains very little which represents the day-to-day lives and experiences of those who live with it. This represents a major empirical and analytical shortcoming of the economic theories that are at work in governing us, and ultimately a serious vulnerability.

A further lesson to be taken from neoliberalism, for the purposes of a critique of neoliberalism, is that restrictive economic practices need to be strategically and inventively targeted and replaced. In the 1930s and 1940s, 'restrictive economic practices' would have implied planning, labour organization and socialism. Today our economic freedoms are restricted in very different ways, which strike at the individual in an intimate way, rather than at individuals collectively. In the twenty-first century, the experience of being an employee or a consumer or a debtor is often one of being ensnared, not one of exercising any choice or strategy. Amidst all of the uncertainty of dynamic capitalism, this sense of being trapped into certain relations seems eminently certain. Releasing individuals from these constraints is a constructive project, as much as a critical one: this is what the example of the early neoliberals demonstrates. Lawyers willing to rewrite the rules of exchange, employment and finance (as, for instance the ordo-liberals redrafted the rules of the market) could be one of the great forces for social progress, if they were ever to mobilize in a concerted way. A form of collective entrepreneurship, which – like individual entrepreneurs – saw economic normativity as fluid and changeable, could produce new forms of political economy, with alternative valuation systems.

The reorganization of state, society, institutions and individuals in terms of competitive dynamics and rules, succeeded to the extent that it did because it offered *both* a vision of the collective *and* a vision of individual agency simultaneously. It can appear impermeable to critique or political transformation, if only challenged on one of these terms. For instance, if a different vision of collective organization is proposed, the neoliberal rejoinder is that this must involve abandoning individual 'choice' or freedom. Or if a different vision of the individual is proposed, the neoliberal rejoinder is that this is unrealistic given the competitive global context. Dispensing with competition, as the template for all politics and political metaphysics, is therefore only possible if theory proceeds anew, with a political-economic idea of individual agency and collective organization, at the same time. What this might allow is a different basis from which to speak of human beings as paradoxically the same yet different. The problem of politics is that individuals are both private, isolated actors, with tastes and choices, and part of a collectivity, with rules and authorities. An alternative answer to this riddle needs to be identified, other than simply more competition and more competitiveness, in which isolated actors take no responsibility for the collective, and the collective is immune to the protestations of those isolated actors.

REFERENCES

Agamben, G. (2005) *State of Exception*. Chicago, IL: University of Chicago Press.

Aglietta, M. (2001) *A Theory of Capitalist Regulation: The U.S. Experience* (new edition). London: Verso.

Aiginger, K. (2005) *Towards a Renewed Industrial Policy in Europe*. Brussels: European Commission.

Aiginger, K. (2006a) Competitiveness: from a dangerous obsession to a welfare creating ability with positive externalities, *Journal of Industry, Competition and Trade*, 6 (2): 161–177.

Aiginger, K. (2006b) Revisiting an evasive concept: introduction to the Special Issue on competitiveness, *Journal of Industry, Competition and Trade*, 6 (2): 63–66.

Alonso, W. & Starr, P. (eds) (1987) *The Politics of Numbers*. New York: Russell Sage Foundation.

Amadae, S.M. (2003) *Rationalizing Capitalist Democracy: The Cold War Origins of Rational Choice*. Chicago, IL: University of Chicago Press.

Amato, G. (1997) *Antitrust and the Bounds of Power: Dilemma of Liberal Democracy in the History of the Market*. Oxford: Hart.

Arendt, H. (1958) *The Human Condition*. Chicago, IL: University of Chicago Press. pp. vi. 332.

Aronczyk, M. (2012) *Branding the Nation: The Global Business of National Identity*. Oxford: Oxford University Press.

Arrighi, G. (2009) *The Long Twentieth Century: Money, Power and the Origins of Our Time* (new edition). London: Verso.

Backhouse, R. (2006) Economics since the Second World War. In *Paper to the History of Postwar Social Science Seminar Series*, London School of Economics, March. Available at http://www2.lse.ac.uk/CPNSS/events/Abstracts/historyofposwarScience/Econsince1945.pdf

Baritz, L. (1960) *The Servants of Power*. Middletown, CT: Wesleyan University Press.

Barley, S. & Kunda, G. (1992) Design and devotion: surges of rational and normative ideologies of control in managerial discourse, *Administrative Science Quarterly*, 37 (3): 363–399.

BBC (2012) 'Bank crisis impact bad as world war', Andrew Haldane says. BBC Online. Available at www.bbc.co.uk/news/business-20585549 (last accessed 3rd May 2013).

Becker, G.S. (1976) *The Economic Approach to Human Behavior*. Chicago, IL: University of Chicago Press.

Beckert, J. (2011) Where Do Prices Come From? Sociological Approaches to Price Formation. MPIfG Discussion Paper 11/3. Stuttgart: Max Planck Institute.

Bergin, A. (2013) *The Great Persuasion: Reinventing the Case for Free Markets Since the Depression*. Cambridge, MA: Harvard University Press.

Berridge, K.C. (2003) Pleasures of the brain, *Brain and Cognition*, *52* (1): 106–128.

Bevir, M. & Rhodes, R.A.W. (2004) Interpretation as method, explanation, and critique, *British Journal of Politics and International Relations*, 6: 156–161.

Biggart, N.W. & Beamish, T.D. (2003) The economic sociology of conventions: habit, custom, practice, and routine in market order, *Annual Review of Sociology*, *29* (1): 443–464.

Black, C. (2008) *Working for a Healthier Tomorrow: Dame Carole Black's Review of the Health of Britain's Working Age Population*. London: TSO.

Blokker, P. (2011) Pragmatic sociology: theoretical evolvement and empirical application, *European Journal of Social Theory*, *14*: 251–261.

Boltanski, L. (2011) *On Critique: A Sociology of Emancipation*. Cambridge: Polity.

Boltanski, L. (2012) *Love and Justice as Competencies: Three Essays on the Sociology of Action*. Cambridge: Polity.

Boltanski, L. & Chiapello, E. (2007) *The New Spirit of Capitalism*. London: Verso.

Boltanski, L. & Thévenot, L. (1999) The sociology of critical capacity, *European Journal of Social Theory*, *2* (3): 359–377.

Boltanski, L. & Thévenot, L. (2000) The reality of moral expectations: a sociology of situated judgement, *Philosophical Explorations*, *3* (3): 208–231.

Boltanski, L. & Thévenot, L. (2006) *On Justification: Economies of Worth*. Princeton: Princeton University Press.

Bonefeld, W. (2012) Freedom and the strong state: on German ordoliberalism. *New Political Economy*, *17* (5): 633–656.

Bonefeld, W. (2013) Human economy & social policy: on ordoliberalism and political authority, *History of the Human Sciences*, *26* (2): 106–125.

Bork, R. (1954) Vertical integration and the Sherman Act: the legal history of an economic misconception, *University of Chicago Law Review*, *22* (1): 157–201.

Bork, R.H. (1978) *The Antitrust Paradox: A Policy at War with Itself*. New York: Basic.

Boyer, R. (1989) *The Regulation School: A Critical Introduction*. New York: Columbia University Press.

Boyer, R. & Saillard, Y. (2001) *Regulation Theory: The State of the Art*. London: Routledge.

Braudel, F. (1979) *Afterthoughts on Material Civilization and Capitalism*. Johns Hopkins University.

Brenner, N. (2004) *New State Spaces: Urban Governance and the Rescaling of Statehood*. Oxford: Oxford University Press.

Brenner, N. & Wachsmuth, D. (2012) Territorial competitiveness: lineages, practices, ideologies. In *Planning Ideas that Matter*. Cambridge, MA: MIT Press.

Brown, W. (2015) *Undoing the Demos: Neoliberalism's Stealth Revolution*. Cambridge, MA: Zone Books.

Bruni, R. & Sugden, L. (2007) The road not taken: how psychology was removed from economics, and how it might be brought back, *Economic Journal, 117* (516): 146–173.

Bryan, D., Martin, R., Montgomerie, J. & Williams, K. (2012) An important failure: knowledge limits and the financial crisis, *Economy and Society*, *41* (3): 299–315.

Buch-Hansen, H. & Wigger, A. (2010) Revisiting 50 years of market-making: the neoliberal transformation of European competition policy, *Review of International Political Economy*, *17* (1): 20–44.

Buchanan, J. (2005) Cost, choice and catalaxy: an evaluation of two related but divergent Virginia paradigms. In F. Parisi & C. Rowley (eds), *The Origins of Law and Economics*. Cheltenham: Elgar.

Cacioppo, J.T. & Patrick, W. (2009) *Loneliness: Human Nature and the Need for Social Connection*. New York: Norton.

Caliskan, K. (2010) *Market Threads: How Cotton Farmers and Traders Create a Global Commodity*. New Jersey: Princeton University Press.

Caliskan, K. & Callon, M. (2009) Economization, part 1: shifting attention from the economy towards processes of economization. *Economy and Society*, *38* (3): 369–398.

Callon, M. (1998) Introduction. *The Laws of the Markets*. Oxford: Blackwell.

Cerny, P.G. (1990) *The Changing Architecture of Politics: Structure, Agency, and the Future of the State*. London: Sage.

Chandler, A.D. (1977) *The Visible Hand: The Managerial Revolution in American Business*. Cambridge, MA: Harvard University Press.

Chiapello, E. (2009) *Die Konstruktion der Wirtschaft durch das Rechnungswesen*. In Diaz-Bone, R. and Krell, G. (eds), *Diskurs und Ökonomie, Diskursanalytische Perspektiven auf Märkte und Organisationen*. Wiesbaden: VS Verlag, 125–149.

Christakis, N.A. & Fowler, J.H. (2011) *Connected: The Surprising Power of Our Social Networks and How They Shape Our Lives – How Your Friends' Friends' Friends Affect Everything You Feel, Think, and Do*. New York: Little, Brown.

Clark, A.E. & Oswald, A.J. (1994) Unhappiness and unemployment, *The Economic Journal*, *104* (424): 648.

Clement, P. (2010) The term 'macroprudential': origins and evolution, *BIS Quarterly Review, March*. Available at http://papers.ssrn.com/sol3/papers.cfm?abstract_id=1561624

Coase, R.H. (1937) The nature of the firm, *Economica*, *4* (16): 386–405.

Coase, R.H. (1960) The problem of social cost, *Journal of Law and Economics*, *3* (1): 1.

Coase, R.H. (1988) *The Firm, the Market and the Law*. Chicago, IL: University of Chicago Press.

Coase, R.H. (1993) Law and economics at Chicago, *Journal of Law and Economics*, *36* (s1): 239.

Coase, R.H. (2005) Transaction costs in the economic analysis of law. In F. Parisi & C. Rowley (eds), *The Origins of Law and Economics*. Cheltenham: Elgar.

Colander, D. (2007) *Edgeworth's Hedonimeter and the Quest to Measure Utility*. Middlebury College, Department of Economics. Available at http://ideas.repec.org/p/mdl/mdlpap/0723.html

Cole, A. (2012) *American Competitiveness: A Matter of National Security*. American Security Project.

Committee on Oversight and Government Reform (2008) Testimony of Dr Alan Greenspan (October).

Competition Commission (2013) Statutory Audit Services Market Investigation (22 February).

Crouch, C. (2011) *The Strange Non-Death of Neoliberalism*. Cambridge: Polity.

Danziger, K. (1997) *Naming the Mind: How Psychology Found Its Language*. London: Sage.

Davies, W. (2010) Economics and the 'nonsense' of law: the case of the Chicago antitrust revolution, *Economy and Society, 39* (1): 64.

Davies, W. (2011a) The political economy of unhappiness, *New Left Review, 71.*

Davies, W. (2011b) Economic advice as a vocation: symbioses of scientific and political authority, *British Journal of Sociology, 62* (2): 304–323.

Davies, W. (2011c) Knowing the unknowable: the epistemological authority of innovation policy experts, *Social Epistemology, 25*: 401–421.

Davies, W. (2012) The emerging neocommunitarianism, *The Political Quarterly, 83* (4): 767–776.

Davies, W. (2013) When is a market not a market? 'Exemption', 'externality' and 'exception' in the case of European state aid rules, *Theory Culture & Society, 30* (2): 23–59.

Davies, W. (2015) *The Happiness Industry: How the government and big business sold us wellbeing*. London: Verso.

Davies, W., Montgomerie, J. & Wallin, S. (2015) *Financial Melancholia: Mental Health and Indebtedness*. London: Political Economy Research Centre.

De Neufville, J. (1975) *Social Indicators and Public Policy: Interactive Processes of Design and Application*. Amsterdam: Elsevier.

Desrosières, A. (1998) *The Politics of Large Numbers: A History of Statistical Reasoning*. Cambridge, MA: Harvard University Press.

Dezalay, Y. & Sugarman, D. (1995) *Professional Competition and Professional Power* (first edn). London: Routledge.

Dolan et al. (2010) *MINDSPACE: Influencing Behaviour through Public Policy*. London: Institute for Government.

Donzelot, J. (1991) The mobilization of society. In G. Burchell et al. (eds), *The Foucault Effect: Studies in Governmentality*. New York: Simon and Schuster.

Dorling, D. (2016) Brexit: The decision of a divided country. *British Medical Journal, 6* July 2016.

Dos Santos Ferreira, R. (2012) Two views of competition: 'Is it peace or war?', *The European Journal of the History of Economic Thought, 19* (6): 852–867.

Du Gay, P. (2000) *In Praise of Bureaucracy: Weber, Organization and Ethics*. London: Sage.

Easterlin, R. (1974) Does economic growth improve the human lot?: Some empirical evidence.

EC (1980) *Tenth Report on Competition Policy*. Brussels: EC.

EC (1990) *Industrial Policy in an Open and Competitive Environment: Guidelines for a Community Approach*. Brussels: EC.

EC (1992) *The Treaty of Rome*. Brussels: EC.

EC (1999) COUNCIL REGULATION (EC) No. 659/1999 of 22 March 1999 laying down detailed rules for the application of Article 93 of the EC Treaty. Brussels: EC.

EC (2004) *A Pro-active Competition Policy for a Competitive Europe*. COM(2004) 293. Brussels: EC.

EC (2005) *Less and Better Targeted State Aid: A Roadmap for State Aid Reform 2005–2009.* COM(2005) 107. Brussels: EC.

EC (2008a) *Common Principles for an Economic Assessment of the Compatibility of State Aid under Article 87.3.* Brussels: EC.

EC (2008b) *The Application of State Aid Rules to Measures Taken in Relation to Financial Institutions in the Context of the Current Global Financial Crisis (2008/C 270/02).* Brussels: EC.

EC (2008c) *Temporary Framework for State Aid Measures to Support Access to Finance in the Current Financial and Economic Crisis.* Brussels: EC.

EC (2010) *The Application of State Aid Rules to Government Guarantee Schemes Covering Bank Debt to be Issued After 30th June 2010.* DG Competition Working Document. Brussels: EC.

Engelen, E. et al. (2011) *After the Great Complacence: Financial Crisis and the Politics of Reform.* Oxford: Oxford University Press.

Espeland, W.N. & Sauder, M. (2007) Rankings and reactivity: how public measures recreate social worlds, *American Journal of Sociology, 113* (1): 1–40.

Espeland, W.N. & Stevens, M.L. (1998) Commensuration as a social process, *Annual Review of Sociology, 24* (1): 313–343.

European Management Forum (1979) *Global Competitiveness Report.* Davos: European Management Forum.

Eyal, G., Szelenyi, I. & Townsley, E. (2003) On irony: an invitation to neoclassical sociology, *Thesis Eleven, 73* (1): 5–41.

Farmer, R. & Richman, B. (1970) *Comparative Management & Economic Progress* (revised edn). Bloomington, IN: Cedarwood.

Farmer, R. & Richman, B. (1971) *International Business: An Operational Theory.* Bloomington, IN: Cedarwood.

Fine, B. (2001) *Social Capital Versus Social Theory: Political Economy and Social Science at the Turn of the Millenium.* London: Routledge.

Fine, B. & Milonakis, D. (2009) *From Economics Imperialism to Freakonomics: The Shifting Boundaries Between Economics and Other Social Sciences.* London: Routledge.

Fischer, F. (2009) *Democracy and Expertise: Reorienting Policy Inquiry.* Oxford: Oxford University Press.

Fitoussi, J. et al. (2009) Report of the Commission on the Measurement of Economic Performance and Social Progress.

Fligstein, N. (2001) *The Architecture of Markets: An Economic Sociology of Twenty-First Century Capitalist Societies.* Princeton, NJ: Princeton University Press.

Foucault, M. (2007) *Security, Territory, Population: Lectures at the College De France, 1977–78.* Basingstoke: Palgrave Macmillan.

Foucault, M. (2008) *The Birth of Biopolitics: Lectures at the Collège De France, 1978–79.* Basingstoke: Palgrave Macmillan.

Fourcade, M. (2011) Cents and sensibility: economic valuation and the nature of 'Nature', *American Journal of Sociology, 116* (6): 1721–1777.

Fourcade, M. & Healy, K. (2007) Moral views of market society, *Annual Review of Sociology, 33*: 285–311.

Fox, E. (2008) The efficiency paradox. In R. Pitofsky (ed.), *How the Chicago School Overshot the Mark*. Oxford: Oxford University Press.

Frank, T. (2007) *What's the Matter with Kansas: How conservatives won the heart of America*. New York: Henry Holt & Company.

Freeman, L. (2004) *The Development of Social Network Analysis: A Study in the Sociology of Science*. Vancouver: Empirical.

Friedman, M. (1962) *Capitalism and Freedom*. Chicago, IL: University of Chicago Press.

Friedman, M. (1953) *Essays in Positive Economics*. Chicago, IL: University of Chicago Press. pp. v. 328.

Friedman, T. (2000) *The Lexus and the Olive Tree*. London: HarperCollins.

Froud, J. et al. (eds) (2006) *Financialization and Strategy: Narrative and Numbers*. London: Routledge.

FTC (2003) FTC History: Bureau of Economics Contributions to Law Enforcement, Research, and Economic Knowledge and Policy. Roundtable with Former Directors of the Bureau of Economics, Washington, DC, 4 September.

Fuller, L.L. (1934) American legal realism, *University of Pennsylvania Law Review*, 82: 429.

Gamble, A. (1996) *Hayek: The Iron Cage of Liberty*. Cambridge: Polity.

Gamble, A. (2009) *The Spectre at the Feast: Capitalist Crisis and the Politics of Recession*. Basingstoke: Palgrave Macmillan.

Garelli, S. (2006) *Top Class Competitors: How Nations, Firms, and Individuals Succeed in the New World of Competitiveness*. Chichester: Wiley.

Garvin, D.A. (2003) Making the case, *Harvard Magazine*, 106 (1): 56–65.

Gavel, D. (2000) Michael Porter named University Professor, *Harvard Gazette*, December 7th 2000.

Gerber, D.J. (1994) Constitutionalizing the economy: German neo-liberalism, competition law and the 'New' Europe, *American Journal of Comparative Law*, 42 (1): 25–84.

Gerber, D.J. (1998) *Law and Competition in Twentieth Century Europe: Protecting Prometheus*. Oxford: Clarendon.

Ghemawat, P. (2000) Competition and business strategy in historical perspective, *Harvard Business School Competition & Strategy Working Paper Series* (798010).

Giddens, A. (1998) *The Third Way: The Renewal of Social Democracy*. Cambridge: Polity.

Goffman, E. (1997) *The Goffman Reader*. Malden, MA: Blackwell.

Graeber, D. (2013) A practical Utopian's guide to the coming collapse, *The Baffler*, No. 22.

Granovetter, M. (1985) Economic action and social structure: the problem of embeddedness, *American Journal of Sociology*, 91 (3): 481.

Gray, J. (1998) *Hayek on Liberty*. London: Routledge.

Grossekettler, H. (1996) Franz Böhm as a pioneering champion of an economic theory of legislative science, *European Journal of Law and Economics*, 3 (4): 309–329.

Guo, J. (2016) 'Death predicts whether people vote for Donald Trump', *The Washington Post*, 4 March 2016.

Hacker, J.S. & Pierson, P. (2010) *Winner-Take-All Politics: How Washington Made the Rich Richer – And Turned its Back on the Middle Class*. New York: Simon and Schuster.

Haldane, A. (2012a) The doom loop, *London Review of Books*, 23 February.

Haldane, A. (2012b) Tales of the Unexpected. Bank of England. Available at www. bankofengland.co.uk/publications/pages/news/2012/058.aspx (last accessed 3 May 2012).

Hall, P. (1986) *Governing the Economy: The Politics of State Intervention in Britain and France*. Cambridge: Polity.

Hall, P. (1989) *The Political Power of Economic Ideas: Keynesianism Across Nations*. Princeton, NJ: Princeton University Press.

Häring, N. & Douglas, N. (2012) *Economists and the Powerful: Convenient Theories, Distorted Facts, Ample Rewards*. London: Anthem.

Harman, C. (2009) *Zombie Capitalism*. London: Bookmarks.

Hart, H.L.A. (1961) *The Concept of Law*. Oxford: Clarendon.

Harvey, D. (2005) *A Brief History of Neoliberalism*. Oxford: Oxford University Press.

Harvey, D. (2011) *The Enigma of Capital: And the Crises of Capitalism*. London: Profile.

Hayek, F.A. von (1942) Scientism and the study of society, Part I, *Economica*, 9 (35): 267–291.

Hayek, F.A. von (1944) *The Road to Serfdom*. London: Routledge.

Hayek, F.A. von (1945) The use of knowledge in society, *American Economic Review*, 35 (4): 519–530.

Hayek, F.A. von (1949) The intellectuals and socialism, *University of Chicago Law Review*, 16 (3): 417–433.

Hayek, F.A. von (1963) The meaning of competition. In *Individualism and Economic Order*. Auburn, AL: Ludwig von Mises Institute.

Hayek, F.A. von (2002) Competition as a discovery process, *Quarterly Journal of Austrian Economics*, 5 (3): 9–23.

Hayek, F.A. von (ed.) (2009) *Collectivist Economic Planning:* Auburn AL: The Ludwig von Mises Institute.

Healy, D. (1997) *The Antidepressant Era*. Cambridge, MA: Harvard University Press.

Heukelom, F. (2006*) Kahneman and Tversky and the Origin of Behavioural Economics*, Tinbergen Institute Discussion Paper.

Heukelom, F. (2010) Measurement and decision making at the University of Michigan in the 1950s and 1960s, *Journal of the History of the Behavioral Sciences*, 46 (2): 189–207.

Heukelom, F. (2011) Building and defining behavioral economics, *Research in the History of Economic Thought and Methodology*, 29 (Part 1): 1–29.

Hirschman, A.O. (1977) *The Passions and the Interests: Political Arguments for Capitalism Before its Triumph*. Princeton: Princeton University Press.

HMT (2013) *The Green Book: Appraisal and Evaluation in Central Government*. London: TSO.

Hood, C. (1991) A public management for all seasons?, *Public Administration*, 69 (1): 3–19.

Hood, C. (1995a) The 'new public management' in the 1980s: variations on a theme, *Accounting, Organizations and Society*, 20 (2–3): 93–109.

Hood, C. (1995b) Contemporary public management: a new global paradigm?, *Public Policy and Administration*, 10 (2): 104–117.

Hood, C. (2007) Public service management by numbers: why does it vary? Where has it come from? What are the gaps and the puzzles?, *Public Money & Management*, 27 (2): 95–102.

Hutton, W. (2010) *Them and Us: Changing Britain – Why We Need A Fair Society*. London: Little, Brown.

Innes, J.E. (1989) *Knowledge and Public Policy: The Search for Meaningful Indicators* (2nd expanded edn). New Brunswick: Transaction.

Jagd, S. (2011) Pragmatic sociology and competing orders of worth in organizations, *European Journal of Social Theory*, 14: 343–359.

Jessop, B. (1990) *State Theory: Putting the Capitalist State in Its Place*. Cambridge: Polity.

Jessop, B. (2002) *The Future of the Capitalist State*. Oxford: Polity.

Jessop, B. (2012) A cultural political economy of competitiveness, *The Knowledge Economy and Lifelong Learning*, 57–83.

Kahneman, D. & Tversky, A. (1979) Prospect theory: an analysis of decision under risk, *Econometrica*, 47 (2): 263–291.

Kant, I. (1970) An Answer to the Question 'What is Enlightenment?'. In H. Reiss (ed.), *Kant's Political Writings* (translated by H.B. Nisbet). Cambridge: Cambridge University Press.

Kant, I. (2007) *Critique of Judgement*. Oxford: Oxford University Press.

Kao, J. (2007) *Innovation Nation: How America is Losing its Competitive Edge, Why It Matters, and What We Can Do To Get It Back*. New York: Simon & Schuster.

Karpik, L. (2010) *Valuing the Unique: The Economics of Singularities*. Princeton, NJ: Princeton University Press.

Kaufman, E. (2016) 'Brexit voters: NOT the left behind', Fabian Society blog, 24 June 2016. www.fabians.org.uk/brexit-voters-not-the-left-behind (accessed 30 September 2016).

Ketels, C. (2003) The development of the cluster concept – present experiences and further developments. Paper prepared for NRW conference on clusters, Duisburg, Germany, 5 December.

Ketels, C. (2006) Michael Porter's Competitiveness Framework – recent learnings and new research priorities, *Journal of Industry, Competition and Trade*, 6: 115–136.

Khurana, R. (2007) *From Higher Aims to Hired Hands: The Social Transformation of American Business Schools and the Unfulfilled Promise of Management as a Profession*. Princeton, NJ: Princeton University Press.

Kitch, E.W. (1983) The rite of truth: a remembrance of law and economics at Chicago, 1932–1970, *Journal of Law and Economics*, 26 (1): 163.

Kitchin, R. (2013) The real time city? Big data and smart urbanism. Paper presented at the 'Smart Urbanism: Utopian Vision or False Dawn?' workshop at University of Durham, 20–21 June.

Knight, F.H. (1935) *The Ethics of Competition, and Other Essays*. London: Allen & Unwin. p. 363.

Knight, F.H. (1957) *Risk, Uncertainty and Profit* (eighth impression). London: London School of Economics and Political Science. pp. lxvi. 381.

Knights, D. & Morgan, G. (2011) 'Corporate strategy, organisations and subjectivity: a critique'. In M. Alvesson, *Classics in Critical Management Studies*. Cheltenham: Elgar.

Krippner, G. (2012) *Capitalizing on Crisis: The Political Origins of the Rise of Finance*. Cambridge, MA: Harvard University Press.

Krugman, P. (1994) Competitiveness: a dangerous obsession, *Foreign Affairs*.

Labrousse, A. & Weisz, J.-D. (2001) *Institutional Economics in France and Germany: German Ordoliberalism versus the French Regulation School*. New York: Springer.

Langley, P. & Leaver, A. (2012) Remaking retirement investors: behavioural economics and defined contribution occupational pensions, *Journal of Cultural Economy*, 5 (4): 473–488.

Lapham, L.H. (1998) *The Agony of Mammon: The Imperial World Economy Explains Itself to the Membership in Davos, Switzerland*. London: Verso.

Latour, B. (2003) What if we talked politics a little?, *Contemporary Political Theory*, 2 (2): 143–164.

Latour, B. (2005) *Reassembling the Social: An Introduction to Actor-Network-Theory*. Oxford: Oxford University Press.

Levinson, J.D. & Peng, K. (2006) *Valuing Cultural Differences in Behavioral Economics*. SSRN eLibrary. Available at http://papers.ssrn.com/sol3/papers.cfm?abstract_id=899688

Lo, A. (2004) The adaptive market hypothesis: market efficiency from an evolutionary perspective, *Journal of Portfolio Management*, 30: 15–29.

Lo, A. (2005) Reconciling efficient markets with behavioral finance: the adaptive markets hypothesis, *Journal of Investment Consulting*, 7 (2): 21–44.

Luengo Hernández de Madrid, G.E. (2007) *Regulation of Subsidies and State Aids in WTO and EC Law: Conflicts in International Trade Law*. Alphen aan den Rijn: Kluwer Law International.

Maas, H. (2005) Jevons, Mill and the private laboratory of the mind, *The Manchester School*, 73 (5): 620–649.

Maas, H. (2009) Disciplining boundaries: Lionel Robbins, Max Weber, and the borderlands of economics, history, and psychology, *Journal of the History of Economic Thought* 31 (04): 500–517.

MacIntyre, A.C. (2013) *After Virtue: A Study in Moral Theory*. London: Bloomsbury Academic.

MacKenzie, D.A. (2006) *An Engine, Not a Camera: How Financial Models Shape Markets*. Cambridge, MA: MIT Press.

MacKenzie, D. (2011) The credit crisis as a problem in the sociology of knowledge, *American Journal of Sociology*, 116 (6): 1778–1841.

MacKenzie, D. et al. (eds) (2007) *Do Economists Make Markets? On the Performativity of Economics*. Princeton, NJ: Princeton University Press.

Manne, H. (2005) How law and economics was marketed. In F. Parisi & C. Rowley (eds), *The Origins of Law and Economics*. Cheltenham: Elgar.

Martin, R. & Sunley, P. (2003) Deconstructing clusters: chaotic concept or policy panacea?, *Journal of Economic Geography*, 3: 5–35.

Massumi, B. (2002) *Parables for the Virtual: Movement, Affect, Sensation*. Durham, NC: Duke University Press.

McCloskey, D.N. (1985) *The Rhetoric of Economics*. Madison, WI: University of Wisconsin Press.

McCraw, T.K. (2007) *Prophet of Innovation: Joseph Schumpeter and Creative Destruction*. Cambridge, MA: Harvard University Press.

McLaren, N. (2011) Using internet search data as economic indicators, *Bank of England Quarterly Bulletin*, Q2.

Medvetz, T. (2012) *Think Tanks in America*. Chicago, IL: University of Chicago Press.

Miller, J. (1989) *The Economist as Reformer: Revamping the FTC, 1981–1985*. Washington, DC: American Enterprise Institute.

Mills, J. (1998) *Control: A History of Behaviorism*. New York: NYU Press.

Mirowski, P. (2005) How positivism made a pact with the postwar social sciences in the United States. In G. Steinmetz (ed.), *The Politics of Method in the Human Sciences: Positivism and its Epistemological Others*. Durham, NC: Duke University Press.

Mirowski, P. (2009) Postface: defining neoliberalism. In P. Mirowski and D. Plehwe (eds), *The Road from Mont Pelerin: The Making of the Neoliberal Thought Collective*. Cambridge, MA: Harvard University Press.

Mirowski, P. (2013) *Never Let a Serious Crisis Go to Waste: How Neoliberalism Survived the Financial Meltdown*. London: Verso.

Mirowski, P. & Plehwe, D. (2009) *The Road from Mont Pelerin: The Making of the Neoliberal Thought Collective*. Cambridge, MA: Harvard University Press.

Mises, L. von (1990) *Economic Calculation in the Socialist Commonwealth*. London: Ludwig von Mises Institute.

Mises, L. von (2009) *Socialism: An Economic and Sociological Analysis*. London: Ludwig von Mises Institute.

Mitchell, T. (1998) Fixing the economy, *Cultural Studies*, 12: 82–101.

Mitchell, T. (2002) *Rule of Experts: Egypt, Techno-Politics, Modernity*. Berkeley, CA: University of California Press.

Montague, P.R. & Berns, G.S. (2002) Neural economics and the biological substrates of valuation, *Neuron*, 36 (2): 265–284.

Mulgan, G. (2012) Government with the people: the outlines of a relational state. In R. Muir and G. Cook (eds), *The Relational State*. Newcastle: IPPR.

Mulholland, J. (2007) Behavioural Economics and the Federal Trade Commission. Presentation to the Australian Productivity Commission Roundtable on behavioural economics and public policy, 8–9 August.

Muniesa, F. & Callon, M. (2007) Economic experiments and the construction of markets. In D. Mackenzie, F. Munniesa and L. Siu (eds), *Do Economists Make Markets? On the Performativity of Economics*. New Jersey: Princeton University Press.

Muris, T. (2003) How history informs practice – understanding the development of modern US competition policy. Prepared remarks before American Bar Association Antitrust Section Fall Forum, Washington, DC, 19 November.

NAO (2009) *Maintaining Financial Sustainability Across the United Kingdom's Banking System*. London: HMSO.

OFT (2010) *What Does Behavioural Economics Mean for Competition Policy?* Working Paper OFT1224. London: OFT.

Parisi, F. & Rowley, C. (eds) (2005) *The Origins of Law and Economics: Essays by the Founding Fathers*. Cheltenham: Elgar.

Pearson, H. (1997) *Origins of Law and Economics: The Economists' New Science of Law, 1830–1930*. Cambridge: Cambridge University Press.

Peck, J. (2008) Remaking laissez-faire, *Progress in Human Geography*, 32 (1): 3–43.

Peck, J. (2010) *Constructions of Neoliberal Reason*. Oxford: Oxford University Press.

Peck, J., Theodore, N. & Brenner, N. (2010) Postneoliberalism and its malcontents, *Antipode*, 41: 94–116.

Perlman, M. (1987) Political purpose and the national accounts. In W. Alonso and P. Starr (eds), *The Politics of Numbers*. New York: Russell Sage Foundation.

Phillips-Fein, K. (2009) *Invisible Hands: The Making of the Conservative Movement from the New Deal to Reagan*. Indonesia: Yayasan Obor.

Pigou, A.C. (1912) *Wealth and Welfare*. Macmillan & Co.: London. pp. xxxi. 493.

Pitofsky, R. (2008) *How the Chicago School Overshot the Mark: The Effect of Conservative Economic Analysis on U.S. Antitrust*. Oxford: Oxford University Press.

Plehwe, D. (2009) Introduction. In P. Mirowski and D. Plehwe (eds),*The Road from Mont Pelerin: The Making of the Neoliberal Thought Collective*. Cambridge, MA: Harvard University Press.

Polanyi, K. (1957) *The Great Transformation: The Political and Economic Origins of Our Time*. Boston, MA: Beacon.

Poovey, M. (1998) *A History of the Modern Fact: Problems of Knowledge in the Sciences of Wealth and Society*. Chicago, IL: University of Chicago Press.

Porter, M.E. (1979) How competitive forces shape strategy, *Harvard Business Review*, March/April.

Porter, M.E. (1990) *The Competitive Advantage of Nations*. New York: Free Press.

Porter, M.E. (1995) The competitive advantage of the inner city, *Harvard Business Review*, September/October.

Porter, M.E. (1998) *On Competition*. Boston, MA: Harvard Business School Publishing.

Porter, T.M. (1995) *Trust in Numbers: The Pursuit of Objectivity in Science and Public Life*. Princeton, NJ: Princeton University Press.

Porter, M. (2001a) *Clusters of Innovation: Regional Foundations of US Competitiveness*. Washington DC: Council on Competitiveness.

Porter, M. (2001b) Competition and Antitrust: A productivity-based approach. *Antitrust Bulletin*. Winter 2001.

Posner, R.A. (1981) *The Economics of Justice*. Cambridge, MA: Harvard University Press.

Posner, R.A. (2002) *Antitrust Law: An Economic Perspective*. Chicago, IL: University of Chicago Press.

Power, M. (1997) *The Audit Society: Rituals of Verification*. Oxford: Oxford University Press.

President's Commission on Industrial Competitiveness (1985) *Global Competition: the New Reality*. Washington, DC: US Government Printing Office.

Priest, G. (2005) The rise of law and economics: a memoir of the early years. In F. Parisi and C. Rowley (eds), *The Origins of Law and Economics: Essays by the Founding Fathers*. Cheltenham: Elgar.

Ptak, R. (2009) Neoliberalism in Germany: revisiting the Ordoliberal Foundations of the Social Market Economy. In P. Mirowski and D. Phlewe (eds), *The Road from Mont Pelerin*. Cambridge, MA: Harvard University Press.

PwC (2012) *Making Executive Pay Work: The Psychology of Incentives*. London: PwC.

Rawls, J. (1972) *A Theory of Justice*. Cambridge, MA: Harvard University Press.

Reinhart, C. & Rogoff, K. (2010) *Growth in a Time of Debt*. NBER Working Paper 15639, January 2010.

Rhodes, R.A.W. (1996) The new governance: governing without government, *Political Studies, XLIV*: 652–667.

Rhodes, R.A.W. (1997) *Understanding Governance: Policy Networks, Governance, Reflexivity and Accountability*. Buckingham: Open University Press.

Roeller, L. & Buigues, P. (2005) The Office of the Chief Competition Economist at the European Commission. Available at http://ec.europa.eu/dgs/competition/officechiefecon_ ec.pdf (last accessed 8 March 2009).

Rose, N. (1990) *Governing the Soul: The Shaping of the Private Self*. London: Routledge.

Rose, N. (1996a) *Inventing Our Selves: Psychology, Power, and Personhood*. Cambridge: Cambridge University Press.

Rose, N. (1996b) The death of the social? Re-figuring the territory of government, *Economy and Society, 25*: 327–356.

Rose, N. (1999) *Powers of Freedom: Reframing Political Thought*. Cambridge: Cambridge University Press.

Rose, N. (2010) 'Screen and intervene': governing risky brains, *History of the Human Sciences, 23* (1): 79–105.

Rose, N. & Miller, P. (2008) *Governing the Present: Administering Economic, Social and Personal Life*. Cambridge: Polity.

Rousseau, J.-J. (1984) *A Discourse on Inequality*. Harmondsworth: Penguin.

Rubinfeld, D. (2008) On the foundations of antitrust law and economics. In R. Pitofsky (ed.), *How the Chicago School Overshot the Mark: The Effect of Conservative Economic Analysis on U.S. Antitrust*. Oxford: Oxford University Press.

Saint-Paul, G. (2011) *The Tyranny of Utility: Behavioral Social Science and the Rise of Paternalism*. Princeton, NJ: Princeton University Press.

Sandel, M.J. (1998) *Liberalism and the Limits of Justice*. Cambridge: Cambridge University Press.

Saporta, V. (2009) The role of macroprudential policy, *Bank of England Discussion Paper*. Available at http://estaticos.expansion.com/estaticas/documentos/2009/11/ doc_banco_inglaterra23112009.pdf

Savage, M. & Burrows, R. (2007) The coming crisis of empirical sociology, *Sociology, 41* (5): 885–899.

Schmalensee, R. (2007) Viewpoint: thoughts on the Chicago legacy in US antitrust, *Competition Policy International*, May.

Schmitt, C. (1996) *The Concept of the Political*. Chicago, IL: University of Chicago Press.

Schumpeter, J.A. (1934) *The Theory of Economic Development: An Inquiry Into Profits, Capital, Credit, Interest, and the Business Cycle*. New Jersey: Transaction.

Schumpeter, J.A. (1954) *History of Economic Analysis*. London: Allen & Unwin.

Schumpeter, J.A. (1976) *Capitalism, Socialism and Democracy* (fifth edn). London: Allen and Unwin.

Schwarzkopf, S. (2011) The political theology of consumer sovereignty: towards an ontology of consumer society, *Theory Culture & Society, 28* (3): 106–129.

Shiller, R. (2008) *The Subprime Solution: How Today's Global Financial Crisis Happened and What To Do About It*. Princeton, NJ: Princeton University Press.

Shizgal, P. (1997) Neural basis of utility estimation, *Current Opinion in Neurobiology*, 7 (2): 198–208.

Simons, H. (1937) *A Positive Program for Laissez-Faire*. Chicago, IL: University of Chicago.

Skeggs, B. & Loveday, V. (2012) Struggles for value: value practices, injustice, judgment, affect and the idea of class, *British Journal of Sociology*, 63 (3): 472–490.

Smith, A. (1999) *The Wealth of Nations: Books I–III* (new edn). Harmondsworth: Penguin.

Spieker, J. (2012) Defending the open society: Foucault, Hayek, and the problem of biopolitical order, *Economy and Society*: 42 (2): 304–321.

Stark, D. (2009) *The Sense of Dissonance: Accounts of Worth in Economic Life*. Princeton, NJ: Princeton University Press.

Stark, D. (2011) What's valuable? In J. Beckert and P. Aspers (eds), *The Worth of Goods: Valuation and Pricing in the Economy*. Oxford: Oxford University Press.

Stedman Jones, D. (2012) *Masters of the Universe: Hayek, Friedman and the Birth of Neoliberal Politics*. New Jersey: Princeton University Press.

Stewart, M. (2010) *The Management Myth: Debunking Modern Business Philosophy*. New York: Norton.

Stigler, G.J. (1992) Law or economics?, *Journal of Law and Economics*, 35 (2): 455.

Suzuki, T. (2003) The epistemology of macroeconomic reality: the Keynesian Revolution from an accounting point of view, *Accounting, Organizations and Society*, 28 (5): 471–517.

Taylor, C. (1992) *Sources of the Self: The Making of the Modern Identity*. Cambridge: Cambridge University Press.

Teles, S.M. (2008) *The Rise of the Conservative Legal Movement: The Battle for Control of the Law*. Princeton, NJ: Princeton University Press.

Thaler, R. & Sunstein, C. (2008) *Nudge: Improving Decisions About Health, Wealth, and Happiness*. New Haven, CT: Yale University Press.

Therborn, G. (2012) Class in the 21st century, *New Left Review*, 78, November-December.

Thorelli, H.B. (1954) *The Federal Antitrust Policy: Origination of an American Tradition*. London: Allen & Unwin. pp. xvi. 658.

Thrift, N.J. (2005) *Knowing Capitalism*. London: Sage.

Thurow, L.C. (1985) *The Zero-Sum Solution: Building a World-Class American Economy*. New York: Simon & Schuster.

Van Horn, R. (2009) Reinventing Monopoly and the role of corporations: the roots of Chicago law and economics. In P. Mirowski and D. Plehwe (eds), *The Road from Mont Pelerin: The Making of the Neoliberal Thought Collective*. Cambridge, MA: Harvard University Press.

Van Horn, R. (2011) Chicago's shifting attitude toward concentrations of business power (1934–1962), *Seattle University Law Review*, 34 (4): 1527.

Van Horn, R. & Mirowski, P. (2009) The rise of the Chicago School of economics and the birth of neoliberalism. In P. Mirowski and D. Plehwe (eds), *The Road from Mont Pelerin: The Making of the Neoliberal Thought Collective*. Cambridge, MA: Harvard University Press.

Van Overtveldt, J. (2006) *The Chicago School: How the University of Chicago Assembled the Thinkers Who Revolutionised Economics and Business*. Chicago, IL: Agate.

Von Neumann, J. & Morgenstern, O. (1953) *Theory of Games and Economic Behavior*. New Jersey: Princeton University Press.

Wagner, P. (1994) Dispute, uncertainty and institution in recent French debates, *Journal of Political Philosophy*, 2 (3): 270–289.

Wagner, P. (1999) After justification: repertoires of evaluation and the sociology of modernity, *European Journal of Social Theory*, 2 (3): 341–357.

Wagner, P. (2001) *A History and Theory of the Social Sciences: Not All That Is Solid Melts into Air*. London: Sage.

Wagner, P. (2008) *Modernity as Experience and Interpretation: A New Sociology of Modernity*. Cambridge: Polity.

Wagner, P. et al. (eds) (1991) *Social Sciences and the Modern States: National Experiences and Theoretical Crossroads*. Cambridge: Cambridge University Press.

Walras, L. (1954) *Elements of Pure Economics*. London: Routledge.

Walzer, M. (1983) *Spheres of Justice: A Defence of Pluralism and Equality*. Oxford: Robertson.

Weber, M. (1978) *Economy and Society: An Outline of Interpretive Sociology*. Berkeley, CA: University of California Press.

Weber, M. (1991a) Science as a vocation. In *From Max Weber: Essays in Sociology* (new edn). London: Routledge.

Weber, M. (1991b) Politics as a vocation. In *From Max Weber: Essays in Sociology* (new edn). London: Routledge.

Weber, M. (2002) *The Protestant Ethic and the 'Spirit' of Capitalism and Other Writings*. London: Penguin.

Wilkinson, J. (1997) A new paradigm for economic analysis?, *Economy and Society*, 26 (3): 335–339.

Wilkinson, R.G. & Pickett, K. (2009) *The Spirit Level: Why More Equal Societies Almost Always Do Better*. London: Allen Lane.

Wittgenstein, L. (1965) I: A lecture on ethics, *The Philosophical Review*, 74 (1): 3.

Wittgenstein, L. (2001) *Philosophical Investigations: The German Text with a Revised English Translation* (third edn). Oxford: Blackwell.

Wright, E.O. (2010) *Envisioning Real Utopias*. London: Verso.

Yanow, D. (2000) *Conducting Interpretive Policy Analysis*. Thousand Oaks, CA: Sage.

Zizek, S. (2011a) Shoplifters of the world unite, *London Review of Books*, 19 August.

Zizek, S. (2011b) Good manners in the age of wikileaks, *London Review of Books*, 20 January.

INDEX